Keep th
need it
your car...

About the American Hotel & Lodging Association (AH&LA)

Founded in 1910, AH&LA is the trade association representing the lodging industry in the United States. AH&LA is a federation of state lodging associations throughout the United States with 11,000 lodging properties worldwide as members. The association offers its members assistance with governmental affairs representation, communications, marketing, hospitality operations, training and education, technology issues, and more. For information, call 202-289-3100.

LODGING, the management magazine of AH&LA, is a "living textbook" for hospitality students that provides timely features, industry news, and vital lodging information.

About the American Hotel & Lodging Educational Institute (EI)

An affiliate of AH&LA, the Educational Institute is the world's largest source of quality training and educational materials for the lodging industry. EI develops textbooks and courses that are used in more than 1,200 colleges and universities worldwide, and also offers courses to individuals through its Distance Learning program. Hotels worldwide rely on EI for training resources that focus on every aspect of lodging operations. Industry-tested videos, CD-ROMs, seminars, and skills guides prepare employees at every skill level. EI also offers professional certification for the industry's top performers. For information about EI's products and services, call 800-349-0299 or 407-999-8100.

About the American Hotel & Lodging Educational Foundation (AH&LEF)

An affiliate of AH&LA, the American Hotel & Lodging Educational Foundation provides financial support that enhances the stability, prosperity, and growth of the lodging industry through educational and research programs. AH&LEF has awarded millions of dollars in scholarship funds for students pursuing higher education in hospitality management. AH&LEF has also funded research projects on topics important to the industry, including occupational safety and health, turnover and diversity, and best practices in the U.S. lodging industry. For information, go to www.ahlef.org.

00885TXT02ENGE
PP-3203

ETHICS IN THE HOSPITALITY AND TOURISM INDUSTRY

Educational Institute Books

ETHICS IN THE HOSPITALITY AND TOURISM INDUSTRY

Second Edition

Karen Lieberman, Ph.D.
Bruce Nissen, Ph.D.

American
Hotel & Lodging
Educational Institute

Disclaimer

This publication is designed to provide accurate and authoritative information in regard to the subject matter covered. It is sold with the understanding that the publisher is not engaged in rendering legal, accounting, or other professional service. If legal advice or other expert assistance is required, the services of a competent professional person should be sought.

— *From the Declaration of Principles jointly adopted by the American Bar Association and a Committee of Publishers and Associations*

The authors, Karen Lieberman and Bruce Nissen, are solely responsible for the contents of this publication. All views expressed herein are solely those of the authors and do not necessarily reflect the views of the American Hotel & Lodging Educational Institute (the Institute) or the American Hotel & Lodging Association (AH&LA).

Nothing contained in this publication shall constitute a standard, an endorsement, or a recommendation of the Institute or AH&LA. The Institute and AH&LA disclaim any liability with respect to the use of any information, procedure, or product, or reliance thereon by any member of the hospitality industry.

©2008
By the AMERICAN HOTEL & LODGING
EDUCATIONAL INSTITUTE
2113 N. High Street
Lansing, Michigan 48906-4221

The American Hotel & Lodging
Educational Institute is a nonprofit
educational foundation.

Printed in the United States of America
6 7 8 9 14   D

ISBN 978-0-86612-328-0

DEDICATION

For
Jared and Karen
and
Leif and Heather

Contents

8 Applying Ethics to the Sales Function **79**

Case Commentary: Utilitarianism • Case Commentary: Kant's Categorical Imperative • Case Commentary: The Ethic of Justice • Case Commentary: Aristotle and the Ethics of Virtue

9 Applying Ethics to the Maintenance Function **87**

Case Commentary: Utilitarianism • Case Commentary: Kant's Categorical Imperative • Case Commentary: The Ethic of Justice • Case Commentary: Aristotle and the Ethics of Virtue

10 Applying Ethics to the Food and Beverage Function **99**

Case Commentary: Utilitarianism • Case Commentary: Kant's Categorical Imperative • Case Commentary: The Ethic of Justice • Case Commentary: Aristotle and the Ethics of Virtue

Preface

Ethics in the hospitality and tourism industry continues to be an important topic around the world. In this second edition of *Ethics in the Hospitality and Tourism Industry*, we try to further the ethical dialog in the classroom. It is our continued hope that the students who study the topic will keep it at the forefront of their industry commitment.

The first edition had 12 chapters; this second edition has 25 chapters. The table of contents now lists five parts: Fundamentals of Theory, Lodging and Food Service Applications, Other Hospitality Applications, International Applications, and Leadership Applications.

Part I: Fundamentals of Theory, is virtually unchanged, as we remain convinced that the best theories to assist us in our ethical studies are utilitarianism, deontological (Kantian) ethics, justice ethics, and virtue (Aristotelian) ethics. Critical thinking is the most important aspect of learning to think about ethical issues. If a student absorbs and understands the theories listed above and develops the ability to use those theories to think through a thorny problem, we will feel that our book has accomplished its purpose.

Part II: Lodging and Food Service Applications contains more inclusive information on the industry. In this new edition, maintenance and housekeeping are in separate chapters. Purchasing, marketing, and sales are also in individual chapters. These new chapters have been expanded with many original case studies covering ethical issues specific to each subject area. Revised chapters on front office management and food and beverage management have also been included in this section.

Additionally, this new edition is more specific to the various hospitality and tourism industry segments. Part III: Other Hospitality Applications incorporates new areas of study including club management, cruise line management, sports management, entertainment management, event management, and meeting management. As the industry becomes more segmented, and students become more precise in their subject areas, it is necessary to look at the specific ethical issues that might arise in these particular areas.

Part IV: International Applications comprises two new chapters, "Ethical Issues for International Managers" and "Managing a Culturally Diverse Workforce." There are two significant reasons for including these chapters. Primarily, hospitality managers today must be prepared to lead a diverse workforce. Knowing and understanding the cultural differences in approach to ethical issues one might confront from the many regions of the world is very important to successful management. Secondly, international opportunities are plentiful in the modern industry. Hospitality students and graduates have more opportunities to study and work abroad than ever before. Understanding and learning how to handle cultural obstacles to ethical understanding and agreement could make the difference in whether or not one has a successful international experience or career.

The final section, Part V: Leadership Applications, has two new chapters, "Ethics in Financial Management" and "Ethical Issues in Research and Academia."

Financial scandals continue to appear in the headlines, demonstrating the importance of ethical training and sensitivity where the temptation of "easy money" leads some astray. This new chapter will assist with reasoning through a problem that might put one's pocketbook in conflict with one's moral outlook. Critically thinking through these problems from theoretical perspectives will help in making an ethical choice.

The last chapter, "Ethical Issues in Research and Academia," has been included because record numbers of hospitality students are continuing on to graduate school for master's and doctoral degrees. Some consider academia almost from the start of their academic careers. There are issues that academics face that are usually not found in industry. Therefore, a separate chapter has been included to cover these concerns.

In closing, we would like to thank the many people in both academia and industry who have contributed case studies to the text. New perspectives through outside authorship add an invaluable dimension. We also would like to thank our friends and family for continued encouragement and support. Without them, it would be more difficult to do the right thing.

About the Authors

Karen Lieberman is Professor and past Chair of the Hospitality College, Johnson & Wales University, Florida campus, North Miami, Florida. She was previously Department Chair and Associate Professor, Purdue University North Central, Westville, Indiana. She holds a B.A. degree from New York University (Near Eastern Languages & Literature), a master's degree from Purdue University (Restaurant, Hotel, Institutional Management and Nutrition) and a Ph.D. from Purdue University (Educational Administration). She is also a Registered Dietitian.

Dr. Lieberman is the author of *Nutrition and Disease* (Garland Publishers), as well as many scholarly articles. In 2003, she was awarded an Emerald Management Review Citation of Excellence. She has been an active member of the International Council on Hotel, Restaurant, and Institutional Education (CHRIE) since 1988 and has served on several CHRIE committees, and as President of Florida/Caribbean CHRIE. She also serves on many civic and community boards in the Miami area.

Bruce Nissen is the Director of Research at the Center for Labor Research and Studies at Florida International University (FIU) in Miami, Florida. He also directs FIU's Research Institute on Social and Economic Policy (RISEP). He holds a B.A. degree from Grinnell College and a Ph.D. in Philosophy (Ethics) from Columbia University.

Dr. Nissen has previously authored or edited seven scholarly books, and is also the author of numerous academic journal articles and book chapters. In 2004, he was awarded FIU's university–wide Excellence in Research award. Dr. Nissen is widely quoted in regional and national media, and has served on boards and commissions of both community organizations and government agencies.

Dr. Lieberman and Dr. Nissen are husband and wife. They are the parents of two grown sons, Leif and Jared. *Ethics in the Hospitality and Tourism Industry* is their first book together, although they often present workshops and seminars together on the topic of hospitality ethics.

(Photo of Drs. Lieberman and Nissen by Barry Greff.)

Part I

Fundamentals of Theory

1

Why Are We Studying Ethics?

Unlike the world of facts, which is concerned with "what is," ethics is concerned with "what ought to be." Ethics is the study of moral principles concerning "rightful" conduct based on our most deeply held values. This book focuses on a particular branch of ethics, business ethics, and, more particularly, ethics within a particular branch of business—the hospitality and tourism industry. We will examine ethical issues that apply to individuals working in the industry and to organizations whose norms and internal cultures encourage ethical or unethical behavior.

The Language of Ethics

Throughout this book, the terms "ethics" and "morality" are used interchangeably. What is ethical is considered moral; what is unethical is considered immoral. Ethical discussions focus on the "right thing to do" or the "wrong thing to do." When used in this way, "right" and "wrong" are ethical terms. However, "right" and "wrong" are not always used in the ethical sense. For example, we could say that the right way to play golf is with a certain kind of swing that hits the ball straight, while the wrong way to play is with a swing that hits the ball so it curves off the fairway. There is no ethical or moral dimension to how we hit a golf ball, but there is when we discuss whether cheating on your golf score is right or wrong.

Other terms that we often use when we think about ethics or morality are "good" and "evil," especially when we use these terms as opposites. We also speak of "moral obligations" or "moral responsibilities" when we refer to what a person or organization ought to do. Sometimes, we say that it is a person's "duty" to behave in a certain way, or that someone "should" behave in a certain way. When we do, we are making a moral or ethical judgment, either about that person's character or about that person's actions. Not all judgments are ethical judgments. For example, it is not an ethical judgment when we judge the color of a restaurant menu as attractive or unattractive.

Another ethical norm that we frequently appeal to is "fairness." If we say that something is not fair, that statement is an ethical or moral judgment. Closely related is the standard of "justice." We want our society and our institutions to be just, and that too is an ethical judgment. Another ethical standard we employ is that of "rights," as when we say that someone's rights were violated and this is wrong and immoral. For example, consider a restaurant chain in which managers and franchisees conspire to limit the number of black employees and to restrict those employed to menial tasks. If a restaurant company engages in practices like

3

these, it is not acting in a fair, moral, or just way toward its employees—their rights are being violated.

Ethical norms differ from other norms or rules in that they are not the result of government legislation or some organizational rule-setting process. They are not the same as laws (although hopefully there is a considerable overlap). Something can be legal yet immoral. For example, slavery is an immoral institution, but it was legal in the United States for a long time. As late as the 1960s, black people were not permitted to eat with whites in many restaurants. Separate facilities existed for white and black people, and blacks were only allowed to sit in the rear of buses. This was all perfectly legal in parts of the United States—but was it moral?

So what exactly puts something in the "moral" or "ethical" category? Ethical or moral norms concern our most deeply held values, the things we most cherish and the things we most despise. As such, they concern actions that we believe either greatly benefit or greatly injure human beings. We believe that ethical or moral norms are more important than other values, such as our own self-interest or material comfort. If there is a conflict between "doing the right thing" and doing something that is wrong, but makes us wealthier or more comfortable—we should do the ethical thing. For example, if our menu says fresh fish, we should serve fresh fish—even if frozen fish could be offered at a much lower cost to the restaurant.

Ethical Understanding

Some believe you cannot teach ethics, nor is it something that you "learn." According to this view, people either have it or they do not. It is certainly true that moral reasoning begins in childhood, and that an upbringing that guides a young person toward ethical behavior is critical to an ethical understanding. A young adult who has not consistently been taught right from wrong will more likely go astray than those who have had a consistent ethical viewpoint given to them from childhood.

However, this does not mean that adults cannot learn and change in this area. Adults are able to change their views, and even more important, to deepen their understanding of ethical or moral issues. The field of social psychology has shown that adults can grow and change in their moral sensitivity and reasoning just as they can in other areas. At the very least, simply subjecting your moral beliefs and intuitions to a systematic look cannot be a bad thing—it can only help you think through the issues more clearly.

A closely related objection is the view that ethics cannot be taught because morality is a private affair. That is, you cannot teach someone ethics any more than you can teach them that something tastes good or bad. Morality is seen as specific to an individual; what is right for me may be wrong for you, and vice versa. Therefore, there is no point in studying ethics because you cannot tell someone what their private belief system should be.

This view may hold in some situations in which no large moral principles are involved. It might be true, for example, that it is right for me to donate to a certain charity but wrong for you to do so because I can afford it but, if you do, your family will suffer. In this case, what is "right" and what is "wrong" for each of us depends a lot on our individual circumstances, and the right choice will depend on many factors that have to be considered. The "right" thing and the "wrong" thing can depend a lot on circumstances. Imagine two hotels, one very large with many conference rooms, the other relatively small with only one conference room. The large hotel donates a conference room to a scout troop once a month. When a second scout troop approaches the smaller hotel, the owner has to deny the scouts because the only conference room must be available for business purposes.

Does this mean, however, that right and wrong, moral and immoral, have no real grounding? Is it up to each individual to decide his or her own moral beliefs any way he or she wishes, with no need to justify the choices? Can it really be true that any set of ethical or moral beliefs is as good as another? If that were true, a person who engaged in murder or rape and who thought this was perfectly okay would be just as moral as one who treated others with respect and compassion. Is it really true that someone who believes Adolf Hitler's genocide of millions is morally acceptable is on just as solid a moral standing as all of the rest of the world, which universally condemns the Holocaust as evil?

By its very nature, ethics or morality cannot be a purely private affair because moral principles are intended to guide our conduct in relationships with each other. We may not reach agreement on ethical or moral principles as easily as we can on "matters of fact," but this does not mean there is no basis for justifying or refuting one's moral or ethical judgments.

It is striking that, with all their differences, the major moral and ethical systems of the world, along with virtually all of the world's great religions, have an enormous overlap in what they condone and condemn. None of them condone, as a matter of principle, murder, rape, genocide, intentional cruelty to other human beings, etc. While delusional or fanatical individuals (whose factual belief systems are also warped beyond recognition) attempt to use a great moral or religious belief system to justify such actions, they simply misinterpret and misapply the belief system. In fact, there is a fairly large convergence among the great ethical and moral theories, which is encouraging evidence that morality or ethics is not merely a matter of individual taste requiring no further justification. We can, and should, justify and defend our ethical beliefs and examine them for indefensible assumptions or reasoning so that we can more intelligently lead an ethical life.

Business Ethics

Even if we grant that ethics is an important area of study and reflection for individuals, some have argued that there is no basis for applying ethics to the world of business. According to this way of thinking, the two do not mix. The cynical view sees business operations as inherently corrupt and beyond redemption. In an era where the news headlines frequently feature corporations that have employed "off-the-balance-sheet," fake subsidiaries to deceive investors; accounting firms that hide financial irregularities; companies that rip off taxpayers by overcharging the government or charging for services never performed; senior managers who enrich themselves while they bankrupt their companies and impoverish their workers; inside traders who become multimillionaires through buying and selling stock on the basis of information kept from ordinary investors; companies apparently "buying" legislation through donations to public officials;

whistleblowers being treated badly instead of the wrongdoers they expose—it is easy to be cynical.

The hospitality industry is no different. Victor Posner, then the majority shareholder of DWG Corporation, which owns Arby's, was known for improperly enriching himself by running public companies as private preserves. Even after he was caught, it was found that DWG (since renamed Triarc Companies) was using company money to clean his private home and do his laundry.[1]

However, cynicism provides nothing constructive to the moral dilemmas we face. In fact, it feeds into the very problems to which it responds. The more cynical people become, the more open the atmosphere becomes to ethical improprieties, which then become a "way of life." A vicious circle sets in, and unethical practices and cynicism mutually reinforce each other. The most cynical societies are those that are the most corrupt. There are both practical and ethical reasons cynicism is not a productive response to the unethical practices you may see in the world around you. A much more useful response is to do what you can to see that practices that poison the business atmosphere are changed.

A much different argument is that business executives and managers have few, if any, ethical obligations to anyone other than their owners. Therefore "business ethics" is a lot of mumbo-jumbo, imposing inappropriate standards on businesses. The best-known exponent of this view was Milton Friedman, the conservative economist who is widely recognized for arguing that businesses have essentially no obligations other than to maximize profits for their owners or shareholders. Friedman argued that the only ethical responsibility of the corporate executive is to the company's owners. That responsibility is to "make as much money as possible while conforming to the basic rules of the society, both those embodied in law and those embodied in ethical custom."[2] Friedman also maintained that the only social responsibility is profit maximization, as long as you stay within the rules of the game, meaning that you compete openly without fraud and deception.

Friedman's argument is an interesting ethical one, but it does not avoid ethical questions. Instead, it strongly asserts one particular ethical viewpoint, the viewpoint that the single-minded pursuit of profit will result in the most ethically advantageous situation for all concerned. This may or may not be true, but it is an ethical assertion in either case. A number of writers have questioned Friedman's belief that pure selfishness of each leads to the best possible outcome for all. Even Friedman argued that business leaders, in addition to maximizing profits, must (1) obey the law and (2) follow ethical custom. We will deal with the relationship between morality and the law later. The addition of "ethical custom" could add a large number of responsibilities onto businesses. For example, does ethical custom require that companies adhere to any standards regarding a fair compensation of employees? Friedman apparently wanted ethical custom to mean very little, and he never referred to any business obligations that arise out of extra-legal ethical concerns again in his article. However, he did acknowledge that they exist, and we need to explore what those obligations are if we wish to arrive at acceptable standards for business conduct.

Another view that attempts to absolve business leaders and personnel from ethical obligations beyond maximizing profits is what Alex Michalos has called the "loyal agent's argument."[3] The argument is that a manager has to be a loyal agent of his or her employer, and therefore has a duty to serve the employer. The employer would like to have his or her self-interest served, and therefore the manager (and presumably other employees as well) has a duty to serve the self-interest of the employer in any manner that will further that self-interest.

There are a number of problems with this argument. It assumes that the loyal agent duty is the only duty of a manager or employee. Are there no limits to this duty? Are there no other duties? Are there no other stakeholders to whom you have any obligations, beyond the shareholders or owners of the company?

The loyal agent argument is morally suspect because it attempts to exempt a person from moral responsibility for his or her actions by hiding behind an organizational barrier. If there is no moral responsibility of individuals running an organization, and if by their very nature organizations are hard to hold morally accountable, this begins to look like an attempt to evade all moral responsibilities altogether. Particularly in the field of business ethics, where the temptation to cut moral corners for the sake of self-gain is great, it is important to be on the lookout for arguments that are simply rationalizations of self-interest that avoid normal ethical responsibilities.

Consider the following loyal agent example within the hospitality and tourism industry. Imagine that you sell tickets for the Daytimer's Cruise Line, owned by Jay McGill. Mr. McGill tells you that he needs money to make improvements on his boat. He orders you to charge 8 percent tax on all tickets, instead of the required 4 percent. If anyone questions this practice, he wants you to tell them that it's a special tourism tax. Mr. McGill plans to use the extra 4 percent for his boat improvements. By agreeing to the deception, you have become a "loyal agent." Is the deception ethical because you are loyally acting as the owner's agent?

Is It Enough to Obey the Law?

Some argue that the only ethical or moral norm a business needs to follow is to obey the law. That is, as long as it is not illegal, it is okay. This is a fairly widespread attitude, but it runs into some real problems if you take it seriously. Equating the law and morality can lead to perspectives that do not seem to square with our ethical views. First, as we have already noted, there are times and places where the law has condoned and even required immoral behavior. The pre–Civil War laws in the South of the United States upheld slavery and required people to turn in runaway slaves. We now know that this was absolutely immoral. In Nazi Germany, anti-Semitic behavior was required, and some non-Jewish Germans were even put to death for speaking out against the Nazi atrocities or for attempting to protect the Jewish population from slaughter. As recently as 45 years ago, the so-called "Jim Crow" laws in the southern United States required racial discrimination, and a black man would sometimes be lynched for simply looking at a white woman or for failing to show a submissive enough attitude toward white people in the street. Even in a democracy, laws can occasionally get off the track morally.

Beyond the extreme examples cited above, legality cannot be equated with morality because many of our laws have little to do with morality. They are actually conventions, or rules, that make our lives more orderly or convenient, but they lack any important moral content. A good example would be the parking laws of a city. There is nothing distinctively moral about this form of regulation, but it does make our lives more orderly. A code regulating upkeep of front yards is a further example. A law declaring a certain day to be a national holiday is another. While all of these may be considered moral issues in the same extended sense that almost everything one does as a human being may have some remote moral consequence, in general, these matters are not considered moral ones, but rather matters of convenience. Just like proper etiquette or good manners are perhaps not serious enough matters to be considered deeply moral, the same is true for many laws.

Equating legality with morality is also faulty because something may be legal but immoral. For example, there is nothing in the law in the United States preventing an employer from firing for no reason whatsoever an employee who has faithfully and loyally done a good job for 15 years. You can fire an employee simply because you found out this morning that he is a cousin to somebody you detest. You can fire people because their new contact lenses make their eyes look brown, and you do not like brown eyes. This freedom to fire is known as the legal "employment-at-will" doctrine; only certain types of hiring and firing discrimination (on the basis of race, gender, skin color, national origin, handicap, etc.) are illegal. Consider the front desk agent who has been a loyal employee for many years. A new general manager would like a job for his nephew. There is nothing in the law preventing the manager from hiring his nephew and firing the long-term employee.

Legal though it may be, the morality of firing a good, long-term, loyal employee for no reason whatsoever (or for a reason that has nothing to do with his or her job performance) is highly questionable. We would say that such a firing, although legal, is unethical or immoral. Similarly, if for some bizarre reason an employer decided in times of layoff to terminate the most needy employees with the largest families first, we would find this to be contrary to our ethical or moral standards, even though it is perfectly legal, absent a union contract or a written policy stating that layoffs will be in order of seniority or some other more rational criterion.

While legality and morality are not identical, there is obviously a large overlap. A good number of our more strongly held moral beliefs are written into law, making their violation a transgression of both our moral standards and the law. Laws everywhere make a number of immoral actions illegal, including murder, rape, assault, theft, fraud, etc. Nonetheless, while some unethical practices and forms of behavior are illegal, not all are, and the law probably cannot be made so detailed that it makes all immoral practices illegal.

Is Ethical Behavior Good for Business?

The distinction between legal and ethical standards suggests the need to categorize different realms of business activity. A useful set of categories for the responsibilities of businesses has been developed by Archie B. Carroll.[4] Two categories are fairly obvious and widely recognized: *economic responsibilities*, whereby the business must achieve satisfactory financial results (for example, make a profit), and *legal responsibilities*, whereby the business must abide by the nation's laws and regulations (for example, pay taxes). *Discretionary responsibilities* are responsibilities that a company may elect in order to meet the expectations of some of its customers or a particular element in society. An example would be philanthropic activities, whereby a company chooses to give to the arts or to donate to certain charities in the local community. A good example of this is the Ronald McDonald House. Beyond these three categories are *ethical responsibilities*, whereby society expects compliance with norms of behavior that may not be written into law but are, nevertheless, necessary for the business to operate properly.

It can be argued that well-managed businesses meet or exceed expectations at economic, legal, and ethical levels. However, there is much debate about whether there might be a conflict of interest between doing well in one area and doing well in another. Some writers stress the potential conflict between the need to do well economically and doing well ethically (or sometimes, even legally). Supporting this view are well-known cases such as Enron, which made itself one of the most economically successful businesses in the United States (at least temporarily), powering a phenomenal ride to the top by massive fraud and other unethical practices. Adelphia, WorldCom, and other businesses that were spectacularly successful economically, until caught in unethical and probably illegal behavior, add further support. A well-known case in hospitality and tourism involved the 2002 Winter Olympics. In their successful bid to host the winter games, Salt Lake City employees bribed Olympic officials with cash and benefits amounting to almost $800,000. After the scandal broke, their defense was that they were "playing by the unwritten rules" for Olympic site selection.[5]

All too often, we see companies and individuals making a lot of money by engaging in practices that seem to contradict our ethical beliefs. We need to ask if being ethical is "good business." Does an ethical approach to business lead to financial success? Those who have looked at this question do not have a definitive answer.

We know that most businesses must abide by at least some minimal legal and ethical standards or we could not conduct business with each other. If all companies routinely lied, cheated, and deceived, commerce would grind to a halt. No one would trust anyone: promises would not be kept, checks would not be accepted. Billing would be impossible because invoices would likely not be paid. Banking would be impossible because bank officials would likely run off with customers' deposits. Loans would never be made and so on. All transactions would have to occur instantaneously, with cash changing hands at exactly the same time that goods or services are delivered.

Therefore, businesses have to abide by certain basic rules of conduct if the system of business is to work at all. Underlying those basic rules of conduct are ethical practices regarding honesty, respect for other human beings, and the like. So, a case can obviously be made that at least minimal standards of ethical behavior are built into the very business practices of a market system.

The difficult question is whether individual businesses (hotels, restaurants, airlines, etc.) or businesspersons can serve their own self-interests best by breaking some of those rules and violating accepted ethical standards. If it is a legal matter, and there are substantial penalties for breaking the law, companies and individuals will not be serving their best self-interest in the long run if they are caught because they will end up in jail and/or with stiff fines. But what if they do not get caught? Or, what if the law has such weak penalties that even if they do get caught,

Exhibit 1   Outcomes in the Prisoner's Dilemma Situation

	Other prisoner denies	Other prisoner confesses
You Deny	**You get one year in jail** Other prisoner gets one year in jail	**You get three years in jail** Other prisoner goes free
You confess	**You go free** Other prisoner gets three years in jail	**You get two years in jail** Other prisoner gets two years in jail

they come out ahead financially and do not go to jail? Even beyond the law, what if they can make substantial sums of money by engaging in deceptive or abusive practices that are not illegal?

In important ways, these questions address the relationship between our individual self-interest and our collective self-interest. The problematic nature of this relationship is posed by philosophers through a puzzle called the "prisoner's dilemma."[6] While there are a number of ways to illustrate the prisoner's dilemma issue, a standard example is as follows:

> Two men are arrested for committing a crime. Secretly, they promise each other that each will deny having committed the crime. The police department separates the two prisoners, and tells them both the same thing. If both men deny having committed the crime, they each will get one year in prison. If both confess, they each will get two years in prison. However, if one confesses while the other denies committing the crime, the person who confesses will be freed but the other will get three years in prison.

If you were one of the prisoners, what would you do? For the purposes of this exercise, put aside any feelings you might have for the other prisoner. You are only to think of your own self-interest; you are to do only what is best for yourself. What would you do? Economic theory for a market system like capitalism assumes that companies and individuals act rationally and strictly in their own self-interest. This theory assumes that all economic or business transactions are carried out for reasons of self-interest—not because we like each other or want to help each other. A for-profit restaurant or hotel, for example, serves its customers with the goal of making a profit, not because it "likes" those customers and wants to give them a gift or do them a favor.

For the purpose of working through the prisoner's dilemma, assume the same attitude. Think through the situation rationally; do what is in your own self-interest. Would you stick to your promise, cooperate with the other prisoner, and deny having committed the crime? Or, would you break the promise to the other prisoner, betray your fellow prisoner, and confess to the crime? To help you think through the alternatives, Exhibit 1 shows the outcomes of each possible decision.

Notice the outcomes for you (printed in bold in Exhibit 1) if you keep your promise and deny committing the crime. In that case, you will get either one year in jail or three years in jail, depending on what the other prisoner does. Notice the outcomes if you break your promise and confess to the crime. You will either go free or get two years in jail. In both sets of outcomes, you are better off breaking your promise, betraying the other prisoner, and confessing to the crime. This holds true no matter what the other prisoner does. You will be worse off, of course, if the other prisoner betrays you and confesses—in that case, you both get two years in jail. Two years jail time beats three, and those are your only two alternatives if the other prisoner betrays you.

Notice that collectively your interests and those of the other prisoner are best served if you both keep your promise to each other and deny having committed the crime. In that case, the collective jail time is two years. If just one of you breaks the promise, the collective jail time goes up to three years; if both of you break the promise, the collective jail time goes up to four years. But the picture changes considerably if you look only at your individual self-interest. From that viewpoint, if you are going to act rationally, you should break the promise and confess.

The prisoner's dilemma is a classic situation where self-interest seems to contradict the collective, or general, interest. If you think about it, we encounter dilemmas similar to the prisoner's dilemma all the time. In general, we would all be better off if everyone followed ethical principles (do not cheat, do not lie, do not steal, do not take advantage of others when the opportunity arises, etc.). However, numerous occasions arise when we can benefit or enrich ourselves if we break those principles while, at the same time, expecting others to adhere to them. Is the prisoner's dilemma example telling us that a rational, self-interested individual should behave unethically in business whenever he or she gains from the behavior?

Perhaps that is not the proper conclusion to draw from this exercise. In most situations, we deal with others (people or businesses) on a repeated basis. Therefore, there are usually additional consequences, beyond the most immediate one, of our actions. If, in fact, unethical behavior causes your restaurant to lose repeat customers or causes suppliers, employees, or lending institutions to shun or sabotage your business because of its bad reputation, even your narrow individual self-interest might very well be best served by your behaving in a more ethical manner.

There is a lot of general evidence showing that reputation and trust count for a lot in most business situations.[7] Treviño and Nelson state it succinctly: "Trust is essential in a service economy where all a firm has is its reputation for dependability and good service."[8] In the case of customers, this is almost so obvious that it hardly bears repeating. Customers who feel abused by a company will very likely avoid doing business with that company in the future. Other stakeholders can also damage a business when they perceive that business to be unjust or immoral. Employees, for example, who believe that their employer engages in unjust decision-making may retaliate through lower productivity, higher absenteeism, higher tardiness and turnover, and demands for higher wages.[9] While there is less research into the behavior of creditors or suppliers, it makes intuitive sense that they too will avoid dealing with a company that they consider to be unethical. Trust is perhaps an underrated ingredient in business relationships. A business that is unable to establish a strong sense of trust with customers, employees, and others faces a large number of obstacles to financial success. Companies that rely on repeat customers and a stable staff will find it important to establish the greatest degree of trust possible with them.

Moving beyond relationships with customers, employees, creditors, and suppliers, it would seem that companies that are perceived as socially responsible are rewarded by investors, and those perceived as socially irresponsible are punished. A number of studies address corporate social responsibility and its relation to financial performance or performance on the stock market and they reach mixed results.[10] While the largest number of studies finds a positive correlation between socially responsible behavior and enhanced financial or stock performance, others find no impact at all. A few studies even find a negative relationship between social responsibility and financial success.

From all of these studies, the most one could say is that a number of them show a correlation between high profitability and socially responsible behavior. However, we must be careful in concluding that high ethical and "social responsibility" standards inevitably or consistently lead to higher profitability. The line of causality could run either way, or perhaps some third factor we have not considered leads to both high profitability and high ethical and socially responsible behavior.

Ethical behavior does not always lead to higher profits in the short run and, in some cases, perhaps not even in the long run. In our view, it depends a great deal upon whether a particular business relies on repeat customers or continuous relationships with other elements in the productive business cycle. Some businesses, including some in the hospitality industry, may be able to do just fine financially without relying on repeat customers or other ongoing relationships. If that is the case, perhaps unethical relationships will lead to the highest profitability. For example, let's assume that the Broadway Restaurant offers all show-goers a discount coupon in their playbill for 20 percent off their dinner entrées. However, when guests show their coupons, they are handed overpriced menus. All prices are inflated by 30 percent, giving the owners a hefty profit. The restaurant might be able to sustain this marketing and pricing strategy if the vast majority of show-goers are out-of-towners.

Most hospitality businesses rely on repeat business and word-of-mouth recommendations to be profitable. While this provides financial support for ethical behavior, a more productive view would be to discourage thinking about ethics solely in the context of financial success. If the only reason to be moral is that it pays off financially, people will abandon ethical behavior when it becomes apparent that more money can be made by the unethical route. We want to encourage the view that ethical accounting is a separate endeavor from financial accounting. Ethics is a sphere separate from finance, and it should be taken seriously—not just because it might lead to greater profitability, but because ethical behavior is important in its own right.

Moral Responsibility

In the event of unethical behavior, who is to blame? Are superiors to be held responsible for the unethical behavior of their subordinates? Are subordinates to be held responsible for carrying out unethical orders from their superiors? Are you responsible even if you can't do anything to prevent the unethical behavior? What if you weren't even aware of the unethical behavior? Is ignorance a defense against responsibility?

It would seem that you are not responsible for a morally reprehensible action if you are unaware of it. You should not be held responsible for something you do not know about. For example, if a restaurant cashier steals, and does an excellent job of covering up, the dining room manager might not be held responsible for the theft. However, there are limits to a defense of ignorance. If you deliberately keep yourself ignorant of something in order to avoid responsibility, you are not blameless. Consider the corporate executive who instructs underlings to not tell him about the results of studies that reveal damaging health effects of the corporation's product. He doesn't want to know because he doesn't want to be liable if the product turns out to be unsafe. Or, consider the restaurant owner who doesn't want to know about the "catch-of-the-day." Does it come from reliable sources where the waters are inspected and verified as safe, or is the catch made by local fishermen in unsafe waters? Deliberate ignorance with the intent to avoid responsibility excuses no one. Additionally, carelessness about keeping yourself reasonably informed about the consequences of your (or your company's) products or actions is also blameworthy. The degree of responsibility would probably depend on the degree of carelessness; extreme carelessness has no excuse at all.

The inability to do anything about an unethical situation could absolve one of responsibility for some morally unacceptable actions. We cannot be made responsible for something over which we have no control. In each situation, of course, there may be a dispute about whether the person could have done anything about the unethical action. Inability has to be proved, not simply asserted. A good example of this would be overcharging hotel guests. Consider a front desk agent who was fully aware that a guest had been overcharged but did nothing to correct it. The agent later claims he or she was unable to make amends. The claim might cite computer program restrictions, or company policy, or a supervisor's strict instructions. Whatever the claim, it would have to be verified before we could find the front desk agent blameless.

There are also circumstances that might lessen our responsibility. We call these "mitigating circumstances." An example would be a situation in which we are unclear or uncertain about the effects of our action, and this uncertainty is at least somewhat reasonable. Another would be a situation in which it is difficult, but not impossible, to do something to correct a morally suspect activity. A third would be a situation where the individual's involvement was minimal, or was far removed from the center of the wrongdoing. In all of these cases, we would say that the person is not blameless, but his or her responsibility is diminished compared to what it would be without the mitigating circumstances.

Within business organizations, assigning moral responsibility for actions becomes complicated by the chain of command. How much blame does a subordinate bear if he or she carries out clearly unethical practices, but does so under the orders of a superior? Is the excuse, "I was only following orders!" a sufficient defense of such behavior?

Imagine that Jane works for Vacationesque, a company that sells timeshares by telephone. Jane's boss, Harvey, instructs her to claim that all vacations are in four-star hotels, when the hotels are really all three-star properties. If the company is legally cited, can Jane claim, "I was only following orders" as her defense?

At best, the argument "I was only following orders" might be a mitigating circumstance. However, the claim cannot absolve you entirely of responsibility for carrying out something that you clearly knew to be immoral. The severity of the moral infraction increases as the degree to which the claim operates as a legitimate mitigating circumstance diminishes. As Manuel Velasquez puts it:

> Moral responsibility requires merely that one act freely and knowingly, and it is irrelevant that one's wrongful act is that of freely and knowingly choosing to follow an order. For example, if I am ordered by my superior to murder a competitor and I do so, I can hardly later claim that I am totally innocent because I was merely "following orders." The fact that my superior ordered me to perform what I knew was an immoral act in no way alters the fact that in performing that act I knew what I was doing and I freely chose to do it anyway and so I am morally responsible for it.[11]

While subordinates do not escape moral responsibility for their behavior simply because they are within a chain of command, it is clear that the larger responsibility falls on decision-makers. For example, a housekeeper does not escape moral responsibility when knowingly stocking guestrooms with shampoo purporting to be a name brand product that actually is a falsely-labeled cheaper product. However, greater moral responsibility for this act of deception resides with the corporate manager who decided to implement the practice throughout the chain's many hotels to achieve a higher profit.

Making Ethical Decisions

What is the basis upon which we make moral or ethical decisions? Many would answer, "The values and rules I was taught as a child." That may or may not be a good basis for moral decision-making. It would depend entirely on the moral understanding of whoever taught you as a child. For some, doing as they were taught as children could mean repeating the moral lapses and mistakes of the adults who taught them. While it may be a good bet that one's parents and other caregivers had good moral values, it is wise to examine for yourself what you believe. Unthinking adherence to someone else's rules is not a smart strategy for living your life. We do, and should, use our moral upbringing as a standard to measure the morality of different actions, but we should not simply leave it at that.

Religion and religious beliefs are another basis for making moral or ethical decisions. The world's major religions have a strong moral or ethical core to them and undoubtedly provide guidance for moral conduct. But this does not automatically resolve all ethical dilemmas. For example, religious teachings can often be applied in many ways, so simple adherence to a religious belief or religious institution may not give absolute answers to all moral questions. Many religions have multiple denominations or branches because of differences over how a commonly followed sacred text is to be understood. A number of the differences between branches or denominations of a particular religious tradition may concern weighty moral issues, such as the morality of war, what constitutes justice for the less fortunate, the morality of abortion, and the like. So, even if you follow a particular religion, you still must determine *how* to follow it and what its teachings really mean in your life. If you do this, you will inevitably be undertaking moral reflection, and you will be thinking carefully about the moral basis for your life. Simply being a devout member of a certain religious tradition does not absolve you of the moral responsibility to think through for yourself the basis of your ethical views.

Feelings are often given as a basis for moral decision-making. Many claim that if it feels good or right, it is moral; if it feels bad or wrong, it is immoral. A "gut check" is probably a good idea when you are faced with an ethical dilemma, but it is doubtful that mere feelings are enough to provide a solid basis for making ethical choices. Feelings are notoriously fickle; they change all the time. Can it really be true that the morality of something changes with your mood swings? Your choice is a moral choice at one point, when you are feeling euphoric and happy about it. Is it possible that it could suddenly become immoral a few minutes later when you feel shamed and remorseful?

Our feelings are an important part of making ethical or moral decisions, but they are inadequate as the sole basis for such decisions. It does not take long to see that this is true. If a person has no conscience and therefore feels perfectly fine about defrauding or abusing other human beings, does their lack of the feelings of shame or remorse make the abusive or fraudulent behavior acceptable? Very few would answer, "Yes."

Some of the world's greatest minds have thought deeply on the moral basis for our actions. Over time, the most influential perspectives have been debated and refined into a few ethical schools of thought. In this book, we will consider the major theories that have lasted through the ages. Each theory is worth serious consideration, because each connects in some fundamental way with our ethical understanding of the world. The four theories we will consider are:

- Utilitarianism

- Kantian ethics

- Justice ethics

- Virtue ethics

These theories have considerable agreement concerning what is morally right or wrong, but there are also areas of disagreement. While the overlap among the theories is interesting and encouraging, it is also important to note the ways in which these theories differ from one another. The next four chapters will explain each theory, noting apparent strengths and potential weaknesses. The rest of the chapters model the kind of analyses you can take to a variety of ethical situations specific to hospitality and tourism. At the end of these chapters, short case studies are provided for your own analysis. A deep, thoughtful consideration of ethical issues can make us all more aware and better able to make wise decisions in the world of work.

Endnotes

1. Steve Brooks, "At the Trials of Chairman Posner," *Restaurant Business,* May 20, 1992, p. 88.

2. Milton Friedman, "The Social Responsibility of Business is to Increase Its Profits," *The New York Times*, September 13, 1970. Reprinted in Shari Collins-Chobanian, ed., *Ethical Challenges to Business as Usual* (Upper Saddle River, N.J.: Pearson/Prentice Hall, 2004), pp. 224–229.

3. See Alex C. Michalos, *A Pragmatic Approach to Business Ethics* (Thousand Oaks, Calif.: Sage Publications, 1995).

4. The following categories are taken from the work of Archie B. Carroll. See Archie B. Carroll, "A Three Dimensional Conceptual Model of Corporate Performance," *Academy of Management Review*, 4, (1979), 497–505. See also Archie B. Carroll, "The Pyramid of Corporate Social Responsibility: Toward the Moral Management of Organizational Stakeholders," *Business Horizons*, 34 (4), (1991), 39–48.

5. *Economist*, January 30, 1999, pp. 42

6. For more on the "prisoner's dilemma" problem, see Anatol Rapaport and A. Chammah, *The Prisoner's Dilemma* (Ann Arbor, Mich.: University of Michigan Press, 1965). For a view of the large volume of research that has been done on the prisoner's dilemma, see William Poundstone, *Prisoner's Dilemma* (New York: Doubleday, 1992).

7. For a good summary of the research backing up this statement, see Manuel Velasquez, "Why Ethics Matters: A Defense of Ethics in Business Organizations," *Business Ethics Quarterly 6*, no. 2 (1996): 201–222.

8. Linda K. Treviño and Katherine A. Nelson, *Managing Business Ethics: Straight Talk About How to Do It Right*, 3d ed. (Hoboken, N.J.: Wiley, 2004), p. 43

9. For some of the research backing up this statement, see Robert H. Frank, "Can Socially Responsible Firms Survive in a Competitive Environment?" in David M. Messick and Ann E. Tenbrunsel, eds., *Research on Negotiations in Organizations* (Greenwich, Conn.: JAI Press, 1997). See also Robert H. Frank, *What Price the Moral High Ground? Ethical Dilemmas in Competitive Environments* (Princeton, N.J.: Princeton University Press, 2003).

10. For one overview of these studies, see Joshua Daniel Margolis and James Patrick Walsh, *People and Profits? The Search for a Link Between a Company's Social and Financial Performance*. Mahwah, N.J.: Erlbaum, 2001). An older review of previous studies, plus a study finding no impact one way or another, is Kenneth E. Alpperle, Archie B. Carroll, and John D. Hatfield, "An Empirical Examination of the Relationship Between Corporate Social Responsibility and Profitability," *Academy of Management Journal* 28 (June 1985): pp. 449–461. A positive correlation is found in Jean B. McGuire, Alison Sundgren, and Thomas Schneeweis, "Corporate Social Responsibility and Firm Financial Performance," *Academy of Management Journal*, 31 (December 1988): pp. 854–872.

11. Manuel Velasquez, *Business Ethics: Concepts and Cases* (Upper Saddle River, N.J.: Prentice Hall, 2002), p. 54.

Chapter Questions

1. What is the loyal agent's argument? Give an example of a loyal agent.

2. What is the difference between individual self-interest and collective self-interest?

3. What is the "prisoner's dilemma"?

4. Is it true that high ethical and social responsibility standards always lead to higher profits? Explain your answer.

5. When might you not be held responsible for unethical behavior?

6. What are mitigating circumstances? Give an example of a mitigating circumstance.

7. People often rely on their "gut reaction" when making a moral decision. Will a gut reaction help you make a moral decision? Why or why not?

Thinking Exercise

Have you ever been in a loyal agent's dilemma? What were the circumstances? What did you do? Would you make the same choice today that you did then? Explain your answer.

2

Utilitarianism:
The Greatest Good

Some ethical theories argue that the *consequences* of an action make it either moral or immoral. Thus, an action that leads to beneficial consequences is right or moral, and one that leads to harmful consequences is wrong or immoral. All theories of this nature are known as consequentialist theories, because of their dependence on consequences as criteria for moral rightness or wrongness.

The most influential consequentialist theory is known as *utilitarianism*. Utilitarianism takes its name from the concept of utility, meaning the use or benefits to be derived from an action or situation. In its most simplified form, utilitarianism holds that an action is morally justified to the extent that it maximizes benefits and minimizes harm or costs. Thus, the one moral thing to do in any situation is that action that can be reasonably seen to provide the greatest *net* benefit for all concerned, when the expected costs are subtracted from the expected benefits. To do something else is to behave unethically, and the more an alternative action maximizes net costs or net harm, the more immoral it becomes. The shorthand phrase often used to describe utilitarianism is that it calls for "the greatest good for the greatest number of people."

It is important to note that utilitarianism does not say that the moral action is the one that maximizes the benefits or happiness *of the person doing the action*. It must be the benefits and happiness of *all*—each person counts equally. Thus, any attempt to use utilitarianism to justify selfish behavior at the expense of the greatest good for the whole society would be a misuse of the doctrine. Another common misconception is the belief that utilitarianism takes into account only the *immediate* consequences of an action. This is wrong—utilitarianism clearly states that *all* consequences must be counted, and this includes both short-term and long-term consequences, to the extent that these can be foreseen.

This certainly seems to make a lot of sense because we generally approve of promoting the general welfare. But there are a number of questions that must be answered before we can be certain that this is a valid and workable ethical theory.

What Is the "Good"?

What is the "good" we are trying to maximize? If different people have different ideas of the "good," we will not get anywhere until we clear that up. Some argue that wealth is the "good." But others believe that wealth can be corrupting and is unworthy of being the ultimate aim in life. Some equate power with the "good." But again, many scorn power and believe that "the good life" has next to nothing to do with having power over others. Similar disagreements occur over other possible candidates for what makes the good life: fame, a good reputation, etc.

Utilitarians usually state that the greatest good means the greatest happiness. They back up this claim by pointing out that everybody wants to be happy—it is the one universal thing that everybody desires and agrees is a good thing.

So if everybody desires happiness, perhaps happiness is the universal good that provides a satisfactory criterion for determining what is ethical or moral and what is unethical or immoral. The moral thing to do is whatever maximizes happiness and minimizes unhappiness; the immoral thing to do is whatever minimizes happiness and maximizes unhappiness.

Jeremy Bentham: Pleasures and Pains

Jeremy Bentham (1748–1832), an English philosopher, is widely credited with founding utilitarianism.[1] Bentham argues that happiness and unhappiness are identical to the amount of *pleasure* or *pain* experienced. A life of pleasure is a happy life; a life of pain is an unhappy one. Bentham determines the morality of an action by measuring the quantity of pleasure and the quantity of pain it will produce. After the two quantities are determined and the smaller is subtracted from the larger, you can then measure it morally against other possible actions. The right (or moral, or ethical) action is the one that provides the highest *net* quantity of pleasure. The more net unhappiness an action produces, the more immoral it is.

A number of major objections have been made to Bentham's argument. First, it is difficult (if not impossible) to quantify or measure "units" of pleasure and pain. Thus, the system is unworkable. Second, it is argued that pleasure and pain are the wrong measures of happiness and unhappiness. For example, could it really be true that you would have a happy or a good life if you felt nothing but pleasure in an unthinking haze as you were hooked to a machine pumping heroin into your addicted body continuously over the course of a long life? What if you lived permanently in an elegant spa resort with no cares or worries, but also with no purpose or goals—just a seemingly aimless existence? Would either of these really be preferable to the life of a thinking, intelligent person who experienced more pain along with the less intense pleasures of a more normal life? Put another way, would you prefer the life of a satisfied pig experiencing pleasure after pleasure to the life of an intelligent human experiencing a greater degree of dissatisfaction and pain, but who accomplishes great things?

Defenders of Bentham answer these objections by noting that it may be difficult to quantify pains and pleasures, or to put a value on them, but it can be done—at least in an approximate way. In fact, it is done all the time in what economists and businesspeople call cost-benefit analyses. Hotels and airlines frequently do cost-benefit analyses to aid in decisions on whether or not to follow a particular course of action. Restaurants that offer "free entrée with purchase of another entrée" probably do so on the basis of a cost-benefit analysis. The cost of the second entrée may be quite small compared to the benefit to be gained from all the additional business (more customers, more spending on appetizers, desserts, drinks, etc.) that results from the special offer.

Insurance companies use a cost-benefit analysis when they try to put a value on intangible things (such as loss of companionship or loss of a family heirloom) to compensate those insured under their policies. Insurance companies also put a value on the loss of a limb, or even the loss of life. While this may be upsetting or repulsive to some people, defenders of the practice argue that it is inescapable if restitution is to be made for loss of a loved one or loss of particular body parts. So, in general, a defender of Bentham would probably say that quantifying all the pleasures and pains in life may be difficult, but it is not impossible in principle. We must simply do the best we can.

This may or may not be a satisfactory answer to the first objection, but the second objection, that "happiness" over the long run means much more than simply pleasure and the absence of pain, is more difficult to answer. Consider the *qualitative* difference between the life of a mentally handicapped adult who laughs continuously at simple pleasures but has no ability to think coherently about the world, and the pleasures of a thinking adult in control of his or her life. Wouldn't we find the life of the latter to be a "happier" life, in the long-term sense of being a "good life" or a "fulfilled life," than that of the former? Would a vegetative state of numerous pleasures and few pains (but little or no thinking) really be preferable to a thoughtful life full of both pleasures and pains?

John Stuart Mill: The Quality of Happiness

This objection to Bentham is a serious problem because most of us find some pleasures and pains to be *qualitatively* superior to others. Nineteenth century utilitarian philosopher John Stuart Mill attempted to answer this objection by incorporating into utilitarianism qualitative differences between pleasures. Mill states:

> It is better to be a human being dissatisfied than a pig satisfied; better to be Socrates dissatisfied than a fool satisfied. And if the fool, or the pig, are of different opinion, it is because they only know their own side of the question. The other party to the comparison knows both sides.[2]

This reply has not satisfied some critics of utilitarianism, who believe that the introduction of "qualitative" pleasures and pains undermines the whole attempt to reduce the good and bad things in life into interchangeable, tradable units. First, they would argue that we cannot really make a meaningful comparison between, say, the pleasure one person gets from watching a pornographic film with the pleasure another person gets from attending an Italian opera or reading a book of philosophy. Put another way, we cannot make a meaningful comparison between the pleasure one person gets from a gourmet steak dinner with the pleasure another person gets from a hamburger, milkshake, and french fries. There is no common unit of measurement that can quantify qualitatively different experiences of pleasure.

Second, they would argue that some things, such as freedom, human rights, justice, and life itself are more precious than any pleasures we could turn into quantifiable units. We should not be willing to trade these things away for a

certain quantity of pleasure, and any ethical theory that tells us to do so is deficient, say these critics.

Most modern utilitarians believe that Bentham's equation of happiness with
simple pleasure and the absence of pain is too narrow. Therefore, they either agree
with Mill by making qualitative distinctions between types of pleasures and pains,
or they view happiness as something more complex than a simple pleasure-pain
calculus. But they do insist that the maximization of human happiness (or human
benefits) and the minimization of human unhappiness (or human harm, or costs)
is the goal of morality. This is the essence of utilitarianism.

Strong Points of Utilitarianism

Despite the objections raised so far, utilitarianism seems to have a lot going for it
as an ethical theory. It makes sense that we have a moral duty to behave in ways
that create as many benefits for human society as possible, and to avoid as much
as possible the harms or costs to the entire society. We frequently justify actions on
this basis. So there is no doubt that utilitarianism has a strong hold on our moral
thinking and reasoning. Decisions are made every day on the basis of utilitarian
calculations, especially when there are trade-offs involved in doing one thing or
another. Should we spend scarce health care resources on buying an extremely
expensive kidney dialysis machine, or should those dollars be spent on flu vacci-
nations for a few thousand children in the public school system? In a hotel, should
we fix the refrigeration unit that seems to be acting up, or should we refurbish the
lobby? By calculating the net benefit of taking one course of action over another,
and then choosing the action that provides the greatest net benefit, we are clearly
using a utilitarian decision-making method.

A Major Criticism of Utilitarianism

There is another extremely serious objection to utilitarianism that many believe
makes it unacceptable as a complete basis for our moral thinking. This objection
is that utilitarianism would justify actions that violate other people's rights and/or
lead to injustices.

For example, consider a situation where a large family decides to enslave an
adopted 12-year-old child and force her to do virtually all of the labor in the family home. She is not allowed to step outside the family house, and is periodically
beaten for not working hard enough. She toils intensively for about sixteen hours
a day, seven days a week. She will not live long because of the overwork, and her
existence is miserable. However, ten family members live in ease and great comfort because of her hard work. They get immense pleasure and happiness from
the situation because they are freed from all work. They read books, develop their
talents, play games, and enjoy a comfortable life of interesting and fun pursuits.
In short, they live "the good life." But it is all done on the basis of enslaving the
adopted daughter.

The enjoyment of the ten family members, if it can be put into measurable
"units," may far outweigh the misery of the one enslaved girl when the units of
happiness and unhappiness are counted up. In this case, utilitarianism would

seem to condone such a family situation. Yet, it is clearly a violation of a person's rights and a great injustice. A person who is enslaved loses the right to control his or her destiny. He or she has lost the most basic human right—the right to be free. It also offends our sense of justice; slavery does not treat people in a just or fair manner. The slave is discriminated against and denied freedom for no morally justified reason. Slavery is inherently exploitative. It can never be morally justified because it denies basic human rights and is inherently unjust.

Thus, a very fundamental objection to utilitarianism is that it counts only the benefits and burdens produced by actions or by social arrangements, *but fails to take into account the distribution* of benefits and burdens. It therefore condones unjust situations where benefits and burdens are distributed unfairly. It also fails to take into account individual entitlements to basic freedom of choice and to well-being, thereby approving violations of basic human rights.

This is a very serious objection, but utilitarians do not find it to be persuasive. One reply is that examples such as the one just given are fanciful and not accurate to any real life situation. A defender of utilitarianism could argue that the benefit to other family members is so small and inconsequential (a little more free time) that, even with their great numbers, the total additional happiness or benefit to them in no way counterbalances the horrible consequences to the enslaved child.

Furthermore, the *long-term* consequences, including indirect consequences, of such an arrangement would be extremely detrimental. Family members who can adapt to a situation of domestic enslavement of one of their own will become insensitive to cruel treatment in general, and will engage in such behavior elsewhere, further increasing the misery in the world and decreasing the sum total of human happiness. In fact, they would argue, the case is obvious: the enslavement does *not* bring about the greatest happiness for the greatest number. Therefore, it is immoral and would never be condoned by a full utilitarian investigation and moral judgment.

This answer may be satisfactory, but it is not clear to many that it will *always* turn out to be the case that violations of an individual's human rights lead to a net decrease in human happiness, or overall human benefit. Might there not be cases where the greatest happiness does come from unjust treatment, or from violating the rights of individuals?

Two Types of Utilitarianism

Some utilitarians have modified their system in an attempt to take more account of individual human rights and of our notion of justice or fairness. The modification distinguishes between the traditional form of utilitarianism that we have been considering, called *act utilitarianism*, and a second type called *rule utilitarianism*. Recall that the traditional form of utilitarianism (act utilitarianism) applies the "greatest good" principle to *individual acts*. Rule utilitarianism applies this principle not to individual acts, but to *moral rules of conduct*.

According to rule utilitarianism, we need to look at which moral rules lead to the greatest happiness for the greatest number. What would the consequences be if everyone were to follow a certain moral rule? If universal acceptance and adherence to the rule would lead to the greatest happiness for the greatest number, it is a justified moral rule and we all should follow it. If we do that, it is argued, we will never justify injustices or violations of human rights.

To see why that is so, consider the child slavery example we have just noted. Which of the following general rules would lead to the greatest happiness for the greatest number: (1) People are allowed to enslave other human beings; or (2) People are forbidden to enslave other human beings? Rule utilitarians would argue that the answer is obvious. As a general rule, Rule #2 will obviously lead to the greater good (more happiness) than Rule #1. Therefore, we must all follow Rule #2.

Rule utilitarians thus answer the objection that utilitarianism fails to account for individual rights or for our notions of justice by limiting the utilitarian calculus of happiness and unhappiness to *the moral rules by which we live, not to individual actions.* And, they argue, we will see that the best rules (that is, the ones that lead to the greatest happiness) are invariably those that respect individual human rights and build in fair and equal treatment of everyone. Individual exceptions, such as a family wishing to enslave or mistreat an adopted daughter, are not allowed because the *universal* adoption of enslavement would definitely lead to less happiness and more unhappiness.

Critics are not necessarily satisfied with this argument. They have two objections. First, they argue that it is not necessarily clear in all instances that rules requiring respect for individual rights or fair and equal treatment of all *do* lead to the greatest quantity of happiness. And if they do not, a utilitarian would condone violations of individual rights or injustices. The critics argue that respect for human rights and just treatment of others is right regardless of the impact on happiness or unhappiness. In other words, they challenge the claim that maximum happiness is the *ultimate* moral goal: human rights and fair treatment are *independent* moral goals that are more important than even happiness.

Second, some critics argue that rule utilitarianism is really no different from act utilitarianism. To understand this objection, ask the following question: do the moral rules in a rule utilitarian system allow for exceptions in some circumstances? If they do (for example, if we adopt the rule, "People are forbidden to enslave other human beings, *except in those cases where the sum total of human happiness is increased by the enslavement,*") we are right back to act utilitarianism. People will still have to sum up the happiness and unhappiness resulting from each act of enslavement, and decide the morality of it on that basis. This is no different from act utilitarianism.

On the other hand, not allowing exceptions to the rule would undermine the very basis of utilitarianism. For example, not allowing any exceptions to the "no slavery" rule might lead to a situation where the greatest happiness for the greatest number of people is not achieved, since exceptional cases may occur where enslavement does lead to the greatest quantity of happiness.

Thus, some critics contend that rule utilitarianism is either act utilitarianism in disguise or an abandonment of utilitarianism altogether. The rule utilitarian who does not allow exceptions to general moral rules will argue, of course, that utilitarianism has not been abandoned, merely modified and applied at the level of *rule-making* rather than the level of *acting.*

Utilitarianism: A Summary

As you can see, there are many controversies surrounding utilitarianism as an ethical system. However, utilitarianism is a very powerful ethical system that fits quite well with many of the ways we make moral decisions. Very few would want to argue that unhappiness is better than happiness, for example. And most would agree that every person's happiness counts equally, so our attempts to promote happiness must take everybody impartially into account, not simply our own individual happiness.

However, there are two major objections to utilitarianism, as we have noted. One is that it attempts to turn everything into a measurable value, and therefore does not deal well with values that are difficult to measure. Are some types of pleasure or happiness *qualitatively* better than others? If so, can this really be accounted for in the utilitarian system? Second, it does not seem to deal well with situations where individual rights or justice matter, although some utilitarians have tried to fix this problem by applying the "greatest happiness" or the "greatest good" evaluation only to rules, not to individual actions.

Now that you are familiar with the arguments for and against utilitarianism, you should think these arguments through and decide if it is a satisfactory ethical system to guide your conduct. Before you can completely make up your mind, however, you should become familiar with other ethical theories.

Endnotes

1. See Jeremy Bentham, *The Principles of Morals and Legislation* (Amherst, N.Y.: Prometheus Books, 1988). This book was originally published in 1789.

2. John Stuart Mill, *Utilitarianism* (1863). Quote taken from selection reprinted in Shari Collins-Chobanian, ed., *Ethical Challenges to Business as Usual* (Upper Saddle River, N.J.: Pearson Prentice Hall, 2005), p. 21.

Chapter Questions

1. When does utilitarianism consider an action to be morally justified?

2. What is the shorthand statement that is often used to characterize utilitarianism?

3. Who is the philosopher credited with founding utilitarianism? What was the argument that he used to determine the morality of one's actions?

4. What was the argument John Stuart Mill used to answer the critics of Bentham's version of utilitarianism?

5. A hotel manager wants to refurbish the dining room but also knows that the ceiling tiles in the hallway must be replaced because of a recently broken pipe (that is now fixed). What factors would make you choose one course of action over the other? Why?

6. Do you agree or disagree with the criticisms of utilitarianism? Explain your answer.

7. What arguments would a utilitarian use against slavery? How would a utilitarian argue for slavery?

8. What is the difference between an act utilitarian and a rule utilitarian? Which is superior to the other? Why?

Thinking Exercise

Apply a utilitarian analysis to ethical issues that arose in a work situation you have experienced. Describe the circumstances. What was the specific problem and how did you handle it? Did your solution coincide with a utilitarian solution? Explain your answer.

3

Kantian Ethics: Duties and Rights

IMMANUEL KANT, an eighteenth century German philosopher (1724–1804), developed an approach to ethics very different from utilitarianism in his famous book, *Foundations of the Metaphysics of Morals* (1785).[1] Kant argued that the consequences of an action are irrelevant to a moral evaluation of that action. Therefore, Kant is not a consequentialist, since he believes consequences to be morally irrelevant. Instead, Kant's ethical theory is a prime example of what we call a *deontological* ethical theory. "Deontological" is taken from the Greek word "deon," which means duty. Deontological ethical theories argue that actions are moral or immoral because of their very nature, not because of their consequences. For Kant, their nature stems from the type of rules they follow, and it is on the basis of the rule followed that we can morally judge an action.

It's the Motive that Counts

To understand this important difference between Kant and a utilitarian, consider the following situation. Two wealthy hotel owners give money to charity. One of them does it because he considers it his duty to do so, having been more fortunate in life than some others who are in desperate need. The other does it only because his name and picture will appear in the media, enhancing his status in the community. This owner seeks maximum exposure and makes sure that his giving is widely publicized. The first owner makes no effort to bring attention to his charitable giving, because he does not consider that relevant to his reasons for giving in the first place.

How would we morally judge the actions of these two individuals? Assuming that their wealth was similar and that their charitable giving was of the same magnitude, if they both gave to the same or similar charities and those charities did an equivalent amount of good for the poor and the suffering with those donations, a utilitarian would say that their actions are morally equal. Since they have identical consequences, they are of exactly the same moral worth. Kant, on the other hand, would say that their actions do not have equal moral worth. He would argue that the consequences of their actions (the good done by the charities with the money they contribute) are morally irrelevant. Instead, Kant would judge the actions of the first owner as moral, because they were done for the right reasons. The actions of the second owner have no moral worth even though they result in good for the world, because they were done for the wrong reasons. The actions of the first owner are by their very nature morally praiseworthy, while those of the second are not, because the self-serving motivation behind them changes their nature into simply another effort at self-promotion (which is not a morally praise-worthy action).

For Kant, it is the motivation behind an action that makes it morally worth praising or condemning. Moral actions are undertaken out of a sense of *duty*—which means you do it because you know that it is the right thing to do.

Actions that are undertaken simply because you enjoy them, for example, do not take on a moral character, even if they result in many positive benefits for others. We may be happy and appreciative when we receive excellent service in a restaurant. Our appreciation is not a moral appreciation. It is more like our appreciation for warm weather, or abundant resources, or other things that make our lives more comfortable but which we do not judge morally—positively or negatively.

What Is Our Duty?

If Kant is right that it is the motivation that counts, and if the motivation must be a desire to do what we feel to be our moral duty, how do we determine what is our duty? Kant argues that this can be derived from our unique nature as human beings. As human beings, we are uniquely rational in a way that all other living creatures on earth are not. We alone can reason, and our ability to reason requires us to be logical and consistent. To be logical and consistent, we have to be able and willing to make the basic rules by which we operate into *universal* rules that every-one could and should follow. If we cannot do that, we are illogical and inconsistent. Furthermore, Kant would argue, we are immoral, because we are not granting to other human beings the same freedom and the same status as a rational human being that we are claiming for ourselves. This general claim is the basis of Kant's ethical system. He formulated this claim in a couple of different ways, and it will be much clearer if we consider two of those formulations.

Categorical Imperative: First Formulation

Kant called his formulations of the basic rule of morality the *categorical imperative.* By an "imperative," he means a command that you must follow if you wish to be moral. By "categorical," he means that the command must be followed no matter what, not merely if it is convenient or if it has a certain set of consequences. There are no "ifs" to a categorical rule or imperative; it must be followed under all cir-cumstances. The categorical imperative is *the* rule, or command, that we all must follow at all times in all places under all circumstances if we wish to act morally.

According to Kant: "Act only on that maxim whereby thou canst at the same time will that it should become a universal law."[2] This means that you must act in such a way that you would want the rule you are following to be a universal one that everyone should follow. For example, if you want to cheat a guest and pocket the money, you have to be able to "will it" (or want it) that everyone cheats. If you want to break a promise (for example, a promise that room numbers will not be given out for any reason), you must will it that everyone breaks promises. If you want to commit robbery, murder, rape, or a number of other actions we think to be immoral, you must be able to will it to be the case that they are universally done.

Kant would argue that you cannot will it to be the case that such actions be universally undertaken. This is true, not necessarily because you would not like the consequences (although that certainly would be true), but because it would be self-contradictory and impossible to actually make these into universal practices. Universal breaking of promises would undermine the very meaning of making a promise, and thus it would destroy the entire practice of promise-making, and thus it is self-contradictory. The same is true for cheating, for deceptive practices, and for robbery, whose universal practice undermines the very meaning of owning property, etc.

Therefore, Kant contends that the categorical imperative supplies the universal rule, or command, that we all must follow to be moral. Those who are familiar with the golden rule (*"Do unto others as you would have them do unto you"*) have probably noticed the very close similarity between it and Kant's categorical imperative. While similar, they are not identical. The golden rule depends on which consequences you want, while Kant claims his categorical imperative does not (although this is a point of some controversy among philosophers). It may not be identical, but the categorical imperative is so close to the golden rule that there would be little, if any, difference in practice.

Categorical Imperative: Second Formulation

Kant has a second formulation of his categorical imperative that highlights another aspect of it. Recall that he derives the categorical imperative from the fact that human beings are unique among animals—we alone have reason and therefore we alone are able (and required) to act rationally. Only a rational creature capable of using reason to decide what to do (and what not to do) is capable of being truly free. Animals who live according to instincts are not free in the same way that we are, because they cannot use reason to freely choose their actions; they must blindly follow their instincts. But human beings, as rational creatures, are by their very nature free because their rationality allows them to contemplate alternative actions and to freely choose the one they will undertake.

Because of the unique status of human beings (i.e., of rational creatures), Kant asserts that they, and they alone, have *unconditional* worth. Every human being, and every human life, is unconditionally valuable in a way that mere objects or tools or plants and other animals are not. We feel free to use tools and objects with little regard to the impact on them. If I damage a tool when I do a job, I can simply throw the tool away and get another one. The tool itself has no moral claims on me, and I have not committed an immoral act if I use the tool merely as a means to accomplish some other end.

Kant asserts that it would be immoral to treat another human being that way. If I fail to see each human being as an end-in-himself or end-in-herself, I am denying that human being the freedom that he or she has by virtue of being a rational (and therefore free) being. I have degraded that person from the status of a human being to the status of a thing, and I have used that person in a manner that is both immoral and contrary to the categorical imperative, since we could not will it to be the case that all human beings degrade and use each other in this manner. Therefore, Kant comes up with a second formulation of the categorical imperative: "So act as to treat humanity, whether in thine own person or in that of any other, in every case as an end withal, never as means only."[3] This means that you must never use a person just for your own purposes. Instead, you must treat every human being as someone of independent moral worth, with an equal claim to freely decide his or her own life choices. To deny this freedom to all is to violate a fundamental duty we have to one another. It would be immoral, and it would be a violation of the first formulation of the categorical imperative since it would be impossible to will it to be the case that everyone universally "used" each other this way. Practical life would be impossible, and it would be a self-contradictory negation to further human (free, independent) life by denying a human being a free, independent life.

Kant and the Concept of Rights

Kant speaks frequently of the duty we owe to each other. The word duty has a counterpart on the other side: if I have a duty toward you, you have a right to demand from me that I fulfill that duty. Thus, the concept of "rights" follows easily from Kant's ethical system. As we have seen previously, utilitarianism seems to have a problem accounting for, or dealing adequately with, our notion of rights. But an ethical theory built on the concept of duty, as is Kant's theory, has no such problem.

What exactly is a right? When we say that someone's rights were violated, what do we mean? To have a right to something means to be *entitled* to it. Rights are individual entitlements.

We are primarily concerned with moral rights in this chapter, but the same meaning of an individual entitlement holds when we refer to legal rights. Legal rights are claims that an individual can make against others, based on the legal system. If I have a legal right to sell my hotel or to order you off my hotel property, these rights are granted by the government's property laws, and I can use the legal system to enforce those legal rights. When we refer to moral rights or human rights, we are referring to entitlements that are grounded in a moral code or system. Kant would say, for instance, that we all have a moral right to not be treated as mere things—we have a right to be treated as free, rational, independent, thinking beings.

Negative Rights and Positive Rights

A right is something that you are entitled to have others observe. Negative rights arise when others may be prohibited or forbidden from interfering with your ability to freely choose a certain course of action. An example would be the right to privacy. If such a moral right exists under certain circumstances, it requires that others observe a moral duty to leave a person alone in those circumstances, if the person wishes to be left alone. Another example would be the disposition of one's property. If I have an absolute property right over something, I have a right to buy it, sell it, change it, destroy it, or do as I please with it, free from external interference.

Negative rights require that we leave people alone to freely choose a course of action, as long as they respect the rights of others to equally choose freely.

The rights that require others to do or provide something are known as positive rights. Examples would be the moral (and possibly legal) right to work, the right to have enough food and shelter to survive, the right to adequate health care, the right to an education at public expense, and the like. Full-time hotel employees can expect to receive compensation and benefits that allow them to live at a decent level. These are examples of positive rights.

A person who has a positive right to something is entitled to expect others to undertake some action or to provide something, not merely to refrain from interfering with something being attempted. There is often controversy about positive rights—some say that there are no such rights at all or that they are very few in number. We will not enter into this controversy here, other than to note that in advanced industrial countries, at least some positive rights are generally conceded—for example, the right of all children to a free public education for a certain number of years, or the right of all citizens to get some type of health care, etc.

Kant's ethical system clearly imposes a duty to respect a number of negative rights. The categorical imperative requires that we treat each human being as free and equal in the pursuit of their interests. Therefore, assault, rape, murder, robbery, lying, fraud, extortion, cheating, and the like are all prohibited as interferences with the right to be treated as a human being (a rational creature) and not a thing. Also, freedom of speech, the right to privacy, freedom of association, and freedom of thought must not be interfered with for the same reason.

Kant's ethical system can also be plausibly interpreted to require respect for certain positive rights. As one philosopher writing on business ethics puts it:

> ...Human beings have a clear interest in being helped by being provided with the work, food, clothing, housing, and medical care they need to live on when they cannot provide these for themselves. Suppose we agree that we would not be willing to have everyone (especially ourselves) deprived of such help when it is needed, and that such help is necessary if a person's capacity to choose freely is to develop and even survive. If so, then no individual should be deprived of such help. That is, human beings have *positive* rights to the work, food, clothing, housing, and medical care they need to live on when they cannot provide these for themselves and when these are available.[4]

Strengths and Criticisms of Kant's System

At this point, we hope you see what a powerful, useful ethical system Kant's theory can be. It definitely coincides with some of our most deeply held moral beliefs: the sanctity of human life, the need to be impartial and to not make exceptions for oneself, and the duty we owe to others to treat each person as a person and not as a thing. It also explains our tendency to morally judge the actions of others on the basis of their intentions or motives, not merely on the basis of the consequences of their actions, as utilitarianism does.

Despite the strengths of Kant's system, it is not without its critics. One of the main criticisms is that it is very hard to apply to actual situations. It does not give us much practical guidance in the most difficult matters. A second criticism is that it may lead to conflicting duties, whereby observing one Kantian duty would require violating another Kantian duty. A third criticism, made by utilitarians, is that Kant's system is simply wrong in ignoring the consequences of actions when making moral judgments.

Applicability

Some critics claim that Kant's system does not really give us much guidance in most difficult situations. For example, suppose a restaurant manager is trying to decide the ethical policy to follow regarding provision of wages, tips, and benefits for each of the restaurant's front- and back-of-the-house employees. From Kant, we know that every employee must be given the moral status of an end-in-himself/herself, which means that each employee cannot be degraded to the status of a thing. Each deserves equal and independent moral status with unconditional worth. Clearly, that would rule out forced labor or paying people less than it requires to survive, but those are the obvious cases. How much provision of benefits is required? What wage is required? Inevitably there will be all kinds of trade-offs in making decisions of this nature, and critics claim that Kant is really not very helpful in making this type of decision.

A defender of Kant would reply that the application of any ethical system is never easy. We saw the same thing with utilitarianism in the objection that quantifying happiness (or benefits) is difficult, if not impossible. Despite the difficulty in making precise judgments for every situation, a Kantian could argue that the basic principles required by Kant's system are clear enough. For example, denying employees, especially the lowest-paid employees like buspersons and new servers, sufficient resources to live a life of freedom and autonomy is immoral. Exactly where to draw the line in terms of pay and benefit levels may be subject to debate, but the basic principle is clear enough.

Conflicting Duties

Kantian duties may conflict with each other. Kant's emphasis on rigid, unwavering duties irrespective of consequences seems to run into difficulties in situations where fulfilling one obligation requires not fulfilling another obligation. An example of this difficulty is the permissibility of being deceitful in certain circumstances. Suppose you know a couple and the husband beats his wife frequently, sometimes severely. One evening, she calls you in a panic and asks if she can stay overnight at your house. She says that her husband is on the rampage and is coming home shortly with the intention of beating her so badly that she fears for her life. You agree to put her up for the night. Later that evening, her husband shows up at your door in an apparent rage, asking if his wife is there. You are fairly certain that if you honestly reply that she is there, the husband will forcibly enter your house (which he will be able to do because he has superior force over whatever weapons or capabilities you have) and drag his wife away for at least a severe beating and possibly permanent injury or death.

Imagine a similar scenario, but placed into a hospitality context. You and Joyce both work at the Bedrock Hotel. Herman, the general manager, continuously sexually harasses Joyce. It gets so bad that Joyce begins to fear for her own safety. She starts looking for another job, but she makes you promise that you won't tell Herman. You promise. The next day Herman asks you, "Is Joyce looking for another job?"

Recall that Kant derives from the categorical imperative a clear rule against lying under any circumstances. Since you cannot make lying into a universal principle, you must always speak honestly. On the other hand, you have a duty to each individual to protect his or her humanity. That means you have a duty to the wife, or to your friend, or to a fellow employee, etc., to protect his or her freedom and autonomy. Certainly it means protecting the wife from imminent attack and possibly death. In either case, which course of action should be followed? Should you lie and tell the husband that his wife is not there? Should you lie and tell the boss that Joyce is not looking for another job? In both cases that would break one Kantian duty. Or should you tell the truth? That means breaking another Kantian duty.

The point of this exercise is to show that we can get into situations where fulfilling one duty requires breaking another. In real life circumstances, there are many such situations, and you can probably come up with a number of other examples. The argument against Kant is that his system provides no guidance when duties conflict with each other. His rigid, unwavering rules (such as a prohibition on lying) provide little leeway in situations with conflicting duties.

One possible reply by a Kantian is that the rule against lying would have to be reformulated in a circumstance such as the one stated above. Could we make it a universal rule that everyone could lie under those circumstances? Perhaps we could if we could determine that the duty to protect the life and well-being of others is more fundamental than the duty to not lie. Such an argument could be made by a Kantian, because the duty to protect life and health is more closely related to the fundamental core principle of the second statement of the categorical imperative: the duty not to deny the humanity (freedom and autonomy) of other human beings. Clearly, you are denying a person's humanity more if you allow them to be beaten and possibly killed than you are if you lie to someone.

This may be a satisfactory answer, but it certainly destroys the initial simplicity of Kant's system. One of the attractions of Kant's system is that it does not allow rationalizations and exceptions to basic moral rules all the time, unlike utilitarianism (at least act utilitarianism), which some claim allows too much leeway to rationalize away immoral behavior. If Kant were to allow numerous exceptions to the basic duties and rules derived from his system ("Don't lie," "Don't cheat," etc.), his system would slip back in the direction of less moral certainty and frequent moral ambiguity. Yet, this may be required if he is to satisfactorily deal with situations where duties appear to conflict with one another.

Are Consequences Irrelevant?

A final objection to Kant's model is that it is just plain wrong when it ignores the consequences of actions while making a moral judgment. Utilitarians, of course, make this criticism. They argue that Kant's emphasis on the rights of individuals goes too far, because it may lead to situations where the welfare of the society as a whole is being sacrificed. A Kantian, of course, would argue that the rights of the individual must be protected against the will of the majority, and that those rights are more precious than any amount of public welfare. This is an issue that appears to be a philosophical difference of opinion.

Libertarianism

Before we leave Kant, we should perhaps note some philosophers who operate from a "rights" perspective that is different from that of Kant. These philosophers, known as *libertarian philosophers*, believe that Kant is on the right track when he uses duties and rights as the basis of his system. However, they have a particular notion of rights that sets them apart. Libertarians accept Kant's claim that all human beings have a right to freedom and autonomy, and, therefore, they endorse negative rights, that is, rights against coercion.

However, libertarians deny that there are any positive rights. We have no obligation to provide anything to anybody else, in this view. Libertarians treat an individual's property as an extension of the person, so one's property is not to be interfered with, and attempts to do so constitute unethical coercion. Therefore, individuals of this persuasion oppose taxes as immoral coercion, since it is an involuntary taking away of one's property. They likewise tend to oppose governmental social welfare programs. They condemn governmental requirements that those with more money or possessions contribute the resources needed to provide for those with less. Any such requirement is seen as an immoral violation of the rights (property rights) of the wealthier person who is being taxed to support those with little or no income.

On a broader scale, this view argues that the only morally permissible transfer of money or possessions between people is voluntary exchanges, or voluntary giving. People can make a "contract" with each other, and agree to buy or sell property, but anything beyond contractual rights that involves the taking of money or property involuntarily would be seen as a violation of the owner's individual rights.

Libertarianism has a certain popular following. Milton Friedman, a well-known economist, expressed a mild version of it. Friedman argued that business executives have no obligation beyond the obligation to make the most money possible for the company's owners, as long as they abide by the society's basic laws and moral standards. Freedom is an attractive goal, and the libertarian claim to uphold freedom has an attraction for many.

Objections to Libertarianism

However, there are two major problems with libertarianism. The first is that it seems to ignore the fact that freedom for one person will mean constraints on others. Freedom for one inevitably means the loss of some kind of freedom for others. Thus, any particular freedom must be justified, since it implies restrictions on the freedom of others. For example, the freedom of a corporation (based on its property rights) to use its property to pollute the atmosphere is a restriction on the freedom (or right) of citizens to breathe unpolluted air, or to have healthy living conditions.

Another example would be a hotel with a disco that brings loud revelers through a residential area until very late hours. Which freedom takes precedence?

Libertarians have a difficult time answering this question. The answer that most people would approve (that our freedom to breathe unpolluted air takes precedence or that we have the right to a quiet environment after certain hours) may begin to unravel the entire libertarian argument. The more involuntary restrictions (particularly restrictions on property rights) that are allowed, the further we move from the state of affairs most cherished by libertarians—few or no restrictions on property rights.

The second problem with libertarianism is the extremely restricted view of freedom that it seems to have. In general, apart from freedom against aggression or bodily assault, the main freedom of concern to libertarians is the freedom to own and control one's property. But this is a very narrow view of freedom. For example, is a destitute individual who is starving to death really free, simply because he or she has the right to own property? This seems to be a very cramped view of what freedom really means. People need to be able to make meaningful choices and to have some power to carry out those choices if they are to be free. They must actually have some control over their lives in order to be free. The freedom to own property is not likely to guarantee every individual the power to make and carry out meaningful choices. It may for some, but it is highly unlikely to do so for all, which is what an ethic of freedom should be able to deliver.

What if the impoverished individual mentioned in the last paragraph is destitute because another set of individuals owns all the property in the area and refuses to let the penniless person have access to any of it? What if they refuse to hire this individual, hoard all the material goods in the area, and watch the needy person slowly die of malnutrition while they allow food and shelter to go to waste because they have much more than they themselves need? Is this really a picture of freedom?

A basic problem with libertarianism is that it conceives of human beings as not being social creatures. From this point of view, human beings have no obligations toward one another aside from those they assume when they form a contract binding them to certain obligations. Absent a contract, no obligations exist. This perspective certainly violates the Kantian perspective, which holds that each individual is owed the conditions necessary to obtain the freedom to choose and to develop his or her capacity to act freely. This would include respect for not only negative rights, but also positive rights necessary for self-development. A starving individual is hardly free to develop himself or herself. Therefore, Kant would find it legitimate that governments may impose taxes, impose limits on the use of property (like environmental regulations), and impose limits on contracts (such as minimum wage or anti-discrimination laws) when these actions are necessary for the welfare or self-development of those not able to support themselves otherwise.

Kantian Ethics: A Summary

Kantian ethics has a lot going for it. It seems to do a better job than utilitarianism does in accounting for individual rights and obligations we hold toward all individuals. It seems to be less prone to sacrifice the individual for the sake of the welfare of the greater society. But, it is not without its own problems. It can be very vague in providing guidance in many practical situations, and it may have a problem dealing with situations where rights seem to be in conflict. Despite these problems, Kant's ethical theory has had an enormous impact on modern thinking about morality.

Endnotes

1. See Immanuel Kant, *Groundwork of the Metaphysics of Morals* (New York: Cambridge University Press, 1998). This book was originally published in 1785. (Note also that different translations of this book from the German original use different words for the first word in the title. In this book we follow some translators in calling it *"Foundations" of the Metaphysics of Morals,* while the translated version in this footnote calls it *"Groundwork" of the Metaphysics of Morals.*)

2. Immanuel Kant, *Foundations of the Metaphysics of Morals* (1785). Quote taken from selection reprinted in Shari Collins-Chobarian, ed., *Ethical Challenges to Business as Usual* (Upper Saddle River, N.J.: Pearson Prentice Hall, 2005), p. 32.

3. Immanuel Kant, *Foundations of the Metaphysics of Morals* (1785). Quote taken from selection reprinted in Shari Collins-Chobarian, ed., *Ethical Challenges to Business as Usual* (Upper Saddle River, N.J.: Pearson Prentice Hall, 2005), p. 33.

4. Manuel G. Velasquez, *Business Ethics: Concepts and Cases* (Upper Saddle River, N.J.: Prentice Hall, 2002), p. 101.

Chapter Questions

1. What is a deontological ethical theory?

2. The local humane society has just called you to ask for a donation. You agree to give a very large donation but only if they include you in their press release to the local newspapers. According to Kant, is this an ethical action on your part? Why or why not?

3. What does Kant mean by universal rules?

4. What is Kant's categorical imperative? How does it differ from the golden rule?

5. Kant states that we must never use a person just for our own purposes. What does this mean? Give an example of how this can happen.

6. What are negative and positive rights? Give examples of each.

7. Is dishonesty ever considered a moral action according to Kant? Explain your answer.

8. What does Kant mean when he says that the rights of the individual must be protected against the will of the majority? Explain your answer.

9. How does libertarian theory differ from Kantian theory? Explain your answer.

10. Why is Milton Friedman considered a libertarian? Explain your answer.

Thinking Exercise

Apply a Kantian analysis to ethical issues that arose in a work situation you have experienced. Describe the circumstances. What was the specific problem and how did you handle it? Did your solution coincide with a Kantian solution? Explain your answer.

4

An Ethic of Justice: Treating Others Fairly

Justice is a word often used when making moral judgments. We believe in justice and oppose injustice, but what exactly do we mean by terms like justice and injustice? Usually, we think of justice as *being fair*. Justice requires that we treat everybody fairly.

What does it mean to treat everybody fairly? In the first place, it requires that we treat like cases alike. Justice is a *comparative* term: it involves comparing cases and making sure that we are not discriminating or treating people differently who are alike in relevant respects. To a certain degree, our notion of justice is based on the notion of individual rights. A violation of an individual's rights is considered an injustice. This is certainly part of our conception of justice, but not all of it.

Aristotle, an ancient Greek philosopher (384–322 B.C.E.), divided the concept of justice into three types: (1) distributive justice, (2) retributive justice, and (3) compensatory justice. Distributive justice, perhaps the most basic kind, concerns the division of benefits and burdens among individuals. These must be distributed fairly. Retributive justice concerns what form of retribution or punishment should be imposed on someone who has done wrong. When we say, "The punishment must fit the crime," we are calling for retributive justice. Finally, compensatory justice refers to what kind and amount of compensation someone should receive if he or she has been wronged. Again, we tend to think that compensation should in some way be proportional to the degree of damage that has been done. The greater the wrong or the greater the damage, the greater should be the compensation.

Distributive Justice

Distributive justice requires that equals be treated as equals; like cases be treated alike. The tricky question is: in what respects are we equal, and in what respects are we unequal? No one argues that all people are exactly alike, or equal, in all respects. We have multiple ways in which we are different: different looks, different genders, different heights, different personalities, etc. For many purposes, we might say that these differences are irrelevant—we share a sameness simply because we are all human beings. For other purposes, however, certain differences may be relevant, and discrimination on the basis of those differences is entirely permissible. For example, differences of skill are obviously relevant to the performance of many jobs. A hospitality or tourism employer is perfectly justified in discriminating against those without the needed skills by hiring only those who have the proper skills for the job.

There is a long history of disputes over what distributive justice (fairness) requires regarding the distribution of benefits and burdens. What principles should govern how we distribute these? One candidate is the principle of *equality*, and those who strongly advance this principle are known as *egalitarians*. Egalitarians start with the basic principle that burdens and benefits should be equally divided among all. The ideal of equality has obvious appeal. The U.S. Declaration of Independence states, "All men are created equal." Societies with highly unequal distributions of income and resources are often criticized for such an arrangement, which is thought to be unjust. Equality of treatment of all persons tends to be a general goal of virtually all societies (especially the advanced industrial ones).

Despite the popularity of equality, it has been criticized as an inadequate basis for distributing benefits and burdens. An important criticism argues that it would be unjust to force total equality on people who are different in so many ways—ways that the critics argue are relevant to distribution of wealth or other positive goods, like power. For example, does it make sense to give exactly the same income to someone who works twice as long as another person at the same job, accomplishing twice as much? Or, to reward equally the industrious person who works hard and the lazy person who refuses to work at all or who works very little? Or, to not give greater medical resources to the very sick individual than we give to the person who is perfectly healthy?

Most egalitarians agree that some inequalities of treatment are justified. But they would argue that, at the very least, every human being is entitled to a certain minimum of income needed to survive at a reasonable standard of living, irrespective of any differences used to justify inequalities. Those who put a lower priority on equality would dispute this claim, of course.

A number of bases for differential incomes have been suggested. One is differential payment according to *effort*. If payment is according to effort, the lazy person will not be rewarded equally with the hard-working individual. In a society that believes in a strong work ethic, rewarding people according to their effort seems to make a lot of sense. However, reward according to effort runs into problems because it ignores the question of whether someone's efforts are actually producing anything of value. Should the person who tries very hard, but who produces next to nothing of any value, be highly rewarded? Most of us would say that effort alone is not enough: something of value must be produced by all that effort.

Another possibility would be payment according to *ability*. Those with greater abilities are likely to produce more of value. People with higher skills tend to be paid higher starting salaries, so there is no doubt that this criterion is used to some degree to determine compensation. However, some would argue that ability is a poor determinant of compensation because it does not necessarily translate into a greater contribution or a more meritorious claim on resources.

For some decisions, the criterion of *need* is used. This principle is built into most health insurance policies: the neediest draw the greatest medical resources, even if they have not put in the most through their insurance premium payments. Government assistance during disasters or assistance to those with disabilities or those unable to otherwise provide for themselves is often distributed according to principles based on need; the greater the need, the greater the assistance. On the other hand, private sector market relations ignore need almost entirely. An employee with a large family (and therefore great needs) does not get paid more than does a single individual doing the same work for the same employer but who has no family. A customer with greater needs generally does not get a discount price, etc.

Yet another possible criterion for determining payment is *productivity*. This is the standard that most private sector firms in a capitalist economy would claim they use to determine pay levels. A more productive employee is paid more; a less productive one less. This raises questions about how to measure productivity, especially in industries where the "product" is something like a service that cannot be easily reduced to units. How does one measure the productivity of a research scientist, an entertainer, an athlete, etc.? Also, if we used only productivity to decide income, can we ignore need entirely and allow the disabled and the mentally handicapped and others to starve to death because of their minimal or nonexistent productivity?

It is apparent that different principles of distribution are used in different contexts. The family, for instance, does not distribute its resources according to productivity. Children and the elderly who contribute no economic wealth are taken care of according to the principle of need. In a market economy like capitalism, distribution is determined by some measure of productivity. In a socialist economy, the goal would be to distribute burdens and benefits according to the famous dictum of Karl Marx (1818–1883): from each according to his (or her) ability; to each according to his (or her) need. Government programs often distribute burdens and benefits according to a changing array of the above factors, depending on the purpose of the program.

Clearly, no one of the above principles (total equality, distribution according to effort, ability, need, productivity, etc.) seems to provide a comprehensive, overall criterion by which we can determine a just, or fair, distribution of burdens and benefits. What is needed is a theory that would be applicable in all cases, one that provides clear guidance as to what is ethical and just.

John Rawls: Justice as Fairness

John Rawls, a twentieth century American philosopher (1921–2002), developed a comprehensive theory of justice that attempts to cover all situations.[1] Rawls argued that the only way to determine what is just or fair is to determine what would be accepted as fair by rational people who would consider all points of view. That is, people who could evaluate whether a particular arrangement or a particular action seems just—whether you are on the giving or receiving end, in the advantaged or disadvantaged position. If it seems just and fair from *all points of view*, it is. If it appears unfair from the point of view of the person who benefits least, it may be an unjust arrangement.

How can we actually look at things from the point of view of everyone? We all know our own position in society, so we will inevitably be looking at things based on what looks fair from our own perspective. To remedy this tendency to see things only from our own point of view, Rawls proposed the following arrangement: suppose people had to decide what are just and fair social arrangements and they had to come to unanimous agreement on what those are. However, the people making the decision will not know which position they may end up occupying in that society. Will you be the hotel general manager or will you be the room attendant? Will you be the restaurant cashier, the line cook, the executive chef, or the restaurant owner?

Each person may end up in the most favored or privileged position, but he or she may also end up in the least favored or most underprivileged position. Not knowing where they will end up, all persons will be forced to take the viewpoint of all the people in the society (or the hotel, restaurant, etc.).

According to Rawls, when people take this viewpoint, they will come up with a just or fair arrangement. They will do so because they will be concerned that their own interests are taken care of and the only way to ensure that is to consider equally everyone's interests and perspectives. From such a universal perspective, the agreements arrived at will be just and fair.

The Original Position and the Veil of Ignorance

Rawls called the position of people who do not know where they will end up in the society the *original position*. Those in the original position are operating behind what he called the veil of ignorance. The veil of ignorance means that people do not know whether they will end up being male or female, light-skin colored or dark-skin colored, more wealthy or less wealthy, able-bodied or disabled, young or old, more intelligent or less intelligent, more ambitious or less ambitious, highly skilled or less skilled, good looking or unattractive, a member of religion A or religion B, a supervisor or a laborer, etc. Thus, they will devise social arrangements (working conditions, for example) that do not discriminate unjustly against any of these groups. They will set up the rules and social arrangements that make sure each of these categories of people (and any other categories) are treated equally, unless their difference is relevant to unequal treatment (and acknowledged by all to be relevant).

Notice that Rawls assumed that people in the original position, operating behind the veil of ignorance, do have a few characteristics. First, they are all rational—that is to say, they will not act irrationally and intentionally choose to adopt rules that violate their own beliefs and interests. Second, they are self-interested. That means they will try to avoid consequences that could harm them. They are interested in their own well-being and their own survival. They will also know enough about society and social arrangements to know what the consequences would be of setting up society according to any particular set of rules. But beyond that, they will not know what their own ultimate characteristics or interests will be, and this will keep them from adopting rules that are racist, sexist, or any other type of "ist" that discriminates in an irrelevant (and thus unjust) way against a group of people.

Strengths of Rawls's System

Rawls's system certainly seems like a fair or just way to set up the rules by which a society or organization should operate. The very process used to arrive at the results seems to ensure that justice will prevail. If Rawls's theory is correct, it provides an important addition to either utilitarianism or Kantian ethics. Recall that one of the main objections to utilitarianism is that it does not provide for a just distribution of benefits—it pays attention only to maximizing the total amount of benefits while possibly ignoring the justice or injustice of how they are distributed. And, while Kant provides for individual rights, he says very little directly about justice or fairness in distribution.

The Basic Principles of Justice

What kind of rules would people adopt if they were in the original position, operating behind the veil of ignorance? Rawls argues that they would be extremely careful to avoid discriminatory consequences because each person would know that he or she may end up being the one discriminated against. As an example, we could use the laws that existed in the southern United States before the civil rights laws were enacted. Would those laws have persisted had the lawmakers not known previously if they were to be black or white? Probably not. People in the original position would assume that their worst enemy was assigning them their final place in society or in the institution whose rules they are deciding.

What principles would people choose under these circumstances? Rawls states that they would choose two basic principles. The first, which has come to be known as the *principle of equal liberty,* states that "each person engaged in an institution or affected by it has an equal right to the most extensive liberty compatible with a like liberty for all."[2] Rawls's second principle has two parts. It concerns the circumstances under which unequal treatment would be permitted. He argues that inequalities would only be allowed if:

(a) It is reasonable to expect that they will work out to everyone's advantage.

(b) The positions and offices to which they attach or from which they may be gained are open to all.[3]

Rawls identified principles (a) and (b) above as the *difference principle* and the *principle of fair equality of opportunity.* Each of these principles are explored in the sections that follow.

Principle of Equal Liberty

At a societal level, the principle of equal liberty means that the liberties of every citizen have to be protected equally, and cannot be infringed upon, even for the sake of greater overall social benefits. The basic liberties included here are such civil liberties as freedom of speech, freedom of religion, freedom from arbitrary arrest, freedom to hold personal property, and the like. Applied to businesses or corporations, this principle implies that it is unjust for a business to invade the privacy of employees, use its political and economic clout to influence legislation, pressure or force managers to engage in a particular kind of political activity, etc. All of these would be an unjust denial of equal personal and political freedoms to others. Likewise, our equal freedom to form contracts with others would be denied if others used force, fraud, or deception in business practices, or if they

Exhibit 1

Distribution A	Distribution B	Distribution C
Person 1 25	Person 1 30	Person 1 40
Person 2 25	Person 2 27	Person 2 28
Person 3 25	Person 3 23	Person 3 22
Person 4 25	Person 4 20	Person 4 12
TOTAL 100	100	102

refused to honor valid contracts. These practices are unethical and are a violation of the principle of equal liberty.[4]

Rawls argues that this principle of equal liberty would be chosen because everybody in the original position would want to protect his or her own civil, personal, and political liberties above all else. Therefore, this first principle takes priority over all others, since it is basic to all other processes that could lead to either just or unjust outcomes.

The Difference Principle

The difference principle requires that an inequality has to benefit the least advantaged as well as those who obviously benefit from the inequality. This means that *everyone* must benefit from the inequality, including the person being given less. How could that ever be the case? Perhaps a simple example will illustrate how this is possible.

Suppose some good or benefit is produced and distributed. Consider three possibilities of how this good could be distributed as shown in Exhibit 1.

Since utilitarianism aims for the greatest overall good, with little regard for how that good is distributed, Distribution A and Distribution B would be ethically identical from a utilitarian perspective. But from Rawls's perspective, A is clearly preferable to B, since the good is distributed more justly. This appears to be a clear difference between utilitarianism and a Rawlsian justice perspective.

The difference becomes even clearer when we consider Distribution C. Recall that utilitarianism aims for the greatest benefit for the greatest number. Since Distribution C produces more of the good (102 units) than either A or B, presumably it is the preferable arrangement from a utilitarian perspective. Yet, from a Rawlsian view of distributive justice, Distribution C cannot be justified. Not only is it worse than Distribution A, but it is also worse than Distribution B, because the least favored individual (Person 4) is being treated unjustly (he or she gets only 12 units of the good, compared to 25 or 20 under the other two arrangements.)

As a result, Rawls would say that Distribution A is ethically most justified, B is next best, and C is least justified. A utilitarian would say that C is ethically most justified, and A and B are morally equivalent since they each produce the same amount of good. Note that in picking A, Rawls is willing to sacrifice the most productive arrangement (Distribution C) because it unjustly distributes the good being produced and harms the least favored person (Person 4).

Exhibit 2

Distribution A	Distribution B	Distribution C	Distribution D
Person 1 25	Person 1 30	Person 1 40	Person 1 41
Person 2 25	Person 2 27	Person 2 28	Person 2 26
Person 3 25	Person 3 23	Person 3 22	Person 3 27
Person 4 25	Person 4 20	Person 4 12	Person 4 28
TOTAL 100	100	102	122

So far, we have been considering situations where greater inequality ends up hurting the least advantaged person. In these situations, Rawls condemns the inequality as unjust. But it is possible that greater inequality could be to the advantage of even the least favored person. Consider the possibilities shown in Exhibit 2. Distributions A, B, and C are the same as before. But, notice Distribution D. It is actually the *second most unequal* distribution of all four possibilities, since the difference between the least favored and the most favored is second largest (15 units). Differences are 0 for A, 10 for B, 28 for C, and 15 for D. Yet, despite this inequality, Rawls would endorse D as the ethically preferable situation, since the least advantaged (in this case, Person 2, even though it ended up being Person 4 in the other three examples), actually does better than the least advantaged in any of the other three situations. (The least favored gets 26 units, compared to 25, 20, and 12 in the other three examples.)

Therefore, Rawls's difference principle justifies inequalities, but only if the least advantaged person gains from the inequality. This is what people in the original position (behind the veil of ignorance) would choose because only this difference principle will protect them if they end up at the bottom of inequalities.

The difference principle extends well beyond simple distribution of whatever gets produced. It also applies to the broader practices of all major institutions in society. In the case of businesses, it asserts that business practices that harm the least advantaged are unethical. Since inefficiency and unproductive diversion of resources to those able to "corner" a market inevitably end up harming the least advantaged who are unable to monopolize markets, all anti-competitive practices such as price fixing and monopolization are unethical. So are environmentally degrading practices, since these practices again always end up costing our society's least advantaged citizens by diverting resources away from their needs to environmental cleanup. In addition, the poorest also tend to be the ones who end up most exposed to environmental hazards, again an injustice under the difference principle. So, polluting the environment for the sake of profit is unjust according to Rawls.

The Principle of Fair Equality of Opportunity

The principle of fair equality of opportunity states that everyone has to get an equal opportunity to obtain the most privileged positions and offices in society or in a just institution. This equal opportunity principle again makes sense to people in the original position operating behind the veil of ignorance. They want an equal chance at the best offered by society or the institution. They will not want to arbitrarily deny an opportunity to a particular group because they may turn out to be a member of that group.

The principle of fair equality of opportunity means that all forms of discrimination are unjust. But, it means more than just that. It also means that everyone must be provided the same opportunities to qualify for the best jobs and positions.

If the competition for good jobs can be compared to a competitive race, it is not enough to simply line everyone up at the same starting line and then claim that all had an equal opportunity to win. If some contestants have been given nutritious food and ample opportunity to train while others are denied the same, we cannot really say that they had an equal opportunity to win. Therefore, everybody must be given access to the training and education necessary to succeed in any competition for favored employment. Equal opportunity must mean equal treatment in all the prerequisites to success, so that any differences in outcome stem only from differences in ability or effort. This is a particularly important point for those who are poorest, because they frequently face numerous conditions in their lives that effectively deny them equal opportunities to rise to the top.

Criticisms of Rawls

Rawls's theory has won great acclaim and a great deal of attention from those who study ethical theories.[5] Despite widespread praise, Rawls has his critics, some of whom find his principles too "liberal" for their liking. Most of the criticism centers on the difference principle, which is seen as too friendly to the interests of the most disadvantaged people.

One criticism is that people in the original position (behind the veil of ignorance) would not choose the principles that Rawls claims they would. Some argue that people in the original position would choose to be much bigger risk-takers than Rawls allows. Perhaps they would choose much more unequal conditions that end up hurting those at the bottom, in the hope that they will be one of the lucky ones who end up in a favored position. If they are willing to take the risk, they might agree to quite unequal societies, far removed from the welfare state Rawls claims is the only just society that those in the original position would pick. Utilitarians, for example, argue that people behind the veil of ignorance would really choose arrangements that maximize overall social welfare (that is, utilitarian arrangements), not necessarily those that protect the most disadvantaged.

Other critics attack the entire notion of a veil of ignorance and an original position. They argue that such a position is not really possible, and that Rawls snuck his own liberal and humanitarian principles behind the ignorance veil, thereby giving a false legitimacy to what were really just his own preferences. Some believe he displayed a bias toward values specific to advanced industrial countries—people in underdeveloped countries would probably be happy to give up the liberties so precious to Rawls if they could gain greater material welfare, these critics argue. Others argue that the different liberties Rawls endorsed may clash with each other, and he gave no basis for how to decide between them.

Readers will have to decide for themselves if any of these criticisms have merit. Whatever the criticisms, Rawls exerted an enormous influence over the thinking of those concerned with ethics in the last 50 years.

Applying Rawls: An Illustration

Before leaving Rawls, let us examine a situation to illustrate his theory. Suppose a hotel chain is facing difficult economic times. The company's top executives have determined that they will have to cut back on their expenditures for pensions for the employees. How should the distribution of the size of the cutbacks be determined? For that matter, how should the size of pensions be determined in the first place?

Rawls would argue that principles of justice require that the company treat its least advantaged employees no less favorably than they do the most advantaged, unless the differential treatment can be shown to actually benefit those at the bottom. On the face of it, this concept of justice challenges the practices of many employers, who may cut back or even eliminate pension payments for their lowest-paid employees. At the same time, they may leave untouched or even increase the pension payments for the top executives.

In this instance, it may be possible to argue that, in fact, the lowest-paid employees actually benefit from this unequal treatment, even though it increases inequality. Such an argument might contend that, had the executives not protected their own pensions, those executives would likely abandon the company, causing it to fail and leaving lower-paid employees without any job at all.

If, in fact, the top executives are indispensable and if they will indeed leave for greener pastures should they be required to share the burden with lower-paid employees, this argument may be correct. However, all of these factual claims must be substantiated before this argument can be accepted, according to Rawls's theory of justice. Without proof that the "least" or the "lowest" benefits from the unequal treatment, such inequality cannot be justified. If taken seriously, this theory would force society and all of its institutions (including businesses) to examine and justify all aspects of any unequal treatment they practice.

Retributive Justice

Retributive justice addresses whether it is right to impose retribution (punishment) on someone who has done wrong, and, if a punishment is proper, what the proper retribution or penalty that someone should pay for that wrong is.

It is universally accepted that punishment can be justly meted out only after certain conditions have been met. First, it must be the case that persons who committed the wrong were aware of what they were doing and that they freely chose to do it. A new line cook who lights a gas stove and accidentally damages restaurant property by doing what he or she normally does on the job cannot justly be punished if the damage happened because of a gas leak that was not within his or her area of responsibility. The cook may have started a fire or a minor explosion but was not aware that he or she was causing a problem and could not have reasonably been expected to know this. Or if a cashier is forced to participate in an immoral act (stealing from the employer by handing over the day's proceeds at gunpoint), he or she cannot be blamed and punished for wrongdoing. Thus, ignorance or an inability to do otherwise excuses one from responsibility. Punishment under such circumstances is unjust.

Second, the person must be aware (or should reasonably be expected to be aware) that what he or she is doing is wrong. People so retarded or mentally ill that they are unable to distinguish right from wrong are not morally responsible, and thus cannot be justly punished for their actions.

Third, the proof of guilt must be substantial. Imposing "collective guilt," and thereby punishing an entire group because you are unable to pinpoint exactly who is the guilty party, is completely unjust. Likewise, incomplete proof or flimsy evidence is not sufficient to impose punishment, and any attempt to impose penalties under these circumstances would be unjust. If sheets and towels are regularly found missing from the linen supply closet of a large hotel, it would be unjust to fire all of the housekeepers on that basis alone.

Finally, the type and severity of the punishment should be proportional to, or appropriate to, the wrong committed. This is the meaning of the familiar saying, "The punishment must fit the crime." More severe infractions merit more serious penalties, and lesser offenses deserve lighter penalties. Beyond that, punishment must be given out in a fair and impartial manner. If a hotel department manager is fired for sexually harassing employees, and then another department manager is found to be sexually harassing employees in a similar manner, the second department manager must also be fired, even if the hotel does not want to lose that department manager.

Like cases must be treated alike. A company cannot justly apply harsh penalties to some for a particular infraction while allowing other favored employees to get off with lighter penalties or no penalty for the same infraction. To do so would be a violation of the principles of retributive justice.

Compensatory Justice

Compensatory justice is concerned with the proper way to "make it up" to someone who has been wronged. In other words, what is the proper restitution for them? How should they be compensated for the wrong done to them?

A general rule is that the person who has harmed another should give back what was improperly taken. For example, if an investment advisor has bilked investors out of thousands of dollars, that advisor must pay the investors back all the money they lost. Or if a person has been unjustly dismissed from his or her job, he or she should receive back pay along with reinstatement.

However, sometimes it is impossible to restore what has been lost. A person who was criminally assaulted on the street and lost the ability to walk cannot be restored the power to walk. In this case, perhaps he should be compensated with the "equivalent value" of his ability to walk. But, of course, it is very difficult, if not impossible, to put a value on something like one's ability to walk. Many other things are equally difficult to value in a monetary sense. For example, if I ruin the reputation of your restaurant by falsely claiming that I contracted food poisoning from food eaten there, how much is your restaurant's reputation worth?

There are a number of difficult problems like this in determining what constitutes proper compensation. However, the general rule seems to be that, to the degree possible, justice demands that people be "made whole" — that is, that they be given back what they have lost or its equivalent.

By far the biggest controversies in recent times in the United States concerning justice and compensation have been about programs that grant preferential treatment to a group that has been unjustly discriminated against in the past. For example, if a racial group has been unjustly discriminated against in the past, and this injustice has resulted in many of its members occupying the lowest rungs of society's economic ladder, is it just to make up for this by giving preference to members of this racial group for education, training, and promotional opportunities?

Programs of this nature are usually referred to as affirmative action programs. Polls show that the term affirmative action is very emotionally laden. Simple use of the term immediately raises heated, vehement opinions. This makes it hard to look at the issue dispassionately; the debate over affirmative action has often generated more heat than light.

Nevertheless, there are important and difficult questions to be worked out in regard to this subject. Does preferential access violate justice by denying equal treatment? Or does it create the conditions for equal treatment, which otherwise would be impossible given a history of past discrimination?

There are a number of complex issues involved in this discussion, and we will not be able to address them here. Consider what each of the ethical theories we have covered would say about this issue. How would utilitarianism resolve it: what would produce the greatest good for the greatest number? How would Kantian ethics evaluate the issue: which perspective upholds the categorical imperative's demand that we treat each individual as an end-in-himself or end-in-herself? What about Rawls's theory of justice: which perspective fulfills the principle of liberty, the difference principle, and the principle of fair equality of opportunity?

Endnotes

1. See John Rawls, "Justice as Fairness," *Philosophical Review* 67, no. 2 (April 1958): 164–194 and John Rawls, "Distributive Justice," in Peter Laslett and W. G. Runciman, eds., *Philosophy, Politics, and Society,* 3d series (New York: Barnes and Noble, 1967), pp. 58–82. See also John Rawls, *A Theory of Justice* (Cambridge, Mass.: Belknap Press, 1971). The final book, *A Theory of Justice,* is Rawls's most famous work.

2. John Rawls, "Distributive Justice." Quote taken from selection reprinted in Shari Collins-Chobarian, ed., *Ethical Challenges to Business as Usual* (Upper Saddle River, N.J.: Pearson Prentice Hall, 2005), p. 57.

3. Ibid.

4. Rawls, pp. 108–114 and 342–350.

5. For some of the literature on Rawls's theory of justice, see Norman Daniels, ed., *Reading Rawls: Critical Studies on Rawls's "A Theory of Justice"* (Stanford, Calif.: Stanford University Press, 1989); Samuel Freeman, ed., *The Cambridge Companion to Rawls* (New York: Cambridge University Press, 2002); and Robert Paul Wolff, ed., *Understanding Rawls* (Princeton, N.J.: Princeton University Press, 1977).

Chapter Questions

1. What are the three types of justice according to Aristotle? Define each one.

2. Does justice require welfare payments to the neediest people? Explain your answer.

3. Does justice require a minimum wage be paid to all working people? Explain your answer.

4. According to Rawls, what is the *original position*?

5. According to Rawls, what is the *veil of ignorance*?

6. What is the principle of equal liberty? Give an example.

7. In business, the difference principle would protect the most disadvantaged person. What does this mean? Give an example and explain your answer.

8. Punishment is an example of what type of justice?

9. Restitution is an example of what type of justice?

10. Affirmative action falls within the realm of what type of justice? Explain your answer.

Thinking Exercise

Apply a justice analysis to ethical issues that arose in a work situation you have experienced. Describe the circumstances. What was the specific problem and how did you handle it? Did your solution coincide with a justice solution? Explain your answer.

5

Virtue Ethics:
Aristotle and the Good Life

THE ETHICAL THEORIES we have considered so far have been concerned with principles or rules to govern our actions. There is, however, another way to look at ethical issues. Instead of concerning ourselves with ethical or unethical actions, we can make ethical judgments about the people undertaking those actions. In this regard, we are judging their *character*, which is what the ethical school of thought known as "virtue ethics" does.

When we judge the morality of people's character as well as the morality of their actions, we are comparing what kind of person they are to what kind of person we believe they *should be*. If we say of someone, "He is evil. He is heartless and cruel," we are not judging his actions but, instead, what sort of person he *is*. The ethical school of thought known as virtue ethics is built around this type of judgment.

Virtue ethics claims that the main task of ethics is not to supply us with rules for what is the right type of action, or what is a "good" action. Rather, virtue ethics aims to reveal the right type of person—the "good" person. What kind of character must a person have to be a moral human being? By examining character rather than actions, virtue ethics does not contradict the theories we have previously studied; it simply offers a different angle into morality. Because a "good" person will engage in "good" actions, and because habitually engaging in good actions leads to the development of a good person of good character, virtue ethics offers a complementary way of looking at morality. It is a unique perspective, and it may well afford us additional insight into moral behavior.

Aristotle: A Virtuous Character

The most famous proponent of virtue ethics is Aristotle, the ancient Greek philosopher.[1] Aristotle claimed that good character could be discovered by learning if a person is morally "virtuous." For Aristotle, a morally virtuous person constantly and habitually acts the way a human being should. He or she displays the virtues and avoids the many vices by which we are so frequently tempted. A lifetime of virtuous living and avoidance of vice forms a morally virtuous character.

For Aristotle, a moral virtue is the disposition or tendency to do the right thing and avoid doing wrong. We develop this disposition over time and through training. In other words, a good character is an achievement, not a natural endowment. "Doing right" becomes second nature to us if we have developed our moral character properly. This is not something that is naturally bred into us; we must strive to achieve a virtuous character, and we do this by constantly practicing the virtues.

The Golden Mean

What exactly is a moral virtue? How can we distinguish it from non-virtuous traits or characteristics? For Aristotle, moral virtues follow from our nature as human beings. Virtues enable human beings to act in accordance with our "essence" or human nature. For Aristotle, the feature that distinguishes humans from all other creatures is our ability to reason. Therefore, the virtues are those traits or characteristics that enable us to act according to reason. We must act in a reasonable fashion.

We act in a reasonable fashion and exercise reason when we choose to act in a way that goes neither to excess nor to deficiency. Excess and deficiency always designate a vice. The middle ground, neither going too far nor not far enough, is where virtue lies. Thus, virtue is a *golden mean* between the vice of deficiency and the vice of excess. To quote Aristotle:

> Virtue then is a state of deliberate moral purpose consisting in a mean that is relative to ourselves, the mean being determined by reason, or as a prudent man would determine it. It is a mean state...lying between two vices, the vice of excess on the one hand, and vice of deficiency on the other...[2]

A person who leads a life of moderation, avoiding deficiencies and excesses, leads a virtuous life. This is the best that human beings can be: living according to the virtuous middle path between the errors or vices of going too far or not far enough. As Aristotle would put it, such a person will engage in the right action, at the right time, in the right manner, with the right goal as determined by reason. This is a difficult achievement, for there is only one way to get it right, while there are many ways to get it wrong. Nevertheless, according to Aristotle, the person who is able to get it right will exhibit a virtuous character and lead a happy, fulfilled life worthy of a human being.

Virtue Examples

All of this may seem rather abstract. Perhaps examples can make it clearer. Aristotle names many virtues, but the four fundamental moral ones are *courage, temperance, justice,* and *prudence.* Courage is the golden mean between the vices of cowardice (deficiency) and recklessness or foolhardiness (excess). A courageous person shows just the right amount of bravery and displays a virtuous character. The coward has too little bravery; a reckless individual has too much. Only reason can tell us what is exactly the right amount of bravery, and once it does, a person must practice and develop the virtue of courage so that acting courageously becomes habitual. For example, if you knew that wrongdoing, such as fraud, was widespread at your place of work, would you be brave enough to report it? Would you be brave enough even if you knew some of your friends would be very angry with you for making the report?

The desire for food and other bodily pleasures is related to the virtue of temperance. Temperance is the golden mean between gluttony (excess) and extreme self-denial, sometimes called asceticism or austerity (deficiency). A virtuous man or woman, according to Aristotle, will neither overindulge nor deny himself or herself the bodily pleasures that come from things like good food and drink. Missing the mark and going to either excess or self-denial makes one a less happy or less fulfilled human being. Both lead to a less virtuous life. For instance, do you know when to stop filling up your plate when you are dining at the local buffet restaurant? Do you know when to stop drinking when you are at a party?

Justice is the virtue of giving other people exactly what they deserve, neither more nor less. It is the golden mean between two forms of injustice: either giving them less than they deserve or giving them more than they deserve. We covered justice in the previous chapter, so it should be apparent that the task of treating others justly is complicated. Aristotle would say that only reason can tell us what is just, and only constant practice in treating others justly can build a virtuous character, so that we habitually treat others in a just manner.

Prudence, or wisdom, is the virtue that helps us to know what is reasonable in different situations. It is an extremely important virtue, because it enables us to avoid excess and deficiency in other areas, and thus is fundamental to avoiding a life of vice and immorality. Only a prudent or wise person will know how to avoid extremes. Imprudence is the vice in opposition to prudence, and it can err in both directions. It is possible to imprudently or unwisely overdo (or underdo) virtually any action, emotion, or desire. An imprudent or unwise person then becomes a slave to his or her emotions or desires and misses the mark of moderation, thereby living a life of vice. Do you know people who fluctuate wildly in their enthusiasms, going from one extreme to another, without ever seeming to find a steady set of interests or goals? According to Aristotle, such a faddish person lacks the virtue of prudence or wisdom.

There are numerous other virtues that could be mentioned, although the four mentioned above are the most central ones to Aristotle. Additional moral virtues include trustworthiness, honesty, generosity, civility, sincerity, gentleness, reliability, warmth, dependability, cooperativeness, empathy, tact, kindness, tolerance, benevolence, etc.

The Relationship of Virtues to Moral Principles

In many ways, virtue ethics is closely related to the rules and principles presented earlier, because a person acting on the basis of the various virtues will, in some ways, behave according to those rules and principles. For example, the virtues of generosity and kindness are fully congruent with utilitarianism. A disposition to act generously and kindly will lead one to maximize benefits for others and minimize their pains and sorrows. Likewise, the virtues of honesty, trustworthiness, justice, and sincerity are fully compatible with Kant's insistence on always treating another human being as an end-in-himself or end-in-herself and to never degrade a person to the level of a thing. And certainly, the virtue of justice is directly related to principles of justice, no matter how they may be discovered and applied. So, virtue ethics should not be thought of as necessarily in conflict with the three theories we covered earlier. Of course, it may not be completely in accord with any or all of them, either; it depends on how the virtues are understood and applied in actual practice.

The Relationship of Virtues to Human Nature

A virtuous person is one who totally fulfills what it means to be a complete human being; those who are less virtuous are less successful at being fully human. This means that one's idea of virtue depends on one's idea of human nature and the purpose of life.

St. Thomas Aquinas, the Christian philosopher in the Middle Ages who became the most important philosopher of the Roman Catholic Church, adopted Aristotle's ethical theory virtually in its entirety. Aquinas agreed with Aristotle that the four fundamental virtues are courage, temperance, justice, and prudence. However, as a Christian, Aquinas felt that the purpose of life was not merely to live according to reason in this life, but to unite with God in a future life. Therefore, Aquinas added three specifically Christian virtues: faith, hope, and charity. These virtues made sense to Aquinas but they would not have made sense to Aristotle, who was not a Christian and did not believe in an afterlife. Thus, the virtues for different followers of this school of thought are not always identical—they will vary according to the view of humanity and purpose of human life held by the particular theorist.

In some cases, the different conceptions of humanity can lead to opposite views of what constitutes a virtue and what constitutes a vice. Aquinas, for example, held that humility is a virtue and pride is a vice, because these views fit with his Christian beliefs and the teachings of his sacred texts. Aristotle, coming from an aristocratic Greek society, felt that pride is a virtue and humility is a vice. Thus, virtue ethics presupposes agreement on some fundamental issues about the nature and purpose of human life. Without that agreement, there will likely be disagreement concerning what are virtues and what are vices.

Despite these differences, there is rather widespread agreement across many differing cultures and religions on a number of basic virtues and vices. Virtually no one, for instance, finds cruelty, arrogance, injustice, cowardice, self-centeredness, dishonesty, insensitivity, etc., to be virtues.

Criticisms of Virtue Ethics

As with all the other theories, virtue ethics has a number of critics. One criticism flows directly from points made earlier. Critics charge that virtue ethics is so dependent on one particular worldview that it is not much use in a multicultural world with a variety of religions and traditions. It is not a usable ethic for all of us, charge these critics—only for those willing to accept a particular understanding of human nature and of the role of humans in this world.

Supporters of virtue ethics could answer this charge in a variety of ways. First, it could be argued that there may be differences at the margins, but in some fundamental ways, we all see certain characteristics as virtuous no matter what cultural background or religious tradition we come from. These "universal" virtues (like justice, honesty, courage, and others) provide a good foundation for judging people's character. Also, the virtues that may be specific to a particular group (such as Aquinas's Christian virtues of faith, hope, and charity) are still useful moral anchors, or reference points, for members of that group, even if a society has decided not to impose those particular values on all of its members. As long as the appropriate values and virtues are applied to the appropriate group (one holding to those values as a basis of social cohesion), there is no fundamental clash between virtue ethics and a multicultural and multi-religious world.

A second criticism is that virtue ethics is not useful because it fails to give us any practical guidance on how we should actually behave when we are faced with difficult circumstances. Critics argue that it is all well and good to admonish people to build their character through virtuous practice, but that does not help much in a genuinely perplexing moral dilemma. For example, suppose a company manager is facing an agonizing decision about whether to fire a loyal, earnest employee who is, at best, marginally competent and definitely not as productive as all others working in her position. Does it help to tell this manager to build his character by practicing a virtuous life?

A defender of virtue ethics would reply that sound guidance can be obtained, even if the route to such guidance seems to be a bit indirect. The morality of an action depends on how it affects a person's character. Those actions that create a morally virtuous (good) character are ethical or moral; those that create a morally vicious character are not. True, this principle does not create a simple set of rules to live by, but that is one of its strengths, not a weakness. Any simple set of rules that says "Do this, don't do that" is bound to be too simplistic to fit all occasions. Wrestling with perplexing moral dilemmas is hard work, but so is developing a virtuous moral character. According to this defense of virtue ethics, the request for simple guidance in morally difficult circumstances is a demand for simplicity where no such easy way out is possible.

Many followers of virtue ethics argue that moral dilemmas are actually artificial creations that a person of good moral character is unlikely to ever encounter. These dilemmas are products of previous poor choices made by a less-than-virtuous person who has gotten himself or herself into such a problematic situation that there is no good way out. A person of good moral character who practices virtuous behavior would never get in such a fix in the first place, they assert. Therefore, the best practical advice is to practice the virtues and lead a morally virtuous life. Doing so will resolve a number of the seemingly insoluble moral dilemmas, because those dilemmas never come up in the first place.

Virtue Ethics and Social Institutions

Those who support virtue ethics assert that the theory can be just as helpful in evaluating our social arrangements and institutions as are utilitarianism, Kantian ethics, and justice ethics. Those institutions or practices that create people of bad moral character are to be condemned, while those that lead people to develop a good moral character are to be praised. For example, a social institution or system that teaches people to be greedy is immoral and should be criticized and changed. The same is true for a social arrangement that encourages laziness or dishonesty. To the follower of virtue ethics, this type of evaluation is just as concrete, practical, and useful as the guidance offered by the utilitarian "greatest happiness" rule, or the Kantian categorical imperative, or the Rawlsian principles of justice.

Applied to social institutions like businesses, Aristotelian virtue ethics would emphasize their character as human communities. Since many of the virtues have to do with our ability to live comfortably together in a community, a corporation or business would be judged by how well it contributes to the development of character (such as integrity, honesty, tolerance, fairness, and cooperation) of its employees and shareholders. Businesses or corporations that fail this test would be judged morally deficient. A corporate culture that emphasizes or encourages dishonesty, intolerance, greed, or deception would definitely be found wanting by this criterion. Numerous other examples could be given. For instance, there are many telemarketing firms that sell vacations that do not deliver on what they promise. These companies would be found ethically deficient according to virtue ethics.

The main point is that virtue ethics requires businesses to further the more social virtues relating to the ways we interact with each other in the community. Virtue ethics is not an ethical viewpoint concerned with isolated individuals; many of the virtues are inherently social in nature, and these are the virtues that will figure most prominently in ethical evaluations of businesses and corporations.

Endnotes

1. See Aristotle, *Nicomachean Ethics*, trans. David Ross (Oxford University Press, 1998). The book was originally published in 350 B.C.E.

2. Aristotle, *Nicomachean Ethics*. Quote taken from selection reprinted in Shari Collins-Chobarian, ed., *Ethical Challenges to Business as Usual* (Upper Saddle River, N.J.: Pearson Prentice Hall, 2005), p.13.

Chapter Questions

1. What is virtue ethics?

2. Who was the first proponent of virtue ethics?

3. What are the four fundamental moral virtues according to Aristotle? Define each one.

4. How would you critique virtue ethics?

Thinking Exercise

Apply a virtue ethics analysis to ethical issues that arose in a work situation you have experienced. Describe the circumstances. What was the specific problem and how did you handle it? Did your solution coincide with a virtue ethics solution? Explain your answer.

Part II

Lodging and Food Service Applications

6

Applying Ethics to the Purchasing Function

As economic inequalities have deepened during the last several decades, the renewed worship of money has bred temptation at all levels. Executives at Enron, WorldCom and other corporations, intoxicated by the heady atmosphere of deregulation, defraud shareholders of billions and get away with little or no punishment. The little guy naturally says: If the big shots get away with it, why not me? So he cheats on his taxes, steals from his company and downloads music without paying for it. —Jackson Leers[1]

MONEY CAN BE a very powerful motivator to engage in unethical behavior. In a society obsessed with wealth, we all need to be aware of this danger. The purchasing function is a monetary function and any time money is involved, there is an opportunity for unethical behavior. People working in this area need to examine their principles on a regular basis because of the potential ethical issues that can arise.

Consider the temptation to enrich yourself in a manner that is harmful, unfair, deceptive, etc., to the organization for which you work. When the temptation arises, analyze the situation by asking yourself, *"Is this the best decision for the organization that I work for?"* Beyond your own organization you must also ask, *"Is this the right decision for everyone involved?"* Self-enrichment at your employer's expense, if it is done without the employer's knowledge, will inevitably be a violation of a number of the ethical principles we have covered earlier. It will almost always turn out to be harmful to the greater good; it will also violate the rights of others and lead to unjust outcomes. Don't rationalize unethical behavior by thinking, *"Even if this is not the best organizational decision, it's not so bad and it would really help me out a lot."* If your actions in some way pilfer from your employer for your own gain, your behavior is unethical and rationalizations of that behavior will not withstand an honest ethical scrutiny. For example, if you purchase unnecessary items for your company or if you purchase items at a higher than usual rate for your own personal reasons (buying from friends so that they can profit, etc.), you are acting in an unethical manner. We find many examples of these types of behaviors in the news today; just because someone else does it does not mean that it is acceptable.

The rest of this chapter models the kind of analyses you can take to a variety of ethical situations that arise in relation to the purchasing function. The case below, "A Trip to Las Vegas," is followed by detailed ethical analyses in relation to each of the ethical theories presented earlier: utilitarianism, Kant's categorical imperative, Rawls's justice ethics, and Aristotle's ethics of virtue. The chapter closes with a series of case studies and questions about the cases that challenge you to analyze ethical issues in the area of purchasing.

Case Study—A Trip to Las Vegas

Mr. Brent Wiggly is the director of purchasing for the Commander Hotel Company, which owns and operates 78 hotels in the western United States. The average Commander Hotel has 200 rooms and suites. Mr. Wiggly purchases linens to service over 15,000 rooms.

Yesterday, Mr. Tom Penney, one of the top salespersons for the Linens of Today Company, arrived for his quarterly sales visit. He was excited because he had a new product to offer, king-sized bed sheets with a 200 thread count for only $8.00 apiece.

Mr. Wiggly treated Mr. Penney in his typically cordial manner. However, at the end of the visit, Mr. Wiggly said, "I'm sorry, Tom, but I am making my next big purchase of sheets with the Advantage Linen Supply Company. A salesman was in here just two days ago. He offered me the exact product you have, but the cost to me would only be $7.90 per sheet. That would be a loss to the Commander Hotel Company of over $1,500 if I bought only one sheet per room."

"But, that's not all I have for you," Mr. Penney countered. He pulled a rather large envelope out of his inside pocket and handed it to Mr. Wiggly. "It's an all-expenses paid vacation for two to Las Vegas. It includes airfare, hotel, and two meals a day," he proudly declared.

Mr. Wiggly opened the envelope. He couldn't believe his eyes. The tickets and the reservations were all there. "Wow," he thought to himself. "My wife would sure love this! And what's an extra $1,500 to the Commander Hotel chain anyway?"

Mr. Wiggly may be absolutely correct in assuming that $1,500 would not mean much to his company. But what would happen if all of the managers felt that way? What would happen if every manager in the Commander Hotel chain spent $1,500 unnecessarily?

Anything that could be considered a bribe or kickback is a conflict of interest and, therefore, is unethical. It does not matter what form it takes. Different types of kickbacks include gifts, entertainment, and discounts on personal items from vendors. Another subtle form of kickback can occur when a person has influence or power within an organization and uses it inappropriately. For example, if your cousin Joe owns a web-hosting firm and you hire him to design the company's website—this could be construed as a conflict of interest. However, if there is bidding for the contract and Joe's firm wins the bid honestly, this should be morally acceptable. In instances such as this, it is advisable for you to exclude yourself from the purchasing process.[2]

The moral basis of business relationships involves trust. Let's look at this in a methodical manner from the point of view of the various philosophers we studied earlier.

Case Commentary: Utilitarianism

From an act utilitarian perspective, we can ask which action brings the greatest good for the greatest number of people? It may seem simple at first: two people will have a wonderful vacation and one person will make a large sale and pocket a good-sized commission. Those would seem to be the pluses if Mr. Wiggly were to accept the Las Vegas trip and to purchase linens from Mr. Penney. However, there are many others who will also be affected by the decision that Mr. Wiggly makes.

Act utilitarianism tells us to look at the consequences for everyone. The principled person will ask, *"What about the other people who work for the company? How is this decision affecting all of the employees in the Commander Hotel Company?"* Should all of the employees subsidize a vacation for Mr. Wiggly, the purchasing director? On a local basis, just at that chain property, $1,500 might have been earmarked for something to benefit other employees such as improvements to employee facilities or benefits. The employees may have to collectively "pay" for Mr. Wiggly's vacation out of something they would otherwise have received. And they would pay for this without their knowledge or consent. If all of the consequences are considered, it is apparent that more harm is done than good.

Another negative impact of these types of actions is lower morale among the employees in the operation. If employees were to learn that others are getting away with accepting bribes, an atmosphere of discontent could flourish. Employees could begin to think, *"If they can get away with it, so should I."* The workplace could become a breeding ground of demoralization.

A utilitarian would ask, *"What are all of the consequences of my actions?"* What about guests? Suppose that $1,500 was intended for new carpeting in an area where the old carpeting is torn and where recently several guests had tripped over the larger rips. What about the shareholders? The shareholders would undoubtedly lose money if actions such as Mr. Wiggly's went unchecked. The shareholders would sustain a loss of income and they would own a less valuable company. In addition, a glimpse at the long-term costs would certainly show us a less efficient organization. Eventually, this would lead to higher costs for consumers. Or, the hotel management may choose to lay off employees to cover the extra "overhead" costs. In any case, when dollars are spent for unbudgeted expenses, properties run less efficiently and less profitably.

A rule utilitarian would ask, *"What if everyone operated this way? What if everyone in the organization considered it suitable to accept bribes?"* The organization would run less profitably if all the managers wangled something extra for themselves at the expense of the company. If managers overspent their budgets while hiding the true causes (perks for themselves), each thinking they were the only one doing it, the bottom line would certainly suffer. This would translate into negative consequences for all stakeholders: employees, customers, owners, etc. Rules condoning universal bribery as a way of doing business could never be seen as promoting the greatest good for the greatest number.

The ethical individual must take this analysis even further. Let's look at this in terms of society as a whole. If we do so, it becomes apparent that a civilization that condones the universal taking of bribes makes for a much less satisfying and productive society. Just think what your day would be like if you had to bribe everyone from whom you asked something. What if you had to bribe your librarian for the book you need, or if you had to bribe your mailperson to deliver your mail? Such a world would not only be difficult to negotiate in, but it would breed widespread mistrust and cynicism as well. The consequences are deeply corrosive. In fact, it is difficult to believe that anyone would prefer a world of universal bribery to one without such practices. Therefore, if we are unable to make bribery a universal rule, we could not accept it as an ethical action. A rule utilitarian would say we could accept this type of action only if it was true that a rule stating everyone could do it would lead to the greatest benefit.

Case Commentary: Kant's Categorical Imperative

Kant states that the consequences of your actions are not the basis for making a moral decision. Instead, he argues that actions are moral or immoral based solely on their nature. If someone acts out of a sense of duty, because they know it is "the right thing to do," then that action is moral. We know the right thing to do by following the categorical imperative. The categorical imperative is the rule, or command, that we all must follow at all times in all places under all circumstances if we wish to act morally.

In the case of Mr. Wiggly and Mr. Penney, Kant would be hard pressed to find anything moral about the decision to accept the vacation. If Mr. Wiggly accepts the vacation, he is doing it simply for the enjoyment both he and his wife will receive. He is not accepting it in an attempt to do his moral duty, but rather he is accepting it because it provides positive benefits for both himself and his wife.

From Kant's perspective, what is Mr. Wiggly's moral duty? What is the most rational decision? How should Mr. Wiggly think this through from a Kantian perspective?

The first step for Mr. Wiggly would be to try to universalize his decision. This means Mr. Wiggly would have to be able to say that his decision to accept the vacation would be a suitable decision for all of the managers and employees of the Commander Hotel Company. If he were to decide that the decision is suitable, then, according to Kant, his decision to accept the vacation could be relayed to all of the other managers and employees of the Commander Hotel Company. Conversely, if Mr. Wiggly is unable to universalize his decision, then the decision must be immoral.

Bear in mind that Kant's first statement of the categorical imperative says that we must be able to make the rule or principle we are following into a universal rule. If that is not possible without being self-contradictory, the action is immoral. Could we make secret bribe-taking a universal rule without contradicting the entire basis of open, straightforward business transactions? We cannot; universal bribe-taking would completely undermine business transactions. It is therefore self-contradictory and immoral to engage in a business operation of any sort and take a bribe. Were he to accept the bribe, Mr. Wiggly would be acting immorally, since the other employees and managers would not be receiving the same freedom (to accept bribes) as he is granting to himself. That means he is violating the categorical imperative; he is acting immorally.

Kant's second formulation of the categorical imperative also condemns deceptive practices like bribery. Whenever you engage in deception in business, you are treating other human beings merely as the means to your private ends, not as ends-in-themselves. You are not granting them the same status you claim for yourself—an autonomous, rational human being free to make decisions according to reason. By withholding information or deceiving others, you degrade them to the status of a thing to be used (perhaps used to make money) and deny them their humanity. This is immoral, and Kant would say that all deceptive and/or dishonest business behavior is immoral. Lying, cheating, bribe-taking, deceiving, and so forth will always mean degrading your fellow human beings—violating the categorical imperative. According to Kant, you must never use a person just for your own purposes. Instead, you must treat every human being as someone of independent moral worth, with an equal claim to freely decide his or her own life choices.

One indication that we all implicitly accept Kant's point is that we feel the need to hide activities such as deception, cheating, taking bribes, etc. If we felt these were moral and acceptable actions, we would not feel the need to conceal such activities. If you have to hide it from your fellow employees, your employer, customers, etc., this is a red flag that the action is probably immoral according to Kant.

Case Commentary: The Ethic of Justice

John Rawls, the twentieth century American philosopher, contended that in order to determine what is fair, rational people must decide what would be accepted as reasonable from all points of view. He contended that people are expected to be self-interested, but they also must consider the issues as if they do not know where they will alight in society. In other words, if you are part of a group making rules for a corporation, you must suggest rules that you would want followed whether you were the lowest-paid clerk or the chief executive officer. If the corporation is deciding on contributions toward retirement funds, should the clerks receive less than the executives? If you did not know what position you would hold in the corporation (the veil of ignorance), you would ensure that everyone received a contribution that seemed fair in order to ensure your fair share.

Consider Mr. Wiggly in our "Trip to Las Vegas" case. To act justly, he would have to behave according to rules that would seem fair to him—no matter what his position within the Commander Hotel Company. What would the rules be if those who established them had no idea what their ultimate post at the Commander Hotel Company would be? Would the rules condone bribery? Would those who are not in the position of purchasing director accept rules giving the person in that position the freedom to accept bribes or gratuities like a trip to Las Vegas in exchange for purchase orders that harm the corporation—even if it is only a slight harm? Would they accept this as a just or fair set of rules? Where do we draw the line?

To even ask the question is to answer it. Rules allowing such behavior would result in numerous injustices. Bribery, according to Rawls, is contrary to the principle of equal liberty, which states that each person engaged in an institution or affected by it has an equal right to the most extensive liberty compatible with a like liberty for all.

Applied to businesses or corporations, this principle implies that it is both unfair and unwarranted for a business to engage in bribery in any form. However, the business ethics writer John Boatright contends that it is not necessarily a conflict of interest if a purchasing agent accepts a gift from a supplier who expects special treatment. He further claims that it depends on the value of the gift, the circumstances, as well as industry practice and whether or not the gift violates any laws.[3] Boatright's position is an illustration of the differences of opinion that exist about issues like this.

Nonetheless, according to Rawls, it would be unjustifiable for Mr. Wiggly to accept the bribe because his deceptive practices deprive numerous other people (fellow employees, company stockholders, customers) of liberty equal to that liberty he is claiming for himself. And he is accepting the bribe solely for his own personal gain.

Case Commentary: Aristotle and the Ethics of Virtue

With Aristotle's ethics of virtue, we judge a person's character. We look at the type of person he or she is to make our judgment. What is Mr. Wiggly's character if he accepts the bribe? Would he be acting in a virtuous manner?

Of the many character virtues, there are a few examples that are relevant to this case. Among Aristotle's four main virtues, the virtue of justice applies most directly here. Mr. Penney is committing an injustice by offering Mr. Wiggly more wealth than he is legitimately entitled to. And, if he should accept the bribe, Mr. Wiggly would be acting unjustly by accepting money (or its equivalent in a free vacation) to which he is not entitled. Both men would be committing an injustice by deceptively diverting resources into their own pockets and away from those to whom they should belong. We would therefore judge them to have a faulty character because they lack the virtue of justice and practice the vice of injustice.

Additionally, the deceitfulness involved in the entire transaction shows that both men have a dishonest character. This is a serious flaw, showing that they lack the virtue of honesty. From Aristotle's perspective, Mr. Wiggly would deserve severe condemnation if he accepts the free vacation. He would have a bad character, full of vice and lacking in important virtuous traits.

Ethical tradition also condemns this type of behavior. Many people turn to religion as their basis for ethical tradition. Religions worldwide are full of examples of the value of honesty in one's business dealings.

Honesty in your business dealings is a continual theme throughout both the Old and New Testaments. On Yom Kippur, which is the holiest day of the year for those of Jewish faith, readings from the Book of Leviticus are integrated into the service. An excerpt from the readings is, *"You must not steal; you must not act deceitfully nor lie to one another."* Also included is a statement on truthfulness regarding measurements, *"Do not pervert justice when you measure length, weight or quantity. You must have honest scales, honest weights, honest dry and liquid measures."*[4] Additionally, the Babylonian Talmud contends that the heavenly court for final judgment asks, *"Did you conduct your business affairs honestly?"*[5]

Christianity also includes many references to honesty in the New Testament. Ephesians 4:25 says, *"Put away falsehood; let everyone speak the truth with his neighbor, for we are members one of another."* Matthew 7:12 states, *"Therefore all things whatsoever ye would that men should do to you, do ye even so to them,"* which is another way of saying, "Do to others as you would have them do to you."

Examples from Islamic culture are also numerous. The Koran states, *"And give full measure when you measure out, and weigh with a true balance; this is fair and better in the end."*

It is evident from just these examples (see Exhibit 1 for more examples) that ethical traditions worldwide condemn this type of behavior. Within most religious

Exhibit 1   Examples of Honesty Cited in World Scripture

Let your conduct be marked by truthfulness in word, deed, and thought.	Hinduism. Taittiriya Upanishad 1.11.1
Be honest like Heaven in conducting your affairs.	Taoism. Tract of the Quiet Way
Straightforwardness and honesty in the activities of one's body, speech, and mind lead to an auspicious path.	Jainism. Tattvarthasutra 6.23
He who utters gentle, instructive, true words, who by his speech gives offense to none—him I call a brahmana.	Buddhism. Dhammapada 406
Master Tseng said, "Every day I examine myself ... In intercourse with my friends, have I always been true to my word?"	Confucianism. Analects 1.3

Source: Andrew Wilson, ed., *World Scripture: A Comparative Anthology of Sacred Texts* (New York: International Religious Foundation, 1991).

traditions, there is nothing debatable about this type of behavior. This case fails ethical tests within all traditions.

Conclusion

The desire for money can be very powerful. It can be so potent that it may distort our perspective and lead us to rationalize unethical behaviors as long as it makes us richer. Some people will do almost anything for money. Within the hospitality industry, it is necessary to develop oversight procedures to ensure that self-gain does not override common ethical decency. Even in a highly competitive environment, ethical standards must be maintained. The more competitive the environment, the more care must be taken to ensure that ethical standards are followed.

There have been various attempts at a "transcultural corporate ethic"[6] as a result of intergovernmental agreements over the last fifty years. Guidelines for business conduct for multinational corporations in areas such as employment policies, consumer protection, environmental protection, political payments, and basic human rights have been included.[7] There are four basic principles involved, one of which is market integrity in business transactions. This includes restrictions on political payments and bribes. The reasoning behind this is that bribes "inject non-market considerations into business transactions."[8]

 ## Case Study—Spilled Coffee

Andy is the owner and manager of Global Coffee House, which offers a selection of coffees from around the world. Andy prides himself on the unique selections and blends of coffee that his store offers. He also takes great satisfaction in the comfortable surroundings of his shop.

For the last week, Andy has been very busy trying to finalize the offers he received to refurbish the coffee house with wireless Internet service. Andy was in and out of his office all week to meet with suppliers and left all operations in the hands of his assistant, John. Andy felt sure that John would be able to do the job in his absence.

During one of his meetings, Andy received an alarming phone call from John. It appeared that Nancy, one of his regular customers, had to be taken to the emergency room at a nearby hospital. As she was picking up her coffee cup, the lid popped off and most of the very hot coffee spilled onto her arm. Andy got the name of the hospital from John and rushed immediately to the emergency room to look for Nancy and offer an apology.

On his way to the hospital, Andy started thinking about what might have led to this incident. The first thing that came to mind was that a couple of weeks ago he had changed his hot cup and lid purveyor to another company in order to cut costs and come up with extra cash to help pay for the Internet service refurbishment. He was not able to think of anything else that might have caused this problem.

Finally, Andy arrived at the hospital emergency room where he found Nancy, her arm covered with a bandage. Andy asked as politely as possible about what had happened. Nancy told him that just as she was reaching for her cup from John, the lid suddenly popped open and the hot coffee spilled onto her arm. The doctors told her that the incident caused first-degree burns. Andy offered his sincere apology and promised to help in any way possible.

Andy returned to the coffee house. John was waiting for him. They sat down to discuss the situation. John told Andy that the quality of the new coffee cups is not the same as the ones they had previously had. John demonstrated this by taking an empty cup with the lid on. He squeezed it just a bit, and as he did, the lid popped off.

Andy was devastated about his cost-saving decision. It was apparent to him that his poor judgment had led to the problem as well as to Nancy's burns. However, he also knew that he had thousands of cups and lids in his storeroom as well as a binding contract with the new purveyor.

Case Questions

1. What would you do in Andy's place?

2. What are the ethical issues involved in this case?

3. Would any of the philosophers tell Andy to keep the cups?

4. Would an act utilitarian's decision regarding this case be different from a rule utilitarian's decision? If so, how? Specify what those decisions would be.

This case was authored by Samer Hassan, Ph.D., Associate Professor of Hospitality Management at Johnson & Wales University, Florida Campus.

 # Case Study—The Head Shipper

Ricky Galway is the head shipper for Gourmet Victuals and Delights, Inc., commonly known as GV&D. The company has been in business since 1952 and has an excellent reputation not only for creative gift baskets but for excellent service as well. The company ships baskets to the entire United States and the Caribbean.

On average, Ricky gets visits from ten to fifteen salespeople per week. They represent companies such as Harry's Hungries, Lady Chocolatier, Friendly Fruits, Cook's Coffees, and more. Each of the salespeople realizes that Ricky does not decide what goes into a Gourmet Victuals and Delights gift basket. However, they respect his value to the company and, as such, they like to acknowledge his importance during the Christmas season. Each year, starting the Monday after Thanksgiving and continuing until early January, Ricky is showered with gifts from salespeople. The gifts usually are bottles of wine or liquor; occasionally he has received fine leather luggage or a gift certificate to a local high-end restaurant.

Last year, Ricky noticed that the gifts were becoming pricier and it made him uncomfortable. When the saleswoman from The Heavenly Nut Company handed him two tickets to Aruba, he knew he had to do something. He spent the day pondering his dilemma.

That night, Ricky discussed his dilemma with a college instructor, Mr. Penn, who gave Ricky an article to read by Vincent Barry. In the article, Mr. Barry suggested that the following factors be considered when evaluating the morality of accepting a gift:[9]

- What is the value of the gift? Will it influence one's decisions?

- What is the purpose of the gift? Is it, in fact, a subtle (or not-so-subtle) bribe?

- Why was the gift offered? Was the gift given openly? Was it given to celebrate a special event (Christmas, a birthday)?

- What is the position of the recipient of the gift? Is the recipient able to influence his own firm's dealing with the giver of the gift?

- What is accepted business practice in the industry? Is the gift typical of open and recognized industry practice?

- What is the company's policy? Does the company allow employees to accept gifts?

- What is the law? Does the law prohibit gifts of this type or for this purpose?

Case Questions

1. According to factors suggested in Mr. Barry's article, has Ricky acted in an ethical manner by accepting the gifts that he already has accepted? Explain your answer.

2. If you were in Ricky's shoes, which of the gifts, if any, would you accept? Explain your answer.

3. Why did Ricky decide to seek advice about the gifts now, when he had been accepting gifts for many years? Explain the difference between the gifts.

4. Would any of the philosophers that we have studied tell Ricky to accept the gifts? Explain your answer.

Case Study—Is This My Responsibility?

Mary Lou Cassidy is the purchasing director for the Hopkins Pancake Chain, which presently consists of 225 stores nationwide and employs over 5,000 people. Mary Lou has worked for Hopkins since she graduated from college eight years ago. She has worked her way up while continuing to go to school.

In one of her recent graduate courses, Mary Lou discovered something very disturbing. All of the uniforms, hats, towels, and other assorted linens that Hopkins purchases from Xandar Linens, Inc., are manufactured in a small, developing country in Africa. The people work under sweatshop conditions for pennies per day. She decided to look up the cost difference if she purchased the materials from a U.S. factory. The cost difference was astronomical.

Mary Lou is in a quandary. She does not like the idea of supporting a business that treats their employees in such a hideous manner. But she has a responsibility to Hopkins as well. And, she asks herself, "Is this my responsibility?"

Case Questions

1. Apply a utilitarian analysis to Mary Lou's situation. What should she do? Lay out a few different courses of action, and argue which one is justified from a utilitarian perspective.

2. Where do we have a responsibility for the welfare of others, and where does that responsibility end? Use Mary Lou's situation to illustrate your answer and your reasoning. What is she responsible for, and to whom?

3. Utilize Rawls's distributive justice framework to decide whether the distribution of resources between Mary Lou and people like her on the one side, and the African workers on the other, is just. What do you conclude? Why?

Endnotes

1. Jackson Leers, "Cheater, Cheater," *In These Times*, June 21, 2004, p. 28.

2. Linda K. Treviño and Katherine A. Nelson, *Managing Business Ethics: Straight Talk About How to Do It Right*, 3d ed. (Hoboken, N.J.: Wiley, 2004), pp. 68–69.

3. John R. Boatright, *Ethics and the Conduct of Business*, 4th ed. (Upper Saddle River, N.J.: Prentice Hall, 2003), p. 144.

4. Lev. 19:11.

5. Quoted in Grant Perry, "The Good Jew who went to Jail," *Reform Judaism* (Winter 2002): 26.

6. W. C. Frederick, "The Moral Authority of Transnational Corporate Codes," *Journal of Business Ethics*, 10: 165–177.

7. Treviño and Nelson, p. 43.

8. Frederick.

9. Vincent E. Barry, *Moral Issues in Business*, (Belmont, Calif.: Wadsworth, 1986), pp. 237–238.

7

Applying Ethics to the Marketing Function

The very first law in advertising is to avoid the concrete promise and cultivate the delightfully vague. —Bill Cosby

IN MARKETING, some of the most important ethical issues arise around dishonesty and deception. There can often be gray areas making it hard to decide how best to resolve the situation. Questions also arise about what and how much one is obliged to tell the public and about what is acceptable to withhold without being deceptive.

Billboards, written copy, and television and radio advertising are some of the more typical methods used to advertise and market today. However, marketing has become so pervasive in our society that it has come to invade almost every aspect of daily life. Advertisements of all types are everywhere. Examples include seeing your favorite actress eating in a fast-food chain restaurant in a popular movie or seeing the local hardware store advertised on your next-door neighbor's Little League cap. People often even wear t-shirts, hats, and other pieces of clothing that they have paid for simply to have the pleasure of advertising someone else's product!

Given such pervasive marketing/advertising, ethical questions arise. One of the more important questions is: *How much should consumers be made aware of the fact that they are being marketed to?* Also, we have to determine if the marketing that is being done is honest and accurate.

In the first case below, students are invited to participate in a fund-raising event that is not all that it appears to be. Put yourself in the students' shoes and consider the options. Think about what you would do if you found out that everything wasn't quite what it was claimed to be.

Case Study—The Charitable Event

The ZXT fraternity and the XTZ sorority often worked hand-in-hand, whether it was throwing a party, having study sessions, tutoring local school children, or even just organizing a hike. Both the fraternity and the sorority were recognized for their fun activities, charitable deeds, and scholastic abilities. It was well known that when they worked together, they created some of the most fabulous events on campus. If they threw a party together, it was the place to be.

At the start of the school year, a local environmental group called EcoWind approached the presidents of both the fraternity and sorority regarding a fund-raising event. Margie of XTZ and Tyler of ZXT listened carefully as Frances, the chair of EcoWind, laid out the basic ideology of the group. "We are two-pronged in our approach to the environment: we encourage ecologically friendly businesses and promote wind power." She also explained the group's fund-raising needs and capabilities. "In the past, we have put on a small concert and dinner. We can make almost $5,000 if we get the word out early enough and people save the date. We haven't had a lot of student participation in the past, though, and we are hoping to do something that will encourage student attendance as well as raise student consciousness about the environment.

"I understand that your groups often work together and that you have a stellar reputation. I also know that you consider the environment to be a very important topic. I spent some time in the university library searching through past fraternity and sorority newsletters and I am very impressed with your actions, especially those that pertain to the environment," Frances said with sincerity. "And I confess I also know that you do at least one huge fund-raising event per academic year for a local non-profit group and I am hoping you will consider EcoWind."

Tyler, Margie, and Frances discussed possibilities for a while. They all liked the idea of a concert, similar to what EcoWind had done previously, but with the possibility of finding some big names to donate their time. It was agreed that they would get back together the following week to see if any of them could come up with any leads. They each left the meeting feeling excited about all of the possibilities.

The next evening at the EcoWind executive board meeting, Frances gave an update on potential fund-raising activities. Stan Harley, the newest board member and a real estate lawyer for Martinson Realty, said he thought he could find a sponsor. Frances was pleased but also surprised. She had been uncomfortable having Harley as a board member in the first place, but he had been elected at the recent EcoWind general meeting. Martinson Realty was known to donate money to many local groups, including EcoWind, and it enjoyed good standing in the community. The company also claimed to be working with Eamons Construction on a new housing development that would incorporate wind power and ecologically friendly landscaping and building materials. So Frances dismissed her concern.

Three months later, the excitement surrounding the upcoming EcoWind fund-raising concert was unbelievable. To Frances, it appeared to have taken on a life of its own. The students had thrown themselves into the preparations. Martinson Realty had truly come through: two big name singers were headlining the concert at the county fairgrounds, to be followed by a party with donated music and refreshments.

One of Frances's favorite aspects of the entire event was the logo that had been created by the Exon Ad Agency that Martinson's employed. Exon had agreed to create a logo for the event free of charge. The logo was a montage of windmills, trees, and plants of all varieties superimposed over a rainbow-colored background. All of the flyers and free advertising for the event were printed with the logo. Frances truly thought she was living a dream when she found out that a documentary was going to be made of the event. One of the star performers, Lana

Walker, commissioned it for posterity. Ms. Walker had created a public relations committee just for the concert.

A month later, on the day before the concert, Stan Harley called a meeting of all the students who had worked on the event. He handed out t-shirts and instructed them all to wear them "so people will know who to ask for anything they need." In addition, he had extra t-shirts for all of the sorority and fraternity students, explaining it was their free pass into the event. Any ZXT fraternity and any XTZ sorority member who was wearing the t-shirt could enter the show at no cost.

Harley also had boxes and boxes of trinkets: key chains, pens, plastic mugs, baseball caps, memo pads, mini backpacks, coin purses, and more—all imprinted with the concert logo. "I want every single item given out by the end of the night," he told the students. "In the last hour, we'll give out hundreds of t-shirts; you'll be given boxes to walk through the crowds with. You can give them to anyone you want. Encourage all of your sorority and fraternity members wearing the t-shirts to help out. It will be a special souvenir for those who stay on until the end."

The night of the event finally arrived. It was rumored that there would be over 8,000 attendees each paying $15. Frances could not believe it; she had never seen so many people in one place in her life. Wherever she looked, she saw t-shirts and baseball caps, all with the concert logo. She also saw three television stations and four radio stations represented. The documentarians were also making their way through the crowds.

The concert went off without a hitch. The party was a huge success. All of the trinkets and t-shirts were given away, and the next day, Frances deposited enough funds to keep EcoWind going for quite a while.

Six weeks after the concert, Frances was cooking dinner. She had her television tuned to the local news station. She smiled to herself as she saw the concert logo on the TV. It was always popping up, and each time she saw it, it made her smile. She received notes at work on memo paper with the logo; she saw t-shirts and caps while she walked around town; she saw children with mini backpacks with the logo; and more.

Then she took a second look. This wasn't someone walking around town with a baseball cap. This was an advertisement for something. This must be some kind of mistake, she thought. The logo, her logo (as she thought of it), was being used to advertise Windemere, a new eco-friendly resort and spa two hours from town.

Frances's thoughts went wild. The documentary, all of the TV and radio exposure, the newspaper articles—these people all knew what they were doing. She wondered who had knowledge and who did not. And she wondered who would think she was in on it.

The next day, Frances spent the entire day tracking down Stan Harley. When she finally got him on the phone, he was very blasé. "We decided that since we spent all that money on free advertising for the concert, we should get something out of it, too. I don't see your problem. You got your funds."

"I never would have agreed to your assistance if I would have known about this."

"I know that; that's why we never said anything about the resort. It's just business, Frances, take it easy. These kinds of things happen all the time. That's the way things are done."

Frances's next phone calls were to Tyler and Margie. Then she called the local newspaper.

Case Commentary

In this case, Stan has pulled a fast one on Frances, Tyler, Margie, and all the fraternity and sorority students who got involved in the concert and party. While they thought they were working on a fund-raiser for EcoWind, they were actually involved in an elaborate advertising scheme for a resort apparently connected to Stan's realty company. Two types of ethical issues arise: the ethics of Stan's behavior and what Frances ought to do now that she has caught on to what has happened.

First, can Stan's behavior be justified from a utilitarian perspective? While he may superficially rationalize his actions and try to claim that the "greatest good" came from them, this is definitely not the case. Clearly, some good came from the concert and party: a lot of money was raised for EcoWind, a good time for attendees, higher visibility for and awareness about a "good cause" (EcoWind's work), and the like. However, these benefits are far outweighed by the damage that has been done to trust and the consequent feelings of betrayal.

Furthermore, it appears that a great many more negative consequences will soon be following, including heavy conflicts, exposure in the newspaper, likely monetary loss to the resort, damage to Stan's own credibility and reputation, damage to the reputation of Frances and EcoWind, etc. A long chain of unfavorable consequences are the almost certain result of Stan's unethical behavior. For the sake of a short-sighted and short-term gain (in publicity for the resort), Stan has created long-lasting damage that far outweighs the benefits. If we apply a rule utilitarian analysis, the case becomes even clearer: we could never justify a general rule approving deceptive advertising like this as conducive to the greatest good for the greatest numbers over the long run. Stan's behavior is to be condemned.

Frances faces an ethical question now: what should she do now that she has discovered the deception? She has chosen to contact the fraternity and sorority involved and to explain the whole situation to them. She is also calling the newspaper to expose the entire ruse to the general public. Is this the best course of action from a utilitarian perspective? It appears it is. By doing so, she minimizes the damage already done and exposes the guilty party so that further similar actions by this party (Stan) will be curtailed. She also salvages her own reputation and the well-being of her organization, EcoWind. Finally, she begins the long, hard process of re-establishing trust with those she interacts with and on whom she depends for the success of her organization.

Some might argue that Frances should just let it go and drop the whole issue. That way, she'll avoid getting into public fights and all the messiness that entails. Furthermore, she got her money. Why not just let sleeping dogs lie? But this way of thinking ignores some of the deepest, most important consequences of looking the other way when you see wrongs being committed. Doing nothing negatively affects you (i.e., deforms your character, as Aristotle would say). It likewise leads to cynicism, distrust, and a general decline in the overall moral climate of a society.

All of these are enormously damaging in a broad, general way. All of these consequences must be considered, and when they are, it becomes apparent that a utilitarian perspective requires Frances to expose Stan's wrongdoing and not become complicit herself.

From a deontological or Kantian perspective, Stan's behavior is inexcusable. He is using others for his own hidden purposes, thus treating them as things rather than persons. This dehumanization is a clear violation of the second formulation of the categorical imperative. He also is violating the first formulation of the categorical imperative, because it would be logically impossible to make a universal rule that business transactions (which depend on transparency and honesty) be done consistently in a dishonest, deceptive manner—that would be self-contradictory. Kant would not hesitate to strongly condemn Stan's actions.

To the extent there are distributive justice issues here, they are buried deeply within the primary story, which concerns deception. It could well be that Stan's actions, if successful and not detected, would redistribute resources away from competitors to his resort, thus changing the distribution of income and resources. To the extent it does so, it does so unjustly, because the redistribution is arrived at by fraudulent means that would never be accepted by people in the original position behind the veil of ignorance. They would never accept fraudulent redistribution of resources, because they realize that in real life they may end up in the position of the one being fraudulently dispossessed of resources.

From the point of view of character ethics, this is an extremely easy case. Stan's character is to be condemned because of his dishonesty. Frances's character is to be lauded because of her courage and her honesty. Aristotle would have no problem praising Frances and condemning Stan.

 ## Case Study—Darla's Choices

Darla Guernsey was doing menu layout for the Johnson's Ice Cream Parlor Café. The previous menu had become quite dated, and the owners, Mr. and Mrs. Mack, felt it was time to update it. Mr. Mack took great pride in his restaurant and he wanted to show it in its best light.

Darla was excited about doing the new menu. She had learned a lot in her menu analysis course at the community college and she was eager to put her knowledge to work. However, while she was at her computer going over the changes, she began to notice some irregularities. "Fish of the day" had become "fresh fish of the day." "Ice cream had become "homemade ice cream." Darla became concerned because she knew that the fish of the day came in frozen over the weekend and that the ice cream was always bought from DairyFresh, the local dairy. She decided to see Mr. Mack regarding her concerns.

She closed down her computer and went in search of Mr. Mack. Darla wasn't particularly worried about speaking with Mr. Mack. She had worked for the Macks for more than four years, since she was a junior in high school, and now she was a community college graduate.

She knocked on Mr. Mack's door. When he saw that it was Darla, he gave her a big smile and said, "Come on in."

Darla explained her reason for stopping by. She ended her comments by saying, "I'm sure no one meant any harm, but it's just not right for us to misrepresent our products." Mr. Mack was quite agreeable. He told Darla that he was glad she had brought it to his attention, and ended his remarks by saying, "I'll take care of everything, Darla. Thanks so much for the help. It's really great to have such a sharp girl on our side."

Darla felt much better after her meeting. However, a few short weeks later, she was dismayed when she opened the new menus for the first time. All of the inaccurate menu items were still there.

Darla quickly found Mr. Mack in his office. "I've just gotten my first glimpse of the new menus, Mr. Mack. They are very attractive. But I think you must have forgotten our conversation about the 'fresh' fish and other items."

"I didn't forget anything, Darla. I took what you said into consideration and then I made an executive decision. But I do appreciate your input and you are welcome to offer suggestions any time you wish."

Case Questions

1. What would you do now if you were Darla? Explain your answer.

2. How would Kant judge this marketing ploy? Explain your answer.

3. Is there any way that a utilitarian could justify what Mack is doing? Why or why not?

 # Case Study—The Dynamo (Part I)

Javier Montoya had been working at FoodSource Distributors, LLC, for almost 30 years. He had risen from stock boy to vice president of marketing during that time. He was considered a company hero. He knew that many of the newer employees looked to him for assistance and that many of the long-term employees counted on him. He was welcome anywhere he went within the company.

Javier had always enjoyed working at FoodSource. He never dreaded going to work when he woke up in the morning. He never felt like calling off or doing something else. For the past 30 years, he took great pleasure in his day-to-day activities. Today he woke up knowing that there was an important executive board meeting and he was looking forward to seeing some colleagues he had not seen in a while. He also knew that the board would be discussing FoodSource's newest, hottest item that had been launched exactly one year ago: the Dynamo. The Dynamo was a pasteurized sports drink that had "antioxidants, phytochemicals, vitamins, and minerals up the wazoo" according to FoodSource's president, Bart McIntyre. Additionally, the taste was superb; it had an appealing appearance and texture; and there were only 40 calories in an eight-ounce serving. The sales reports were going to be finalized and discussed. Javier knew that his group had done a superb job on the marketing effort and he was eager to hear the results. He had great plans for celebrating what he expected to be excellent sales results with his group.

Javier dressed in his lucky navy blue pinstriped suit with his favorite red power tie. He arrived at the meeting 15 minutes early. He was surprised to see not only the other executive committee members but the director of food science as well. Eunice Bronson was a no-nonsense, no-fun science type in Javier's opinion, but he had a great deal of respect for her abilities. She had an Ivy League Ph.D. and had been in the field for 20 years. She had been with FoodSource for little more than one year but had proven to be a hard worker and a good colleague.

The meeting started at exactly 9:00 A.M. President McIntyre welcomed everyone and turned the meeting over to Odetta Graves, vice president of operations, who conducted the meeting for the next hour. Shortly after 10:00 A.M., McIntyre took over the meeting again. He became serious and said he had some important findings that had to be discussed with the group and, unfortunately, it would have a bearing on the future marketing activity for the Dynamo.

McIntyre looked directly at Javier and said, "The results of your marketing work with the Dynamo this past year have been outstanding and you will receive a copy of them after the meeting. However, some recent findings by the food science department are more important to discuss at this time. The challenges your group will be facing may be insurmountable." With that, McIntyre called on Eunice Bronson to proceed.

"I will make this short and to the point. Just recently, and accidentally, I might add, one of our food scientists discovered that the caloric content of the Dynamo eight-ounce serving is actually 100 calories. At this point, it has been tested and retested more than one dozen times and it comes out the same each time. We cannot continue to market this as a 40-calorie drink."

Javier was stunned. He could not even imagine how his team was going to take this information. He did not look forward to returning to his office for that discussion any time soon.

Case Questions

1. If you were Javier, what would you do? Explain your answer.

2. If you were Mr. McIntyre, what would you do? Explain your answer.

3. Sometimes what seems practical is not the same as what appears to be moral or ethical. Is there a difference in this case regarding what Javier should do?

4. Concerning the statement in question three above, is there a difference in this case regarding what Mr. McIntyre should do?

 ## Case Study—The Dynamo (Part II)

The following afternoon, Javier pulled his group together for a marketing pep talk and serious discussion. They had all been given the bad news the afternoon before and were told to put their thinking caps on for a full 24 hours and come back with some useful solutions.

The marketing team, comprising Henrietta, Raul, Simon, and Wesley, was huddled around the small conference table when Javier entered. All eyes turned to him immediately.

As the meeting progressed, it became apparent that there were two divergent lines of thinking within his group, and no one saw any way to bring them together. Henrietta and Raul felt that the new marketing scenario should claim that a new 100-calorie edition of the Dynamo has just come out and that the old one would be back on the market soon. The idea was to keep the old one off the market long enough for people to get used to the new one. Also, the new one would come in a longer, slimmer container; the group would jazz the container up so that it looked like a larger serving. "And," Henrietta added, "lots and lots of coupons and specials for the second edition."

"What would you do about bringing the old one back on the market?" Javier asked.

Raul answered for the pair. "We would change the serving size, also put it in a smaller bottle, a very jazzy one. The label would say 'new and improved' so we could change the calorie content without making a big deal over it. With a smaller serving size and a slimmer bottle, it would probably work out to about 60 calories per serving. No one will squawk about that."

"Well, that's all something to think about. What have you two got?" Javier asked as he turned to Simon and Wesley.

Wesley answered, "We want to take a different approach. We want to be honest with the public, apologize, and send out rebates for new purchases. We want to take the entire inventory of old product off the shelf or have distributors put a label on it, stating the actual calorie content. We feel that this is the best way to regain the public's trust and we won't have to look over our shoulder thinking someone might discover our mistake and consequent cover-up. We will probably lose a lot of money up front, but we can gain customer loyalty back by accepting responsibility for our actions and asking for another chance. And don't forget, we do have a great product that the public loves. That means something."

Javier looked from one group to the other. "Thank you all. I know you have put a lot of effort into this quagmire. I'll take this up with Mr. McIntyre and I will get back with you as soon as I know which direction we plan to go.

Case Questions

1. If you looked at this problem from a strictly ethical point of view, which plan is the one to follow: Henrietta and Raul, or Wesley and Simon? Explain your answer.

2. If you looked at this problem from a strictly business point of view, which plan is the one to follow: Henrietta and Raul, or Wesley and Simon? Explain your answer.

3. If you were Javier, which plan would you advocate with Mr. McIntyre?

4. How would Kant view the two plans?

5. How would a utilitarian view the two plans?

Case Study—The Dynamo (Part III) —————————

That day, somewhere else in the building, McIntyre and Bronson were having a meeting.

"Well, Bronson, how did this happen?"

"Mr. McIntyre, as you well know, I was only here a few weeks when the Dynamo was launched. All testing had been done and approved by the time I started," said Bronson.

"You also were privileged to know that we were firing your predecessor for some of his unusual scientific methods, or lack thereof. I must say I am very disappointed. You knew this product was of the utmost importance to us. You should have been all over it like a fly on honey," said McIntyre.

"If you wanted me to re-check everything, you should have said so," Bronson answered belligerently.

"So, now I have to tell you how to do your job?" McIntyre retorted. Then he took a big breath and added, "This isn't getting us anywhere. I'll get back to you when I know what I'm going to do." McIntyre stood up to signal that the meeting was over.

Case Questions

1. Should Bronson be responsible for checking the work of her predecessor since she knew he had been fired because of his "unusual scientific methods, or lack thereof"? Explain your answer.

2. Was McIntyre fair in his expectations of Bronson? Explain your answer.

3. Should the company be responsible for informing the new employee that a re-check of previous work should be done? Explain your answer.

8

Applying Ethics
to the Sales Function

He that is of the opinion money will do everything may well be suspected of doing everything for money — Benjamin Franklin

WORKING IN SALES TODAY is more competitive than ever. Stealing clients and undermining colleagues are examples of unprincipled practices some employees may feel pressured to do. Making the sale through any means necessary may not lead you down an ethical path. In sales, the tendency toward unethical behavior sometimes originates within the company and sometimes within the individual employee.

If your organization, in an effort to achieve its own best advantage, should require you to engage in conduct that principled reasoning tells you is unethical, you should do the right thing — *even if it puts you at odds with your employer.* Consider the following example in which an employer attempts to protect his financial self-interest by pressuring an employee to stretch ethical boundaries.

You work for the All Aboard Travel Agency. You are told to promote Carson Cruise Lines' three-day cruises to the Caribbean that feature a day on their private island. You also know that the private island was devastated during last year's hurricane season and that most of it is still under repair. You are told to assure all potential customers that everything has been repaired and that they can expect a delightful, fun-filled day on the island. What do you do?

Or consider a much more difficult problem with serious implications. You are working on a farm in Wyoming for the summer. Part of your job is to bring the cows in from the field in the evening. Last night, you saw two "downers" (animals that are unable to stand) when you went out to the field. You know from your food safety course that this could mean big trouble in the form of mad cow disease. You immediately go to your boss, who tells you that the animals are "just tired" and that he will handle the situation. He also tells you not to mention the down cows to anyone.

The employer's decision to gloss over such a potentially dangerous situation is unconscionable. In a case such as this, an ethical person would find himself or herself at odds with the employer. The cows should be tested for mad cow disease; if they are not tested, an outbreak could occur. You would be putting innocent people at risk of contracting the fatal brain-wasting condition known as Creutzfeldt-Jakob disease, which can result from eating meat infected with mad cow disease.

You know that there is no way this meat should be sold. You also know that a lot more must be done because the disease can spread.

Even after you have decided that something must be done to ensure that no one is exposed to the risk of contracting this horrendous disease, there are further ethical issues you must resolve. What exactly should you do? Handling this situation in a manner that is both ethically principled and practical will require a great deal of thought and soul-searching. Analyzing the issues with the help of the different philosophical theories presented earlier should help a great deal.

Case Study—The Vacation

Randall and Christopher work in the sales office at the Milliken Resort selling vacation packages. They are in stiff competition this month because the boss, Mr. Milliken, has offered a one-week, all-expenses-paid vacation to whoever reaches $100,000 in sales first. Each of them usually reaches $60,000–$70,000, so it is not too much of a stretch to get to the $100,000 mark. If they both reach $100,000, they will each get the vacation, but the first one will get an additional bonus.

Randall has been working on one of his favorite clients, Mrs. Dortmund, who has brought her church group to the Milliken Resort for the past five years. He knows that if he can finalize this sale he will be over the $100,000 mark.

Just as he is about to call Mrs. Dortmund to finalize her group's arrangements, Mr. Milliken steps into the office that Randall and Christopher share. Mr. Milliken asks Randall to join him for just a moment; one of Randall's clients is on the phone and Mr. Milliken needs his input.

While Randall is gone, Christopher calls Mrs. Dortmund and offers to finalize the arrangements for her church group's visit to the Milliken Resort. Mrs. Dortmund is expecting Randall to call back, but Christopher sounds like such a nice guy, she decides to go ahead and finalize the sale.

Case Commentary: Utilitarianism

A utilitarian analysis of this situation would look at the consequences of what has occurred. As is often the case with utilitarianism, it is easy to misuse the doctrine by looking only *selectively* at *some* of the consequences. This would be incorrect, however: you must consider *all* of the consequences, including all of the harms and benefits to everyone concerned to decide what is the ethical choice.

Christopher may rationalize his actions by claiming that no real harm has been done by his sudden incursion into Randall's sale. After all, Mrs. Dortmund and her church group are getting their vacation, and very promptly too—quicker than if he had waited for Randall to do it. Second, he's helping himself by making the sale, because it may lead him to the coveted free vacation. Third, it may even benefit Randall by getting him to work harder to win the prize—in fact, Christopher may argue that he and Randall will likely benefit from his taking over this sale, because it will spur them both to make even more sales over the course of the month. Everybody benefits because they get more sold and make higher commissions. Finally, it is good for the company because it increases sales and the "competitive spirit" among employees that keeps them performing at their peak.

However, this reasoning is a self-serving rationalization that is a severe misuse of utilitarianism; it is contrary to what an honest and full utilitarian analysis would conclude. First of all, it is a very selective reading of what the full consequences are likely to be. It completely ignores many of the negative consequences that will follow from Christopher's action. By stealing Randall's sale, Christopher has done enormous damage to his relationship with Randall who, after all, had the preexisting relationship with Mrs. Dortmund and did the preliminary work on this sale. Hard feelings and nasty backbiting at the office are almost certain to ensue. This will have negative consequences for both employees. Furthermore, it will likely have negative consequences for the company as well: a company with unhappy, feuding employees is likely to operate poorly. In fact, these negative consequences, which are highly likely, are almost certain to overwhelm any fanciful positive consequences that Christopher has rationalized for himself in the previous paragraph.

From a rule utilitarian perspective, the case against Christopher's action is even clearer. A rule that allows employees to steal each other's business without permission is so obviously going to lead to destructive and negative consequences that companies routinely prohibit such conduct. The case is clear if we consider the consequences for *all concerned*, not simply Christopher and his desire to win the prize. Utilitarianism, whether of the act utilitarian or the rule utilitarian type, would condemn Christopher's action and deem it unethical.

Case Commentary: Kant's Categorical Imperative

For Kant, the question is not what consequences follow from Christopher's action, but rather the motive behind the action. The motive must be ethical, which requires that it pass the test of Kant's categorical imperative in its different formulations.

Could Christopher meet the first formulation of the categorical imperative? Could it be made a universal rule that employees can take each other's business without permission? While it might be theoretically possible for a company to set up such a rule, to do so would be self-contradictory in any practical sense. Doing business with one another relies on a set of understandings and rules (both written and unwritten) that require us to keep faith with each other by acting honestly, in an open and aboveboard manner. If we do not act that way, business cannot be conducted because universal mistrust would destroy our ability to work together. Thus, it would be self-contradictory to have a universal rule allowing deceptive or hidden practices for self-gain. That is one reason Kant is *always* opposed to deception or dishonesty. Since Christopher's action here is a variety of deceptive and dishonest behavior, Kant would condemn it.

This becomes even more apparent when we analyze the case from the point of view of the second formulation of the categorical imperative: Never treat another human being as a thing rather than a person, using them for your own self-gain. Yet that is exactly what Christopher has done to Randall here. Randall has been turned into a stepping stone for Christopher to use in his quest for the prize, rather than a person who has a special moral status as a human being. Human beings are free and rational creatures who deserve to be treated as such. Deception and sneaky behavior conducted behind their backs are always violations of their rights.

Kantian or deontological ethics would absolutely condemn Christopher's behavior. By denying Randall's personhood and by using him for his own selfish goal of winning the prize, Christopher has acted unethically. Just as the golden rule would condemn Christopher's behavior, so would Kant because Christopher is denying Randall his humanity by taking the fruits of Randall's previous labor behind his back.

Case Commentary: The Ethic of Justice

We can also ask if Christopher's conduct is fair to Randall. Is it just for him to receive the commission and potential prize that goes with this particular sale? Again, recall that John Rawls asserts that just or fair arrangements are those that disinterested persons standing behind the veil of ignorance would consider fair or just. Would a person who understood all points of view, and who did not know if he or she would end up being either Christopher or Randall in this situation, consider it fair and just that Christopher takes this sale and its potential benefits?

Clearly not. Knowing that they individually might end up being the "Randall" in situations like this, people would condemn a set-up perpetuating or condoning this type of unauthorized taking of the fruits of other people's labor. They would consider it unjust and would demand that the rules be set up so that Randall gets to keep the benefits of his work with Mrs. Dortmund. Christopher's action would be criticized as an unjust distribution.

Given Christopher's wrongdoing, justice ethics might also address the question of compensatory justice, namely, what type of compensation Christopher should make to Randall for what he did. At minimum, it appears that Randall should be made whole, meaning that he should be given any commission from the sale and credit for the sale in the prize competition. Whether additional compensation is due to Randall is a murkier question; in general, it probably shades off into another justice question, namely, what sort of retribution or penalty Christopher should pay for his wrongdoing?

Retributive justice would ask the question of what punishment Christopher should face for his wrongdoing. Depending on a variety of circumstances, including the existence and clarity of company rules against stealing each other's work, greater or lesser degrees of punishment may be appropriate. Generally, an ethical employer will take into account a variety of circumstances, including the totality of conduct of the individual involved (is there a pattern here?), the company's own responsibility for setting a clear and consistent ethical culture within the firm, and the severity of the harm done.

Case Commentary: Aristotle and the Ethics of Virtue

Aristotle and others who employ character ethics or virtue ethics norms would ask about the character of Christopher in this instance. In general, this incident would be seen to cast a poor light on Christopher's character. He would be seen as deficient in more than one area of virtue or character. And he would be seen as needing to improve his character.

First, he is lacking in the virtue of honesty. He has a dishonest character, as seen by his taking a fellow worker's rewards behind his back. This is a severe character flaw if it exemplifies the habitual behavior of Christopher.

Second, he is acting unjustly, and thus we see he lacks one of Aristotle's four main virtues: justice. By not giving Randall his due, Christopher is exhibiting the vice of injustice. Again, this is a serious character flaw.

Thus, when we look at Christopher's behavior or character as exemplified by this behavior, we have a clean sweep: all ethical traditions condemn Christopher's actions and Christopher himself for what he did. This is not an ambiguous or gray case: ethical thinkers of all traditions condemn what Christopher has done.

Case Study—Theresa the Telemarketer

Theresa Grady works for the Blissful Beat Telemarketing Company. Blissful Beat specializes in selling vacation packages by phone. Most potential buyers appear on Blissful Beat's call list because they signed up in shopping malls across the country for the opportunity to win a free cruise. Since they willingly offered their name, address, and phone numbers to Ready Resorts, Inc., which owns Blissful Beat, they are legally on the list even if they signed up for the national Do Not Call list.

Theresa received two 6-hour days of telemarketing training (for which she was not paid). Blissful Beat explained that it was the "opportunity cost" for being hired and for being allowed to earn the high commissions that they offer for the sale of each vacation package. In training, Theresa was offered the following advice:[1]

1. Be as friendly as your target allows.

2. After friendliness is established, challenge the target's ego. Encourage the target to impress you, but make it difficult. For example, ask the target if he or she is a risk-taker and, if they say yes, encourage them to provide illustrations.

3. After gently putting down one or two of the illustrations, ask if the target trusts you. Encourage back and forth discussion until you can get a "yes" or as close as you can come to a "yes" regarding trust.

4. The next lines could look something like this:

   > "Why don't you want to purchase this vacation? Either you trust me or you don't and I'm telling you it's a great deal. I'll also let you in on a secret. If folks don't buy this package, it is for only one of two reasons—either because they don't trust me or they can't afford it. Which one is it?"

5. The next important step is to get the target to take out his or her credit card. A few questions that usually help are: "Does your middle initial appear on your credit card? What is the date of expiration on your credit card? Does your credit card have a gold seal on the front?" Use whatever you think will work with your target. You will be the expert at that point.

6. And, *voilà*—you have sealed the deal. At this point, you can count on pocketing your commission!

Theresa, a single mother, was thrilled to find this job. It was close to home and she could work the hours she wanted. She was also told that she might be able to work at home in the evening after she becomes established with the company.

However, after two weeks, Theresa is becoming increasingly uncomfortable. She feels like she is fooling people, because she knows that the vacation is really one big advertisement for Ready Resorts, Inc. During the vacation, the guests are continually bombarded with information about Ready Resorts timeshares. The first night, they are offered a free steak dinner (wine included). But they are not told that during the dinner there will be a presentation.

Theresa would like to resign from her job, but has not even been paid to date. After working for one week, she had made a grand total of $150 and, of that money, she will not see $75 for another three months because the company has a policy that places a hold on your first three sales.

Case Questions

1. In your opinion, did Blissful Beat have the right to conceal the fact that they would try to sell timeshares with Ready Resorts to their customers?

2. Look over the five preparation suggestions that Theresa received in her training class. Explain each suggestion individually according to the different philosophical theories we have studied: utilitarianism, categorical imperative, justice, and virtue.

3. Does the company have the right to hold Theresa's wages? If it is legal, is it also ethical? Why or why not?

4. What would you do if you were in Theresa's shoes?

Case Study—The Advertisement Exchange (Part I)

Elvira Quigley is the owner of the small but chic Lavender Boutique Hotel on the Shawnee River. It is located on the outskirts of downtown Middletown, a popular Midwest destination.

Elvira had been searching for ways to reach out to more distant audiences. But she also wanted to improve her name-recognition within her own five-county region. Finally she hit upon the idea of trying to negotiate a cooperative advertising arrangement. She spoke with various newspapers and radio stations. She even approached a television station. Finally, she found a possibility in Mr. Omar Wrath, a radio announcer employed by local station WKRN in Evers County, about 30 miles from Middletown. Mr. Wrath had a sophisticated show and Elvira thought she had found the perfect solution in her search for cooperative advertising.

Elvira invited Omar to have lunch at the Lavender. After they enjoyed a delicious meal, she showed him around the hotel and grounds. The deal they struck was that in exchange for an all-inclusive free weekend for two during Pirate Month, one of the most popular times of the year on the Shawnee River in Middletown, Wrath would give Elvira three 30-second commercial plugs during the three weeks following his stay.

Elvira was delighted. After negotiations concluded, she showed him out to his car and they shook hands on the deal.

A month later, during Pirate Month, Omar Wrath and a guest took full advantage of their free weekend. Elvira had saved one of her top rooms for Wrath and his guest, and instructed the hotel dining room to serve Wrath and his guest whatever they ordered from either the kitchen or the bar. If paying guests had produced the same bill, the profit would have been astronomical, but Elvira thought the exchange was well worth it.

During the next month, Elvira listened each and every day to Wrath's three-hour radio show, but never once did she hear mention of The Lavender. Finally she decided to call Wrath by phone. She had a very hard time connecting with him, but she was persistent. When she finally got him on the phone and asked about her advertisement, he said, "Well, I didn't really enjoy my stay at your hotel, so I don't feel the need to give you the advertisement."

"But we made a deal. We shook hands on it," Elvira answered.

"There's nothing in writing. Look, I'm very busy. I gotta go." And he hung up the phone.

Case Questions

1. From a utilitarian perspective, tally the benefits and harms of what Mr. Wrath has done.

2. Apply rule utilitarianism to Wrath's actions: what would the consequences be of making it a general rule to break verbal agreements?

3. What would Kant say about Wrath's behavior?

Case Study—The Advertisement Exchange (Part II)

Elvira was furious. She was not going to take Wrath's pilfering, sneaky, conniving ways sitting down. She went straight to the Internet and looked up WKRN to find out if there was someone she might contact regarding Wrath. She found that WKRN was a small, local concern; it appeared to have no national affiliation. As she searched further, she found that Leon Hardy was the manager of the station. Further reading showed that Hardy had operated the station for only a short time. Previously, the station had been in bankruptcy proceedings. She easily concluded that the station did not have a lot of money, but that was no reason why they could not keep up Wrath's part of the agreement.

Elvira tried to phone Hardy several times. She finally reached him late on a Friday afternoon. He sounded cranky and tired, but she proceeded with her story.

His answer was brusque and unfriendly. "But he didn't have the right to offer you an advertisement. You got scammed, lady, plain and simple. I'm sorry for your loss. But look, there is absolutely nothing I can do."

"What would it cost you to give me the advertisement? Nothing!" she complained.

"You're wrong there," he countered. "If I give you a free advertisement, it means I have to put off a paying advertisement. Look, time is money and you cannot have any of my time. This conversation is over." And he hung up.

Case Questions

1. What is Wrath's responsibility in the situation? Explain your answer.

2. What is Hardy's responsibility in the situation? Explain your answer.

3. If you were Hardy, would you take any action against Wrath? Why or why not?

4. How would you view Wrath's character? Explain your answer.

5. How would Aristotle view Wrath's character? Hardy's character? Explain your answers.

6. In denying assistance to Elvira, is Hardy breaking Kant's categorical imperative? Explain your answer.

7. Is Hardy's behavior leading to the greatest good for the greatest number of people? Explain your answer.

 ## Case Study—The Advertisement Exchange (Part III)

Elvira was persistent. After much research, she found that even though WKRN had no national affiliation, the main radio station in Capitol City owned and operated it. In desperation, she decided to contact several town representatives who had participated in a retreat at the Lavender the year before. She knew that every one of them had a wonderful experience at the hotel.

One day several months later, she found herself in Capitol City sitting in the radio station president's office. Horatio Billingsly, the president, had agreed to see Elvira after being contacted by many of the town representatives. Elvira laid out her story in as clear and concise a manner as she could.

When she finished, Billingsly said, "Hardy is not the owner. We own the radio station. We have a lease arrangement with him."

"But is there anything you can do?"

"I'm going to investigate the situation over the next week and get back to you one week from today or sooner."

Case Questions

1. What would you do if you were Billingsly? Why?

2. How would you apportion responsibility between Wrath, Hardy, and Billingsly?

3. How would a utilitarian view the situation? Explain your answer.

4. How would Kant view the situation? Explain your answer.

5. From a justice perspective, what compensation is owed to Elvira, if any? Explain your answer.

6. What disciplinary actions, if any, are merited for Wrath and/or Hardy?

 ## Endnote

1. Ideas for this exchange were taken from an article in *The New Times*, January 8–14, 2004, pp. 7–10.

9

Applying Ethics to the Maintenance Function

Engineering is the practice of safe and economic application of the scientific laws governing the forces and materials of nature by means of organization, design and construction, for the general benefit of mankind. —S.E. Lindsay, 1920

THE UPKEEP OF A PROPERTY is a major responsibility. Safety and security are of paramount importance to any visitor who stays in a hotel or who eats at a food service establishment. Whether guests are businessmen, families with small children, single women, or elderly couples—everyone wants to feel secure in a clean and comfortable environment. They want to enjoy the amenities promised.

From a well-lit walkway to a hallway night-light, maintenance employees must consider the guest and work accordingly. These behind-the-scenes tasks come to the fore only when there is a problem. The smoother these back-of-the-house activities function, the more comfortable guests are and this translates into a good business reputation and repeat visitors. Problems occur when matters other than the safety, security, and comfort of the guest overshadow the necessary work of maintaining a property.

The safety of the employees is an important matter as well. In 1970, the Occupational Safety and Health Administration (OSHA) was created to protect workers from hazards in the workplace and to also ensure that they be informed of hazards at the workplace.[1] In maintenance, this could refer to the use of dangerous chemicals and to working with hazardous machinery.

The following case, "On the Edge," is followed by detailed ethical analyses in relation to each of the ethical theories presented earlier: utilitarianism, Kant's categorical imperative, Rawls's justice ethics, and Aristotle's ethics of virtue. The chapter closes with a series of case studies and questions about the cases that challenge you to analyze ethical issues in the area of maintenance.

Case Study—On the Edge

The Edgewater Hotel Group is so-named because it selects hotel sites that are near or adjacent to large bodies of water. It is a substantial hotel group with 110 properties worldwide, 95 of which are in the United States and 15 of which are in Western Europe. Because they are such a sizeable hotel concern, they have always received an excellent liability insurance rate. Their insurance company was recently sold to Commensality, Inc., one of the largest insurance companies in the world. The new owners have been reviewing all insurance rates and have decided that the Edgewater Hotel Group is underpaying for its liability insurance, because there have been several deaths, severe injuries, and large claim payouts over the last five years. All disbursements have been related to the swimming and boating areas.

Marcus Birch, President and CEO of the Edgewater Hotel Group, received a letter from Commensality, Inc., stating that Edgewater's insurance liability rates would be rising, on average, $5,000 per property per year ($550,000 a year) unless Edgewater updated and modernized many of its safety features. Commensality, Inc., included statistics and research reports showing how each new safety measure would improve the overall safety standards for Edgewater. Birch was rather surprised as he read from the report that the inclusion of one or more of the following would bring great savings on Edgewater's liability insurance rates.

1. Higher life-guard stands
   a. Allows for greater visibility on large bodies of water
   b. Cost = $300 per lifeguard stand located on large body of water
   c. Shown to decrease death and serious injuries by 80 percent; Shown to decrease claim expenditures by 18 percent

2. Test water for *E. coli* and other microorganisms on a daily basis
   a. Microorganism contamination of swimming waters causes foodborne illness outbreaks (swallowing contaminated waters)
   b. Cost includes testing of each body of water every day; average cost estimated at $12/day per property
   c. Shown to decrease death and illness by 65 percent; Shown to decrease claim expenditures by 10 percent

3. Erect a barrier to swimming near coastal bluffs
   a. Coastal bluffs are a dangerous natural hazard found along any coastline; estimated annual deaths total approximately 80 per year
   b. Average cost associated with building a fence able to keep swimmers out of dangerous areas is estimated at $2,000 per property
   c. Shown to decrease death and serious injuries by 88 percent; Shown to decrease claim expenditures by 32 percent

As he read, Birch realized that each improvement came at a cost to the Edgewater Hotel Group. After much deliberation, he called in his maintenance chief, Mr. Richard Brick. Birch gave Brick a copy of the letter, highlighting the above excerpt. He also included the following assignment in writing:

> "Send out bids for the three suggested safety improvements noted above. Based on the lowest bid that comes in, check with accounting to see if it will be worth our while to make the recommended improvements. Inform accounting that it is necessary to include all breakeven points. For

example, it is estimated that Property #26 will expend $400,000 in injury and death claims over the next five years. If the suggested improvements are made to Property #26, will it cost more or less than $400,000? I would like this information on my desk three weeks from today."

What appears to be Mr. Birch's main concern? Is the consideration of a break-even point an ethical matter when the safety of guests is concerned? An article appeared in *The New York Times* on January 29, 1995, entitled, "How Much for a Life? Try $3 Million to $5 Million."[2] The article quotes Kip Viscusi, an economist at Duke University, who estimated that if the entire gross national product were devoted to making life safe, there would be only $55 million available to prevent each accidental death.[3] Does that mean that we should spend money on safety only as long as there is enough left over for everything else we want to do? Should we test water for *E. coli* and other microorganisms on a daily basis or reupholster the lobby furniture? If the cost to the company is exactly the same for each item, but there is only enough money for a single expenditure, does the question become which will bring in more guests and, therefore, more income?

When thinking about safety and security, a hospitality entity has a responsibility to the guest. However, it also has a responsibility to its shareholders. In many instances the decision will become *is it worth the cost to the company?*

Case Commentary: Utilitarianism

A utilitarian would approach this dilemma by identifying the alternative actions and their consequences for all stakeholders. For example, if expenditures for improvements at property #37 will be $800,000, but savings in insurance payments are estimated to be only $400,000, then Edgewater should not make the improvements. This is an example of comparing the harms to the benefits for the company. The utilitarian approach can be extremely practical when thinking through this type of ethical dilemma. But it can also be unwieldy to calculate the harms and benefits to each and every Edgewater property and base the decision for that particular property solely on the calculations.

In addition, we have to consider if, when using this strictly consequentialist method, we are really evaluating all of the consequences for all of the stakeholders. Are we thinking about the pain and grief that will unquestionably occur if even one fatality were to take place? Have we taken into consideration all of the stakeholders that would be affected in that regard—all of the family, friends, co-workers, neighbors, etc., of the deceased?

A utilitarian might also look at this problem from the view of maximizing societal welfare. In this case, the decision would still involve money because if the dollars were not used for safety and security, they might be used for other improvements that could also benefit society. For example, if the hotel does not purchase the higher lifeguard stands, management would have the money to hire three new front desk agents. This would not only ease the check-in and check-out lines, but would bring three new jobs, with benefits, to the community. This approach would still involve costing out the benefits and the harms to the society and choosing the approach that would bring the most benefit.

Another way utilitarianism would look at maximizing social welfare would be by calculating the total harms to all of society from the accidents and deaths if improvements are not made. While the insurance costs of an accidental injury may be "X" dollars, the total costs to all of society (ongoing medical costs, lost contribution from a formerly productive worker, etc.) might be four or five times "X" dollars. This could change the balance decisively regarding whether the expenditure for an improvement was worthwhile. However, it would probably also change the calculation for who should be paying for which share of the total cost, since we are now calculating costs and benefits to the entire society, not simply to the Edgewater Hotel Group. Consequently, it is possible society as a whole (through government expenditures, for example) should pick up some of the costs for an improvement proportionate to its share of lowered costs if the improvements are made.

Case Commentary: Kant's Categorical Imperative

Kant would offer a different view of potential solutions. A deontologist would certainly say it is one's duty to protect his fellow man. More specifically, the officials of the Edgewater administration would search their consciences asking, "What is my duty now that I know of the potential harm to my guests?" A Kantian thinker's decision would be based on the formulation of broad, universal principles that relate specifically to the Edgewater dilemma, such as the right to safety and security, compassion for all humanity, respect for the sanctity of life, and so on.

Deontological thinkers often use reasoning very close to the golden rule, which says to treat others the way you would like to be treated. The golden rule would ask, if Marcus Birch were to go to a hotel with his wife and children, wouldn't he want the safety of his family members assured? How much would he pay for what amount of safety? Whatever that amount is, he should provide the same degree of safety at all Edgewater properties.

But the Kantian perspective is slightly different. The golden rule still relies on consequences of actions as the basis for ethical decisions and, as such, it is still a variation of, or closely related to, utilitarianism. Kant would tell us to ignore the consequences when making a moral judgment, but to instead pay attention to the principle or rule being followed if you adopt one course of action or another. Could you make the principle into a universal rule? The universal rule, "Do whatever is cost-effective regarding safety measures," is not obviously self-contradictory, so simply following a utilitarian cost-benefit analysis of safety issues may pass the test posed by the first formulation of Kant's categorical imperative (be able to make the principle of your action into a universal rule).

However, the second formulation of the categorical imperative poses the question a little more sharply: are you turning another human being into a mere means (degrading him or her from being a person into a mere thing), rather than treating human beings as ends-in-themselves? Are you risking a death or a serious injury simply for the sake of a profit margin? On the other hand, you cannot make a property absolutely safe in all respects. So, Mr. Birch will have to decide at which point he is denying "personhood" to others if he chooses not to institute safety measures because of financial consideration. Going past that point is immoral, according to Kant.

Deciding when you are crossing the boundary and treating other human beings merely as means to your own goals (i.e., turning them into things) is not always easy. Perhaps a good rule to follow is to apply that old stand-by, the golden rule. If you would not want others to do it to you, you are probably acting unethically by degrading others to the status of a means, not an end. That is why the golden rule is so closely related to Kantian ethics. If Mr. Birch is to act morally according to Kantian ethics, he will need to institute all safety measures he would want for himself if he were a guest. This may require more expenditure than a utilitarian cost-benefit analysis would justify. Kantian ethics may be stricter than utilitarian ethics in cases such as this.

Case Commentary: The Ethic of Justice

How would an ethic of justice apply to this case? Clearly, if guests are exposed to abnormally hazardous conditions at Edgewater properties without fair warning, an injustice will occur. This violates Rawls's principle of equal liberty: each person in an institution has an equal right to the most extensive liberty compatible with a like liberty for all. On the other hand, if Edgewater properties have safety practices that seem reasonably fair to even those most likely to be injured or killed (e.g., guests and some categories of employees), they are probably just.

Rawls would say that the decision regarding the justice or injustice of Edgewater's safety practices is best made behind the veil of ignorance. That is, make the decision without knowing if you are going to end up as a customer, an Edgewater shareholder, Mr. Birch, a maintenance worker, a lifeguard, the concierge, etc. This way, you will probably be conscientious about safety because you may end up being the person most exposed to danger. But, at the same time, you would not push safety to absurd lengths where you end up harming most people merely for a minuscule, marginal improvement in safety outcomes.

In practice, Rawls's ethic of justice in this case would probably come to conclusions quite close to those of a Kantian. Both would be remarkably close to an application of the golden rule, because both would put primary emphasis on protection of the interests of the most vulnerable, although neither would push this to absurd lengths. But both ethical theories might be more stringent and demanding on Mr. Birch and the Edgewater Hotel Group than utilitarianism, which may require only a cost-benefit analysis.

One aspect where an ethic of justice may be particularly applicable is at the level of public policy and public regulation. For example, which regulations should be in place to *require* Edgewater and similar institutions to provide a safe environment for its guests and its employees? Rather than leaving it up to the individual business, society may wish to require all enterprises in a particular line of business to abide by certain regulations. For example, warning signs may be required. Lifeguards in some places during certain hours may be required. In deciding what is or is not warranted in the form of required legal regulations, the Rawlsian *original position* behind the veil of ignorance may be a most useful perspective to use. Justice ethics can be easily applied in public policy discussions.

Case Commentary: Aristotle and the Ethics of Virtue

The virtue ethics approach focuses more on the integrity of the decision-maker than on the ethical act itself. A virtue ethics perspective primarily considers a person's character.

Which decision would indicate a virtuous character? Several virtues are relevant here. Justice, as already noted, is one. Prudence, or wisdom, would be another. Compassion and sensitivity would be two more. Aristotle would call on Mr. Birch to practice these virtues and to make a decision in accordance with them. If Mr. Birch's decision were unjust, imprudent, lacking in compassion, or insensitive, we would judge him accordingly.

While it is impossible to set up rigid rules to follow, people of good character will have little difficulty in making a judgment. An individual's community becomes their guide. What is the accepted practice within that community? In the case of the Edgewater Hotel Chain, the community is a professional community, but one that also includes guests as well as employees.

If you, the hotel manager, were to make a decision based on virtue ethics, you could ask yourself, within my community, would I be proud to bring up the decision openly? As a hotel manager, would I publicize the fact that I chose to purchase new furniture for the lobby instead of purchasing higher lifeguard stands that would ensure greater safety? Would I be proud to tell fellow businessmen at the next chamber of commerce meeting about my decision? Would I be proud to tell my decision to the parents at the Girl Scout meeting held on property this afternoon? Would I be proud to tell my decision to my extended family at our upcoming Thanksgiving dinner? If the answer to all or some of these questions is no, we can assume the action, according to virtue ethics, may be morally problematic.

Consider the Edgewater Hotel Group specifically. If Mr. Birch decides not to make the safety improvements in order to use the money in some other manner, would he be willing to see that information publicized on the front page of all the local newspapers in the cities where Edgewater has properties? If he is not willing to see this information made public, then he has doubts about the virtue of his character as demonstrated by this decision.

 ## Case Study—The VIP

It was a beautiful, sunny Florida day with blue skies, scattered clouds, and low humidity—a perfect day for the beach. No one could be happier than Richard Jackson, the general manager of the Great Escapes Beach Resort. He had a full house in the hotel and he was expecting a famous celebrity to arrive that day. All the preparations were in place as requested by J.J. Morony, the famous basketball player.

Richard Jackson personally went about ensuring that all the amenities, as well as the necessities, were in the suite. He was being quite particular as Mr. Morony insisted on having the Sportsman Deluxe Suite, the only one of its kind in South Florida. He was also being quite particular because he was a bit worried. The hotel sprinkler system had been acting up recently. It had unexpectedly gone off in the Sportsman Suite just two weeks ago. Thankfully, no one had been occupying it at the time. He had been assured by Deluxe Maintenance Inc. that the problem was a faulty heating switch and everything was now in perfect working order. But the hotel's director of maintenance, Mr. Wilder, was not convinced that the problem was just the faulty heating switch. He thought the entire system was in need of an overhaul and continually told Mr. Jackson that this was the case.

Mr. Jackson listened respectfully to Mr. Wilder. Then he explained, "We cannot give up the extra dollars that the Sportsman Suite will bring us. The revenue from that suite alone is more than four times the revenue of a normal room."

The Great Escapes Beach Resort is a four-star, 320-room hotel boasting three restaurants and a luxurious spa. The resort has a stunning view of the Gulf Coast. Over the last 25 years, the resort has earned a great reputation with both its guests and the community. In recent months, the resort has undergone a number of minor renovations in the lobby and on some of the guest floors. The property is scheduled for major renovations toward the end of summer that will last for several months.

During last month's executive meeting, which included all department heads, a final report was handed to Mr. Jackson highlighting several major problems that needed to be addressed as soon as possible. Especially alarming was the report from the engineering department about the operational status of the fire sprinkler system in all the guestrooms.

Mr. Jackson assured everyone present that all repairs would be taken care of at the end of the season. He also mentioned that they would have several celebrities visiting over the next two months and all repairs would have to wait. He did not want to have the celebrities inconvenienced. He wanted their repeat business as well. Mr. Jackson also stated that he was already in receipt of the estimates necessary for the upcoming repairs to the sprinkler system, and that work would begin promptly when the season was finished. At the end of the meeting, during his summary statement, Mr. Jackson urged everyone present to all work together as one team and help each other until the renovation was completed.

Mr. Jackson was in his office when he received a call from the front office announcing the arrival of J.J. Morony. He immediately went to the lobby where he greeted his guest and his family. After a tour of the resort, Mr. Jackson escorted them to their suite. As he was leaving the room, Mr. Jackson suggested Mr. Morony visit the beach. "This is one of the best days I've seen here in a long time. You and your family should definitely take advantage of the opportunity."

A few hours later, Richard Jackson received a call from Mr. Edwards, the beach hut manager, saying that Mr. Morony and his family took his advice. "They're all on the beach and seem to be having a fine time," Edwards told Jackson.

Later that day, Mr. Jackson was having lunch with several of his business partners at a restaurant located about a mile from the resort. During the luncheon, he received a call from Mr. Plotkin, the head of the security department at the resort. Mr. Plotkin told Mr. Jackson that there was a faulty fire sprinkler on the fifth floor in the west wing where all the full Gulf view suites are located. This included the celebrity's suite. The initial report was that all of the guests' belongings were either damaged or thoroughly soaked as a result of the sprinklers.

Case Questions

1. What are the ethical issues in this case? Explain your answer.
2. Why does Mr. Jackson find himself in such an untenable situation?
3. What should Mr. Jackson have done differently?
4. How should the Great Escapes Beach Resort compensate J.J. Morony?
5. How would someone who is operating from behind the veil of ignorance view this situation? Explain your answer.
6. What ethical rule or rules should Mr. Jackson consider for the future?

This case was authored by Samer Hassan, Ph.D., Associate Professor of Hospitality Management at Johnson & Wales University, Florida Campus.

 ## Case Study—Dissatisfaction ─────────────────

The Chalworth Hotel is located on 50 acres of prime property in eastern suburban Long Island. The hotel was built in 1935 when the area was mostly farmland and it has continued to expand, slowly but surely. The main building is registered as an historic landmark. In fact, the local historical society is planning a celebration for the hotel's 75th birthday. Plans are already underway.

The owners of the original Chalworth Hotel were Margaret and John Chalworth of London, England. They were uncomfortable with the politics in Europe at the time and brought over their very large family: four sons and two daughters, along with both his and her parents. The hotel, worked mostly by family members, had become well known not only for its excellent European service, but for afternoon tea as well. Family members owned the hotel until 1998, when the last remaining Chalworth decided to sell to the international hotel corporation, the S-Group. The hotel has been owned and managed by the S-Group since the 1998 purchase.

At the time of sale, occupancy was at an all-time low; the average annual occupancy rate for the previous five years had been 55 percent. However, from 1945 to 1975, occupancy averaged close to 90 percent per year.

Originally a 12-room hotel, The Chalworth now has 72 guestrooms in three buildings, a heated indoor-outdoor swimming pool, two lighted tennis courts, and many private park-like seating areas around the grounds.

This past September, the Graff family decided to revisit the hotel. Bernie and Betty Graff had honeymooned there in September 1965 and were celebrating their 40th anniversary. They noted quite a few changes, many of them to their dissatisfaction. Bernie decided to write the following letter to Mr. Rogers, the present general manager of the Chalworth Hotel:

> Dear Mr. Rogers:
>
> I have been a guest at the Chalworth Hotel many times over the past 40 years. I have never been as disappointed as I was with this last visit. I will detail for you some of the reasons for my dissatisfaction.
>
> I was unable to swim because the "heated" water in the swimming pool was very cold (no more than 75 degrees F.). The air in the indoor

pool area was too cold as well; my wife and I were even too uncomfortable to sit in that pool area without wearing a sweater.

There was a cracked window in our guestroom. The paint on the walls was peeling. The gardens were overgrown. The benches were chipped. And where were all the bird feeders?

On our first evening at the Chalworth, my wife and I went out to play tennis but the lights were not on. When we inquired at the front desk, we were told that the courts were only lit during July and August. It was a lovely September evening and we were quite disappointed.

I am writing to you because I want to enjoy future visits at the Chalworth Hotel. I fear, now that the hotel is no longer family-owned, the place will become nondescript. I am also writing because your most recent advertisement in the Sunday New York Times states: "heated pool, lighted tennis courts, beautifully manicured grounds, refurbished rooms—all in an atmosphere our guests have come to expect over the years." It is my opinion that you must deliver what you claim or not advertise like this any longer.

Sincerely, Bernie Graff

Mr. Rogers mulled over Mr. Graff's letter. He decided to call in his director of maintenance, Arnold Spencer. When Mr. Spencer arrived, Mr. Rogers handed him the note. Spencer read it through carefully. When he was finished he looked up and waited expectantly.

"Well?" Mr. Rogers inquired. "What have you to say for yourself?"

"You put us on a very tight budget three months ago. You cut our electricity budget in half. You 'trimmed'—your words—my workforce. Every time I have come to you with a maintenance budget request, you have turned me down. You wouldn't even allow us to replace the very old, very broken riding mower. How do you expect 50 acres of grounds to be kept manicured without a decent mower? You told me to make do with what I have. And that is what I have been doing—to the best of my ability."

Case Questions

1. What are the ethical issues in this case? Explain your answer.

2. In their approaches to this case, how would a rule utilitarian differ from an act utilitarian? Explain your answer.

3. How would a justice ethicist resolve this case?

4. If you were in command of this hotel, what would you do? Why?

 Case Study—The Renovation

John Owens is the owner and general manger of the Beach View Hotel. This contemporary 300-room hotel was built in the late 1980s and overlooks a white sandy beach. In recent years, the hotel has built an excellent reputation with its guests. The Beach View Hotel enjoys 80 percent occupancy year round. The best time for business is during summer, when occupancy reaches 100 percent.

For the last few years, Mr. Owens has been considering a major renovation to the property, but he has continually postponed the project for different reasons. Last week, while he was in a meeting with his executive team discussing final preparations for the summer season, the housekeeping director, Mrs. Smithson, told him that a number of rooms on the fifth floor were flooded because of a roof leak. Mrs. Smithson reminded Mr. Owens that during previous meetings she had told him of the stifling smell in some of the rooms on the fifth floor and that guests also had complained several times. The director of engineering, Mr. Landsman, spoke up immediately. He stated that according to previous roof inspections, the recommendation was that the hotel needed a new roof.

Mr. Owens acknowledged that he had been told about the roof in earlier meetings, but he wanted to wait until after the busy summer season so as not to disturb his guests. He further stated that replacing the roof would not be an easy task, and that the workers and equipment in the hotel would definitely create a disturbance. However, shortly after the meeting, Mr. Owens started calling a number of roofing companies to get estimates. The prices varied greatly, but each company agreed that it would take approximately six to eight weeks to get the job done.

The hotel's advertisements all stated *"a peaceful, quiet location on the beach."* Mr. Owens thought about the summer season and the many guests that would be visiting the Beach View Hotel: "What will I tell the guests when they arrive? Should I inform the guests who have existing reservations? When new guests call for reservations, should I mention the construction? Maybe I should just cancel the summer season?"

Mr. Owens thought about his dilemma for a few days. Finally, he decided not to mention anything to either the already existing reservations or to potential guests when they called to book for summer. He would give each guest a note upon arrival, stating that the hotel was undergoing emergency repairs and that he was very sorry for the inconvenience. He would also offer $100 dining credit in the hotel's restaurant.

Case Questions

1. Is Mr. Owens acting in an ethical manner? Explain your answer.

2. How would you handle the situation that Mr. Owens is facing? Explain your answer.

This case was authored by Samer Hassan, Ph.D., Associate Professor of Hospitality Management at Johnson & Wales University, Florida Campus.

 # Case Study—It's All in the Numbers

Freddy Bruner, Jr., owned the Bruner Hotel and Resort in Marbella, New Jersey. His father had opened the hotel in 1935 during the Depression. He had been able to pay very low wages then because people were desperate for jobs. Freddy Sr. had managed to keep out the unions by giving out little bonuses, added breaks, or other little extras to keep his workers satisfied every time union people came around.

Freddy Jr. had his own method of keeping wages low. He had become adept at securing Social Security numbers. He had a real system for doing so. Every day he read several local daily papers online from around the country. He would select a group of people from the obituary columns who were in the age range of 20–55 years old and had died within the last few days. Aside from age, Freddy's main criterion was whether the obituary included the town where the person was born. He would then write to the local city hall asking for a copy of the birth certificate. He was successful approximately half of the time and therefore had quite a collection of birth certificates. He would then write to the Social Security Administration, saying he lost his card and using the birth certificate as proof of identity. This ruse enabled him to employ as many undocumented workers as he wanted.

Emilio Montoya was the hotel manager. Emilio knew about the ruse, but he also felt like he was helping undocumented workers who could not otherwise work. It was easy to give maintenance jobs to these new undocumented workers, most of them to fix just about anything, and they were very appreciative of the work. Emilio didn't hide anything from the employees. He explained how the Social Security numbers were obtained and told each new hire that if they got caught, the boss was not taking the fall. It was very rare that an undocumented worker turned down the job. The jobs always paid the current minimum wage. There were no benefits included for the undocumented workers.

One day, three weeks after the last group of workers was hired, U.S. Marshals showed up at the hotel. They arrested Freddy Jr., Emilio, and 15 undocumented workers. However, that night, both Freddy and Emilio were out of jail after paying a fine. The undocumented workers remained in jail.

Case Questions

1. Sort out the main ethical issues you see in this case. What are they?

2. What would enter into a utilitarian analysis of Freddy's behavior? How should he be judged? What about Emilio? What about one of the undocumented workers?

3. Would you analyze the situation differently if the undocumented workers had obtained their own Social Security numbers, and Freddy, although well aware of their probably illegal status, simply looked the other way? Why would it, or would it not, be different?

4. Analyze the justice of the differential treatment of Freddy and Emilio compared with the treatment of the undocumented workers. What's your conclusion and how do you justify it?

Endnotes

1. Linda K. Treviño and Katherine A. Nelson, *Managing Business Ethics: Straight Talk About How to Do It Right*, 3d ed. (Hoboken, N.J.: Wiley, 2004), p. 208.

2. Peter Passell, "How Much for a Life? Try $3 Million to $5 Million," *The New York Times*, January 29, 1995, sec. 3, p. 3.

3. Ibid.

10

Applying Ethics to the Food and Beverage Function

The art of dining well is no slight art, the pleasure not a slight pleasure.— Michel de Montaigne

WHENEVER GUESTS enter a restaurant, they have the right to be served safe food prepared under sanitary conditions. When discussing the ethics involved in a food service operation, matters such as these are central. Sanitation concerns such as "use-by" dates are one example. Is it permissible to take the attitude, "Oh, that's only two days past the 'use-by' date—it's perfectly okay!"? Other examples of irresponsible behavior are serving food held at inappropriate temperatures and allowing unsanitary conditions in kitchen areas. The pressures of daily operations can quickly complicate ethical issues. What would you do if your supervisor ordered you to serve food that you knew had been kept in the temperature danger zone for more than four hours?

Just as serious are cases involving outright cheating of guests. Guests have the right to receive what they order. This involves not only the ingredients of items described on the menu, but advertised portion sizes as well. Salespeople are known to exaggerate the qualities of their products. But is it acceptable for a restaurateur to exaggerate so much that guests think they are eating fresh fish when, in fact, the fish has been frozen? Is it acceptable to lead guests to believe that they are eating an organic product when they are not? When skirting the truth about a product is more than just hype, it is unethical. Similar to product safety, truth in advertising, which includes truth in menu, is an issue for both organizations and individuals.[1] Truth in menu is an ethical issue because it involves fairness, honesty, and respect for others.

There are plenty of opportunities for cheating, stealing, and other wrongful behaviors within a food and beverage operation. However, guests have the right to expect safe food when they dine out. Additionally, it is a basic consumer right to be told the truth concerning the products and services purchased. This includes full disclosure regarding food and beverage products. One of the fastest ways to lose customers is to be dishonest with them.

The next case, "A Good Job Pays Your Bills," is followed by ethical analyses in relation to utilitarianism, Kant's categorical imperative, Rawls's justice ethics, and Aristotle's ethics of virtue. The chapter closes with a series of case studies and questions about the cases that challenge you to analyze ethical issues that arise in food and beverage operations.

Case Study—A Good Job Pays Your Bills

Mr. Mason is the food and beverage manager of the 550-room Gem Hotel in the Catskill Mountains of New York. As part of his job, every three months, he prepares a "forecasted income statement" for the hotel's food and beverage department.

This past September, when preparing the statement, he was costing out the menu for the winter season and realized that the price of meat products had gone up by 8 to 12 percent. He questioned the purveyor, Best Deal Food, Inc. The purveyor's reason for the price hike was the heavy snow en route to the Catskills from New York. He clarified further by explaining that the delivery trucks that brought the products from New York were also charging higher prices.

Mr. Mason brought his findings to Mr. Maxwell, the owner of the hotel. Mr. Maxwell looked Mr. Mason straight in the eye and said, "Fix it, that's your job. The bottom line pays your good salary and bonus."

In as measured a tone as he could muster, Mr. Mason replied, "I will have to print new menus with a price increase." Mr. Maxwell stared at him in disbelief, put his arm around Mr. Mason's shoulder and said, "Printing new leather-bound menus is expensive, and many of our regular customers will be offended with a price increase. You are a food man—just reduce the portion size, but leave on the old price. Give them a great plate presentation!"

Mr. Mason immediately realized that Mr. Maxwell wanted him to shortchange customers by camouflaging the main entrée with starches and vegetables so they would never know it was a 10-ounce steak instead of the 12-ounce steak on the menu. He would have to do the same thing with all of the meat, chicken, and fish products.*

Federal and state laws apply to this case. Both the federal law and the law of virtually every state include statutes that prohibit the use of deceptive or unfair trade practices. The Federal Trade Commission (FTC), the principal federal agency protecting consumer interests, enforces the law. Under this federal law, the capacity to deceive, and not actual deception, is prohibited. Therefore, the FTC is not required to prove that deception actually occurred. If an advertisement, statement, or brochure fails to disclose important information, there may be a violation.

In addition, most states have now adopted either the Uniform Deceptive Trade Practices Act or their own similar laws. These laws protect consumers and other businesses. The Uniform Deceptive Trade Practices Act provides that a person or business has engaged in an illegal deceptive trade practice when (in addition to many other things) goods or services are represented as of a particular standard, quality, or grade or of a particular style or model when they are not.

Clearly, there are legal dimensions that apply to many ethical situations. However, legal decisions or outcomes are not necessarily ethical decisions or outcomes. If prosecuted for deceptive business practices, Mr. Mason and Mr. Maxwell would hire attorneys who would defend them in relation to the rules of law. The following

---

*This case was authored by Jude Ferreira, Assistant Professor of Hospitality Management, Johnson & Wales University, Florida Campus.

sections view the situation of Mr. Mason and Mr. Maxwell from strictly ethical points of view and seek to judge them not in the legal terms of guilt or innocence, but in moral terms of right or wrong.

Case Commentary: Utilitarianism

Utilitarianism looks at the consequences of our actions. There will be consequences for all of the stakeholders involved if Mr. Mason follows Mr. Maxwell's orders to decrease portion sizes and deceive guests into thinking they are getting the same amount of food promised by the menu. Who exactly are the stakeholders? They are Mr. Maxwell, Mr. Mason, all of the kitchen employees who would be involved in the deception and, of course, the guests.

Mr. Maxwell is cheating many people in order to enrich himself. The losses of the many outweigh the gains to a few, and because of this, act utilitarians would say he is behaving in an unethical manner. Additionally, rule utilitarians would say that the deception is morally unacceptable because rules of conduct allowing such deceptive behaviors will lead to more harm than good. A rule utilitarian would ask, "What would be the consequences if all restaurants lied about portion sizes on their menus?" Or, "What would be the consequences if everyone cheated in their business dealings?"

Mr. Maxwell is breaking a moral rule of society (to tell the truth) if he lies on his menu. What about Mr. Mason? He is only following orders. If he does not follow orders, he will lose his job. Is it acceptable for Mr. Mason to cheat the guests? Mr. Mason needs to ask himself which moral rules he is willing to live by. A rule utilitarian would suggest to Mr. Mason that, in this case, the rule he should follow is the rule that says we all should treat each other fairly and honestly.

Of course, this case is not a simple matter. Suppose Mr. Mason is the sole support of his family. Suppose jobs are scarce. Suppose he has a huge mortgage and other monthly payments to make. However, at the end of the day, he has to live with his own actions. Is he willing to expose himself as a con artist to all of the kitchen employees? If he did, he would also be telling them that it is acceptable to defraud guests.

Case Commentary: Kant's Categorical Imperative

Kant would examine the behaviors of both Mr. Maxwell and Mr. Mason. Remember, Kant judges a person based on the reason for their actions. Kant would find Mr. Maxwell's actions unethical because cheating of this nature violates the categorical imperative to always treat other human beings as ends, not merely as means for your own purposes. Do you think Kant would be just as quick to condemn Mr. Mason, whose job might be at stake? You might think he would be more lenient because Mr. Mason has so much to lose, but remember that Kant's categorical imperative states that there are rules that we always must follow—not only when it is convenient.

Therefore, Mr. Mason should not cheat because he could not make it a universal rule that everyone can cheat. If Mr. Mason attempted to universalize his decision, he would have to ask himself if his choice to deceive the guests by camouflaging the entrées would be a suitable decision for all of the other managers and employees of the hotel. According to Kant, if Mr. Mason thought that his decision was appropriate and that he was treating others as humans (ends) rather than as things (means), then it would be suitable to broadcast it to the other managers and employees of the hotel. In other words, it would be acceptable for all managers and employees to deceive the hotel guests. Front desk clerks could sell deluxe rooms, but place guests in regular rooms. Bell staff could carry guests' luggage to their rooms and then falsely state that there is a charge. Servers could add tips to customers' credit card charges, and so forth. Conversely, if Mr. Mason is unable to universalize his decision, then the decision must be immoral.

Kant also asserts that we should not use a person for our own purposes. Both Mr. Maxwell and Mr. Mason would be doing just that. Mr. Maxwell would be doing it to save money and Mr. Mason would be doing it to save his job. If everyone collectively exploited each other this way, each and every person would universally be denied their own humanity. Every person deserves to be treated as a person and not as a thing.

Case Commentary: The Ethic of Justice

Justice ethics requires that we treat each other fairly. Neither Mr. Maxwell nor Mr. Mason would be treating the guests fairly. They would not be treating the employees fairly either if they required them to cheat the guests.

Rawls argues that we can determine what is fair, or just, by determining what rational people, who considered every point of view, would accept as fair. Remember the veil of ignorance? It would easily apply in this case. What would Mr. Maxwell do regarding the portion sizes if he did not know where he would wind up in the situation? Would Mr. Maxwell say it is acceptable to cheat the customer if he knew he was to be the customer and not the owner? The same would apply to Mr. Mason.

This case is an example of how crucial certain details can be. A critical fact in this case is that the menu states that the steak is 12 ounces. Reducing the portion size to ten ounces involves defrauding and deceiving the customer. According to some legal applications, the author of a deceptive advertisement must:

1. Intend to have the audience believe something false.

2. Know it is false.

3. Deliberately lead the audience into believing the falsehood.[2]

However, consider the differences to our ethical analysis if the menu did not specify the weight of the steak? Would reducing the size of the portion then be ethically permissible? Absolutely. There is no ethical obligation to provide large portions. Deciding to reduce portion size in response to increased costs is perfectly acceptable. What is not ethically permissible is falsely advertising one size and then providing a smaller one. One little detail makes all the difference.

Retributive justice states that the person who committed the wrong must be aware of what they are doing and freely choose to do it. Second, the person must be aware that what they are doing is wrong. Third, the guilt must be substantiated. Finally, the punishment must match the crime. In this case, both Mr. Maxwell and

Mr. Mason are fully aware of what they are doing and they both should know it is wrong. Their guilt would be easy to prove.

A punishment that might properly fit the crime would be a fine levied under the truth-in-menu laws. That might be the institutional punishment levied against the restaurant, perhaps augmented by public exposure of the misdeed, which could harm future profitability a great deal. Punishment of the two individuals involved is a separate matter. Criminal charges against Maxwell and Mason might be brought under the legal system. An action of this type would be unlikely unless they were also involved in more widespread fraudulent criminal behavior.

What type of compensatory justice would be proper? If a civil suit were filed, they might be forced to pay back all of the guests whom they had cheated. This might be levied as a fine or as community service at (for example) a kitchen for the homeless. They certainly would not be jailed for lengthy periods of time because the gravity of the offense would not warrant such a severe punishment.

However, Mr. Maxwell may be considered "more guilty" than Mr. Mason, since he is the ultimate boss. The extenuating circumstance that Mr. Mason is being directly ordered to commit the unethical act may make his appropriate punishment less severe—although it will not absolve him completely. "I was just following orders" does not absolve one of wrongdoing if the unethical behavior was done knowingly.

Case Commentary: Aristotle and the Ethics of Virtue

Beyond the morality of the actions, we can also judge each man's character. Aristotle would look at their deceptive behavior and determine that neither Mr. Maxwell nor Mr. Mason has a virtuous character because neither acts the way a human being should act.

Aristotle named four fundamental virtues that are necessary to moral behavior: courage, temperance, justice, and prudence. Mr. Mason has shown a definite lack of courage because he would not resist Mr. Maxwell. Neither man is exhibiting the virtue of justice. Neither man is showing prudence (wisdom) because they could easily be caught and penalized. Just think how many employees in the kitchen will know that Mr. Mason and Mr. Maxwell are cheating the guests. One's concept of humanity will dictate what that person believes is virtuous. If one believes that honesty is a virtue, one will treat everyone in an honest manner and expect the same in return.

 Case Study—Sound Business Practices?

Mary recently graduated with a master's degree in hospitality from a prestigious college in the United States. She has been hired as the central purchasing agent for the Manley Arms, a family-owned chain of small but luxurious resorts in the British Virgin Islands.

The chain's strategic differentiation from other hotel chains in the immediate area is twofold. First, their concept is all-inclusive, meaning that guests pay only once for all of the main amenities of their stay (lodging, food and beverage, transportation, entertainment, and recreation). Second, the resorts are marketed as the only chain in the Islands that makes indigenous food and beverage products available to guests any day of the week, any time of the day or night. As a result, there is extreme pressure on the purchasing departments of the individual hotels to always have the most popularly requested products (especially local alcoholic beverages) in stock.

There are seven main distilleries and bottlers of local alcoholic beverages in the chain's region. Being a power player in the Islands, Manley Arms has accounts with all seven in order to ensure the most competitive pricing.

Every resort, prior to Mary's employ, had a purchasing agent on site who independently received weekly bids from each supplier and then ordered the majority of that week's products from the lowest bidder. Beverage managers at each resort were sent a copy of the week's purchase order so they would know which products the resort would have in stock. The managers ran specials for the week, highlighting drinks made with those products. This system had been in place for the past nine years with very few complaints from either guests or employees.

The owner of the resort recently expressed interest in opening at least two more resorts over the next three years. He wants to keep the same operational system, but, given the importance of economies of scale, he also wants to centralize the purchasing function and eliminate the need for onsite purchasing agents. He hired Mary to execute his strategy with both the existing and proposed properties.

None of this information was a secret and word reached the distributors for the distillers and bottlers. Mary was soon flooded with calls and visits. Some came with small "reminders" of their products such as calendars, pens, and wine glasses—all embossed with their companies' logos. Some representatives arranged for samples so that Mary, along with the company's executive chef and food and beverage director, could taste new product lines. Three representatives of the largest distilleries called Mary's office directly (bypassing both the executive chef and food and beverage director) to arrange private tastings at her home.

At the end of one of these private tastings, the representative left four cases of the company's most expensive wines on Mary's kitchen counter and flatly announced, "I'm sure that we could make this a habit if my company receives the majority of Manley's purchases from now on."

That same weekend, a rather handsome vice president from the most well known bottling company invited Mary to dinner to discuss future business possibilities. His company also had numerous outlets in the United States. During the dinner meeting, the vice president continuously flirted with Mary and she enjoyed the attention. The only discussion of business at this two-hour dinner was a conditional offer to hire Mary as an executive in his company after two years—if she made sure that his company received a no-bid contract for all local beers and malt beverages.

The next week, during a meeting with a third company's sales representative (who just happened to be the brother-in-law of the owner's wife) Mary was flatly offered a 10 percent kick-back on every $1,000 of product ordered from his company during the next six months. He explained that he was retiring soon and that his income was based mainly on commissions.

Mary was thoroughly confused and decided to call a former classmate who she knew had attended high school in the British Virgin Islands. The classmate just laughed and said, "Don't sweat it. That's how business is done in the Islands. Just do what's best for you."

Case Questions

1. What are the major ethical issues you find in this case?

2. Is the location, the British Virgin Islands, ethically relevant? Why or why not?

3. If you were Mary, exactly what would you do? Ethically justify your choice of action.

4. Which ethical tradition (utilitarianism, Kantian ethics, Rawlsian justice ethics, or Aristotelian virtue ethics) was most helpful in making your decision about what to do? Explain your answer.

This case was authored by Dwayne Mackey, an international food and beverage business consultant.

 ## Case Study—Stolen Lobster Tails

Munford was the dishwasher at the Heavenly Rest Truck Stop outside of Scranton, Pennsylvania. He had worked there for three months and had just passed his probationary period. He enjoyed the job a great deal, especially when a number of relatives on his wife's side began staying at their home.

Once a month, Heavenly Rest has a special lobster tail dinner. Truckers arrange to make their stop at the Heavenly Rest just so they can have that dinner special. To prepare, the restaurant orders dozens of cases of lobster tails. Most of the time, they run out before the evening is over.

There was a blizzard on one particular lobster special evening and only about half of the expected guests showed up. Marvin, the assistant manager, was not too worried because the tails freeze well. He had done it before when inclement weather hit. He knew they would just sell out the next month. He inventoried the tails, noting he had 22 full cases.

Later that same evening, during a slight dinner rush, Munford stepped into the freezer to retrieve a bag of ice for one of the servers. He noticed all the leftover lobster tails and thought about what a lovely New Year's Eve dinner they would make for his wife and her extended family who were visiting with them over the winter holiday season.

At the end of the night, while Marvin was finishing up the books in his office, Munford snuck two cases of the lobster tails out to his car. He threw an old blanket over the cases so no one would see his stolen goods.

The next day when Marvin went into the freezer, he immediately realized that two cases of lobster tails were missing. "It's theft, plain and simple," he said to himself. He walked back to his office and shut the door. He wanted to think through the matter without any disturbance.

Marvin soon came to realize that Munford was probably the thief. He decided to approach him and ask him outright. Munford was surprised that he had been so easily caught. He confessed and begged Marvin to give him a second chance. He told him how much he enjoyed the job. He also told Marvin that he was under terrific stress at home with all the visitors.

Case Questions

1. What would you do if you were Marvin? Why?

2. Would your decision be any different if Munford were a 15-year employee with a wonderful work record? Why or why not?

3. Would it change your mind in any way about what should be done with Munford if you found out that Marvin's superior, Jake, the restaurant manager, routinely took home food of equal value to the two cases of lobster tails, and nothing was ever done about it? Why or why not?

 ## Case Study—To Drive or Not to Drive?

Wolf Burger was the night bartender at the Lazy Nights Saloon in Bliston, North Dakota. On this particular evening, Arthur Oakley was sitting at the bar. By 9 P.M., Wolf thought that he had served Arthur one too many drinks and refused to provide him with another.

About fifteen minutes later, Arthur decided to leave the Lazy Nights Saloon. As Arthur was saying his good-byes to all his buddies, Wolf thought to himself, "I should not let this guy leave. He's too drunk to drive. And the road conditions are not the best either."

Wolf didn't stop Arthur from leaving. Arthur got in his car and when driving home, he hit another car, killing a family of three: the father, the mother, and their eight-year old son. Arthur was hospitalized with a few broken bones.

Case Questions

1. Who should be held responsible for the deaths? Explain your answer using act and rule utilitarianism, justice ethics, and virtue ethics.

2. What universal rule could be written from this incident?

3. How does the veil of ignorance apply to this situation? Explain your answer.

4. If you owned the Lazy Nights Saloon, what policy would you institute that would cover situations like this? Draw up a statement of your policy and justify it as the ethically correct policy.

 ## Case Study—Clean as a Whistle!

Jamie, the executive chef at the Atmore Deluxe Restaurant, was preparing dinner for more than 100 people that evening. There were 75 reservations listed and it was Wednesday, a typically busy night at the restaurant. She had prepped the roasts, given assignments regarding the vegetables and salads, and was now waiting for Rachel, the sous chef, to arrive.

When Rachel walked into the kitchen she looked terrible. She was sneezing and coughing. The chef knew she had to send Rachel home, but she needed her desperately.

Jamie considered her options. "I'll just put Rachel on the cash register, away from food, and bring Carly inside. She is a culinary graduate and she has been dying for a shot at the kitchen." Jamie was satisfied with herself but she knew she was taking a chance. Rachel could still infect people if she was contagious. "I know I should send her home, but I need her," she kept thinking. Finally she decided to take a chance.

The dinner went off smoothly; Carly did a wonderful job. Rachel was fine out by the cash register. One of the regular guests came back to the kitchen, as he often did, to thank Jamie. He told her he loved eating at the Atmore because he knew that the kitchen was *clean as a whistle.*

The next day, however, Mr. Gershon, the Atmore's owner, stomped into the restaurant, nearly causing Jamie's soufflé to drop. "What in blazes went on here last night?" he shouted loudly.

Jamie was baffled until she heard Mr. Gershon's explanation. Twenty-two people who had eaten dinner at the Atmore Deluxe Restaurant were hospitalized with *Staph Aureus* food poisoning early that morning. Jamie immediately knew that Rachel had passed on her infection to guests, probably by handling money.

Case Questions

1. How responsible is Jamie for the food poisoning of the guests? Explain your answer. Is this really a moral issue, or merely a question of good or bad judgment about how sick or contagious someone is? Explain how you came to your conclusion.

2. What is the ethically right thing to do now? Nothing, or something? If something, what? Ethically justify your answer.

 # Case Study—Ratting

Alex Robertson was a line cook at Josephine's Fine Dining, a high-priced restaurant located in Lincoln, Nebraska. One night while Alex was on a break, he stepped out to the back alley and found his friend Mike Norman, a fellow line cook, smoking marijuana. Mike offered some pot to Alex. Mike told Alex that he smoked pot almost every night because it made the time go faster.

Alex politely refused, but when he did so, Mike asked him not to "rat" on him. They both knew it was against company policy and cause for immediate dismissal. Alex promised not to turn him in because Mike was not only a good friend, but also a very good co-worker.

A week later, the restaurant manager, Brandon Richman, called Alex into his office. He told Alex that he heard rumors that kitchen employees were smoking marijuana while on the job. He asked Alex if he knew of any such doings. Brandon also asked Alex if he knew who could be doing it.

Alex felt like a deer caught in the headlights. He tried to think clearly. He considered himself a good friend, but he also considered himself an exemplary employee. He made a quick decision. He said, "I'll keep my eyes peeled for any wrong-doing, Mr. Richman."

Two weeks later, Brandon Richman found out who had been smoking marijuana, and also who was covering up for him. He planned to fire Mike immediately because he had proof of his pot smoking at work. Even though he was fully aware that Alex did not smoke marijuana while at work, he decided to fire him anyway in order to make an example to the other employees.

Case Questions

1. What would you have done in Alex's place when Mike asked him not to "rat"? What is the ethically correct thing to do? Explain your answer.

2. What are the ethical issues involved?

3. Was Alex's behavior ethical? Explain your answer.

4. Was Mike's behavior ethical? Explain your answer.

5. Did Brandon Richman make an ethical decision? Explain your answer.

 ## Case Study—Tip Reporting

Freddy was a waiter at the London Port Steak House in Greenwich. He earned over $150 a night in tips, as well as a small salary. He knew that he was required by the Internal Revenue Service to report those tips. However, Freddy did not think it was fair that he should have to pay taxes on his tips; he felt that the restaurant ought to pay those taxes for him.

Consequently, Freddy reported only $25 per night. Mr. Quinlan, his immediate supervisor at the restaurant, knew that Freddy was being dishonest about his tip reporting. But Mr. Quinlan felt it was Freddy's responsibility, not his, to ensure that the IRS got its due.

As luck would have it, Freddy was audited that year. He immediately went to Mr. Quinlan, his supervisor, telling him about his woes with the Internal Revenue Service and asking for assistance.

"Would you please back me up about the $25 per night? I'll make it worth your while in the future," he added.

Case Questions

1. If you were Mr. Quinlan, what exactly would you do? Explain why.

2. Evaluate the ethics of misreporting your income to the federal government in order to pay fewer taxes. List arguments that could be made stating that it is acceptable and list the counter arguments stating that it is not acceptable.

Case Study—Your Heart's Delight

June was a regular customer at the Heart's Delight Restaurant and Delicatessen. June always celebrated her birthday at Heart's Delight, so everyone knew she was 80 years old. She ate at the restaurant twice a week, usually on Mondays and Thursdays. She always ordered the daily special and took home more than half of the meal as a take-out. Then, like clockwork, every Friday, June returned her mostly-eaten leftovers, claiming that they were spoiled by the time she got home.

Everyone at the restaurant knew that June had reduced economic circumstances and the countermen always gave her something to take home for the weekend to "replace" the leftovers.

After the new manager, Bryce Higgins, saw this happen twice, he approached Michael, the counterman, and asked him what was going on. Michael explained the circumstances and was quite surprised to hear Bryce say that no one was to give June "replacement" food any longer.

Case Questions

1. What are the ethical issues in this case?

2. What would you do if you were the manager of Heart's Delight? Why? Explain your answer using act and rule utilitarianism, justice ethics, and virtue ethics.

 # Case Study—Something for Nothing

Jack Moss and his friend Joanne were dining at *Le Fleur,* one of the newest upscale establishments in Dayton, Ohio. Jack had offered to take Joanne out for a fine dining experience to celebrate their newly formed partnership.

Toward the end of the meal, Jack slipped a tiny piece of glass from his jacket pocket onto his plate (Joanne saw him do it, but Jack did not know that Joanne had seen him). Jack immediately called the waiter, Bryan, over to the table. In a whisper, Jack told him to look on his plate. Jack pointed directly at the glass and asked to see the manager immediately.

Bryan agreed to get the manager, but, unbeknownst to Jack, Bryan had also seen Jack slip the glass onto the plate. Bryan found the manager, Ms. Baum, in the kitchen under harried circumstances. One of the chefs had to be sent home due to illness and orders were backed up in the kitchen. Ms. Baum was doing her best to assist.

As quickly as possible, Bryan explained the situation to Ms. Baum, including the fact that the guest had slipped the glass onto his own plate. Ms. Baum left the kitchen to speak with Jack. Jack insisted that the dinners should be complimentary because of the glass. When Ms. Baum did not immediately agree, Jack started to raise his voice, causing a disturbance in the otherwise quiet dining room. Guests began looking in their direction; Ms. Baum was mortified and tried to get control of the situation.

Case Questions

1. What are all of the ethical issues in this case? Explain your answer.

2. What would you do if you were Joanne? Explain your answer.

3. What would you do if you were Ms. Baum? Explain your answer.

4. Apply each of the ethical theories we have studied to this case. Explain each of your applications.

Case Study—Juanita in the Kitchen

Juanita Rivera was 22 years old. She had been living in East Chicago, Indiana, for five years. She had illegally crossed the border into the United States when she was ten years old with her parents and younger brother. For several years, her parents were employed as seasonal farm workers, each year making their way a little farther north until they reached East Chicago five years ago. They had relatives there, Victor and Carolina Rivera, who owned a restaurant and promised help for the family.

Juanita and her brother, Roberto, had managed to get a high school education. Their Uncle Victor was a legalized citizen and he was able to enroll them in school. Juanita had been a good student, and she wanted to go to the community college, but there had been a recent crackdown on immigrants who were in the country without legal authorization, and her parents were afraid of getting caught. None of them had papers granting them a legal status to be in the country. They had a decent life. They worked in Victor's restaurant; they were paid well, but everything was "off the books." It was as if they did not really exist officially.

Case Questions

1. Name the main ethical issues involved in this case.

2. What should Uncle Victor do? Why?

3. What should Juanita do? Why?

4. Suppose you happen to patronize Victor's restaurant and you find out about Juanita's undocumented status and her "off the books" employment. What would you do? Why?

Endnotes

1. Linda K. Treviño and Katherine A. Nelson, *Managing Business Ethics: Straight Talk About How to Do It Right*, 3d ed. (Hoboken, N.J.: Wiley, 2004), p. 72.

2. Manuel G. Velasquez, *Business Ethics: Concepts and Cases*, 5th ed. (Upper Saddle River, N.J.: Prentice Hall, 2002), p. 362.

11

Applying Ethics to the Hotel Front Office Function

A strong positive mental attitude will create more miracles than any wonder drug. —Patricia Neal

THE FRONT OFFICE is the most visible department in a hotel and the focal point of the front office is the front desk. The front desk is the hub of any hotel, whether a small roadside operation or a five-star luxury resort. Often, the first encounter a guest has with a hotel is with the front desk staff. Guests come to the front desk to register, to receive room assignments, to obtain information about services, facilities, and the community, and to settle their accounts and check out. Whenever problems or questions arise, guests generally pick up the phone and call the front desk. Front desk employees have a great deal of influence and responsibility. They need to know who to contact for the various problems that arise.

Front office operations cover more than just the interactions at the front desk. Functions include reservations, communications (telephone switchboard), uniformed service, and security responsibilities. Money can be a very powerful motivator to engage in unethical behavior. Many hotels average hundreds of cash and credit card transactions each day, giving rise to opportunities for theft and other unethical behavior. Other areas of concern may arise in relation to a property's reservation practices (overbooking), employees overcharging for services, violations of guest privacy, and many other situations.

The following case addresses overbooking and is followed by ethical analyses in relation to utilitarianism, Kant's categorical imperative, Rawls's justice ethics, and Aristotle's ethics of virtue. The chapter closes with a series of case studies and questions about the cases that challenge you to analyze ethical issues that arise in front office operations.

Case Study—Things Go Bump in the Night

Two weeks before her niece's wedding, Esther Barnes negotiated a room rate with the Panda Bear Inn. She received a reservation confirmation number for a double room for two people for two nights. When Esther and her husband arrived at the Panda Bear Inn, much to their dismay, they were told that their room was not available because the Inn had overbooked and they would be put up in a different hotel only five miles away.

They had been traveling most of the day and were very tired. Mrs. Barnes felt a little better when she was told that the Panda Bear Inn would pay for the

111

room at the Lion's Gate Inn. Driving another five miles didn't seem too much of an inconvenience. However, when the front desk manager told her that the Panda Bear Inn would not host them for the two nights at Lion's Gate, she became a little irritated. The manager further explained that Panda Bear Inn had openings for the second night and Mr. and Mrs. Barnes would have to return to the Inn for the second night.

Since Esther wanted to retain the room rate she had negotiated, she agreed and they left to stay at the Lion's Gate for their first night in town. After checking in at the Lions' Gate, they had to completely unpack and ready their clothes for the morning breakfast at her sister's house. The next day, they had to leave the family function and return to the Lion's Gate, repack their belongings, check out, and drive to the Panda Bear Inn. Once there, they again checked in, unpacked, and rushed to get ready for the late afternoon ceremony and the evening reception.

The next morning Esther and her husband felt like they spent more of their time packing and unpacking than they did visiting and celebrating with their relatives. During their trip home, Esther told her husband that their experience reminded her of getting bumped off a flight by an airline—but, in this case, they were not compensated for their inconvenience. She also questioned the legality of overbooking. She asked, "What good is a confirmation number, when there is no guarantee of a room?" Esther decided to write a letter to the corporate headquarters of the Panda Bear Inn hotel chain.

Do no-shows and late cancellations justify overbooking? Do the operational advantages of overbooking outweigh the inconvenience to guests? Were the Barneses treated properly? How would you feel if this happened to you?

Consider an analogous situation. Imagine going to your hairstylist for a late Tuesday afternoon appointment. You expect to be there for two hours. You are very excited because that evening you are going to an important business function where you will meet many significant people in your field. However, when you arrive, you are told that Eva, your favorite hairstylist, is overbooked and the salon has arranged for you to have your hair done at the XYZ Salon, a half hour away. They explain to you that Tuesdays average three cancellations, so the salon always overbooks. On your Tuesday, however, there were no cancellations. Would you consider this acceptable behavior on the part of the salon?

Case Commentary: Utilitarianism

The act utilitarian point of view on the Barneses' situation asks, "Was the greatest good achieved for the greatest number of people?" Possibly—the only ones inconvenienced were Mr. and Mrs. Barnes. The hotel owners certainly achieved their greatest good, at least in the short run. They made the most money possible by having sold all the rooms. However, allowing guests to think their rooms are guaranteed when they really are not may have numerous harmful consequences for the hotel owners, both short-term and long-term. The corporation is using the guest to achieve the highest possible profit for that day, while paying less attention to the guest's needs and comfort.

What are the consequences if a hotel develops a reputation for consistently overbooking? What are the consequences if employees see overbooking as management's inconsiderate treatment of guests? Employees often take their cue from their supervisors. The housekeeper might decide that the bathroom looks "clean enough" for guests. The bellperson might decide to charge a guest for calling a taxi.

An act utilitarian considers all of the consequences of the action. There are also consequences to never overbooking: lost revenue for the hotel owners and empty rooms denied to travelers in need of lodging.

For act utilitarianism, deciding the morality of an action is a balancing act: you weigh the total benefits against the total harms likely to result from a specific act. You are ethically obligated to undertake the action that results in the greatest net benefit for all concerned.

In the case of overbooking, the many factors you must balance can make the calculation fairly complicated. If a hotel overbooks by only X percent of rooms, and the X percent overbooking rate very seldom results in any guest being "walked," the net harm is relatively small. Since the benefits of a full hotel are many, act utilitarianism may find this level of overbooking ethically acceptable, because the benefits outweigh the harms.

However, it is also a question of how injurious the harms are. If a guest who is denied a room because of overbooking is greatly harmed (forced to travel a great distance for alternative accommodations, or forced to accept inferior accommodations, etc.), then the weight may swing in the direction of making overbooking unethical. Another factor that would affect the balance (and, hence, the morality of overbooking) is how much overbooking is practiced. If, instead of X percent of rooms being overbooked, three times X percent are overbooked, and this higher rate means that guests are frequently denied the rooms they reserved, then the amount of harm increases significantly. Thus, act utilitarianism may condone a certain level of overbooking, but not higher levels. It is all a matter of examining the amount of benefit and harm done, and choosing the course of action most likely to maximize the net benefit for all concerned.

Rule utilitarianism applies the principle of greatest good to rules of conduct, not to individual acts. So the question is: can a rule allowing overbooking be morally justified? It is apparent that rules allowing frequent denial of reserved service would not produce the greatest happiness for the greatest number, and thus they would be considered unethical. But it is quite possible that mild forms of overbooking, those that result in very few denials of reserved service and/or in small inconveniences, would be judged ethically acceptable.

Case Commentary: Kant's Categorical Imperative

Kant would view overbooking differently from the utilitarian perspective. He would be primarily concerned with the individual rights of the person denied what they were promised. If the hotel had overbooked because there had been a natural disaster in the area and they were trying to accommodate as many people as possible, Kant would maintain that this might be acceptable because of the motive behind the action. The overbooking was done out of a sense of duty to one's fellow man; it, therefore, may be the right thing to do. However from a Kantian ethical perspective, it would be much harder to justify overbooking as a routine business practice ensuring higher daily profits.

Consider the two formulations of Kant's categorical imperative that we have studied. First, we should act in a way that whatever rule we follow, we could will this to be a universal rule. Since a reservation is a promise to deliver a service (room, airline flight, etc.), denial of that service is breaking a promise. As with all forms of promising, Kant would condemn breaking the promise because breaking promises destroys the very basis of making a promise in the first place. It is self-contradictory to make a promise and break that promise; hence it is irrational and immoral. Thus, the first formulation of Kant's categorical imperative would condemn any overbooking that actually resulted in the denial of a promised service.

The second form of the categorical imperative stipulates that one must not use people for his or her own purposes. On the face of it, the practice of overbooking appears to do just that. Guests are used to ensure higher profits for the corporation without regard for the humanity or autonomy of those guests. Essentially, the guest has been "used" because he or she was, in effect, lied to when the reservation was made.

To illustrate this, consider the following situation. You arrive at your destination hotel after ten very long hours of traveling, including a number of airplane changes, delays, bad weather, and lost luggage—only to find out that your room reservation was not honored. Imagine that you had guaranteed your late arrival and even called just a few hours earlier and were assured a room. Now imagine that you have to taxi to another location and you have the further inconvenience of informing the airline to deliver your lost luggage to this other destination. Would you feel used? Would you have been degraded from the status of a human being to that of a thing used for someone else's convenience?

There may be, however, another way that overbooking could be made compatible with Kantian ethics. If the guest or passenger is made aware, *at the time the reservation is made*, that a reservation does not actually guarantee a room or flight, but rather only a very high likelihood of its availability, then no promise has been made. No deception would have occurred in the event of denial of reserved service. The guest or passenger would not have been used because he or she was aware in advance that there is at least a slight possibility of denial of service. He or she would then be able to rationally make a decision about what to do, and no deception or denial of humanity has occurred.

These appear to be the only circumstances where Kant would find overbooking to be morally acceptable. This is an example of a practice where Kantian ethics is much stricter than utilitarian ethics, which may find overbooking ethically acceptable in a larger number of circumstances than would Kant.

Case Commentary: The Ethic of Justice

Justice ethics states that we should treat each other fairly and asks us to look at the situation from behind the veil of ignorance. Imagine that you do not know if you will be the front desk manager (who earns a bonus based on profit and daily occupancy rates) or the weary traveler who discovers that the "guaranteed" room reservation was, in fact, not guaranteed. If everyone involved in making the decision were both rational and interested in their own well-being, many of the more permissive forms of overbooking would not be tolerated. A rational person would set up rules protecting the interests of the traveler, since he or she may end up being that traveler. Even if mild forms of overbooking were to be allowed, a justice ethic would place strong and effective restrictions on the practice.

Compensatory justice would also dictate that the wronged guest must be compensated for the loss and inconvenience. Some suggest that a guest might expect a free night at a nearby hotel of the same or better quality, a free phone call to notify friends or family of the hotel change, and a free upgrade on a future visit. Is this enough compensation for the traveler? Is this fair to the traveler? What if the person never expects to be in the area again? What good would the future upgrade do? In considering what is fair, you must ask questions such as: what has the hotel lost and what has the guest lost? What is the compensation costing the hotel? What is the denial of a room costing the potential guest?

Case Commentary: Aristotle and the Ethics of Virtue

Virtue ethics would view the hotel as a human community and ask how well the hotel contributes to the development of its employees' character traits? The traits or virtues include honesty, integrity, tolerance, fairness, and cooperation. Overbooking raises concerns about how well a hotel fosters honesty, integrity, and fairness if it does not keep its word to its guests. Any enterprise that engages in overbooking needs to be sure that this practice is honest and open and it does not promote an ethic of deception or irresponsibility in its employees. Virtue ethics requires businesses to foster values that relate to the way it interacts with its community. A business has to display a solid ethical culture in order to be respected by its community.

 ## Case Study—The Wedding Party

For the past five years, Hadley Greerson has been the front desk manager at the Eternal Bliss Hotel in Perpetual City. Previously, she had been the assistant front desk manager at the Honeymoon Heaven Hotel in the adjacent town of Andover.

More than a decade ago, the Eternal Bliss Hotel became recognized as a premier honeymoon spot. It is one of the many well-known honeymoon hotels in this area of the country. At least one wedding is held at the hotel each weekend all year long. The honeymoon couple often stays at least a few days after the wedding. The hotel has 300 guestrooms, six honeymoon suites, and eight ballrooms.

Amanda and Hal Butts have just arrived from Andover. They are in the bridal party for Rose and Richard Wooster, a wedding that is to take place in the hotel that evening. Jill Everley, the front desk agent on duty at Eternal Bliss, welcomes Amanda and Hal to the hotel. Jill has been working at this hotel for just under a year. The Buttses ask to have the keys to the room of the bridal couple. They want to leave champagne, flowers, and hors d'oeuvres in the bridal suite.

Jill knows the policy of the hotel. She is not allowed to give out room numbers of guests, let alone keys to guestrooms or bridal suites. Politely, Jill informs the Buttses that she cannot give them the keys.

The Buttses persist and argue persuasively. They point out that the couple hasn't even checked in yet. If only they are given the keys, anyone on the hotel staff can come with them and check everything out that they do. In fact, they insist the hotel can help, and they are willing to pay anybody who is willing to assist them.

Case Questions

1. What would you do if you were Jill Everley? Why?

2. If you were Hadley Greerson and you became aware of the request, how would you handle it? List all the things that you would do and explain why you would do them.

3. Can you think of any differences in what a utilitarian, a Kantian, a Rawlsian, or an Aristotelian would tell Jill or Hadley to do? Explain your answer.

 ## Case Study—Nobody Will Ever Know

John Flowers is the senior stylist at Happy Locks Salon located on property at the Marvella Resort, near Pensacola, Florida. Mr. Flowers recently approached Ms. Sheila Meriwether about lowering the monthly rent on his salon space, as business had been slow in recent months. Ms. Meriwether denied his request, adding that they did not raise his rent during other months when Mr. Flowers was busier than usual. She also told him that the salon was slow in general and they needed the income for overhead expenses.

Since Mr. Flowers felt that his work was in great demand at the Marvella, he assumed that he should go over Ms. Meriwether's head and speak with the hotel's general manager, Esther Soloff. Mrs. Soloff was sympathetic to Mr. Flowers, but also insisted that they would not lower his rent.

Mr. Flowers was not happy. He was determined to earn at least another $50 per week. Later that evening, he broached the subject with Evan, his friend who was on the night shift at the Marvella front desk. Evan was also sympathetic but said to John, "Look, it's tough all over. You'll just have to bite the bullet. It will get busy again. In the meantime, maybe you can cry a little to your best customers and squeeze out a bit more in tips."

John started to object, but then he got a gleam in his eye. He thought Evan's remarks over and said, "You know, Evan, you may just have something there." And he walked away with a bounce, looking much happier than he did earlier.

I wonder what he's up to, Evan thought to himself.

Three months later, Evan was at the front desk when the phone rang. It was Mrs. Hoolihan, a very irate customer. She demanded to speak to the general manager immediately.

"I'm sorry, ma'am, she's not here. Can I help you in any way?" Evan asked in an understanding tone of voice.

"Who are you? Are you a manager of some type?" Mrs. Hoolihan asked.

"My name is Evan, ma'am, and I manage complaints in the evening."

"Well, I certainly have a complaint, young man. I received my credit card bill and your hotel overcharged me."

"I'm sure I can help you with that. How exactly were you overcharged?"

"In the salon. I had my hair colored, cut, and blown dry. It came to a total of $125. I still have the receipt. But the charge from the Happy Locks Salon is for $135. I am furious, young man. Money does not grow on trees, you know!"

Evan pulled up the account history and immediately saw the problem. A tip of $10 had been added to the charge. He casually asked Mrs. Hoolihan about a tip and she told him that she distinctly remembers that she gave the stylist a cash tip of $10. "I would have given him more, but all he did was whine about money. I did not like that at all," she added.

Evan assured her that he would credit the $10 to her charge card. After he hung up, he looked over other salon fees and he began to discern a pattern. He remembered the conversation he had had with John Flowers. He suspected that John was helping himself to the customer's money. If that was true, he knew it was outright theft. He decided he would talk to John first before reporting the discrepancy. However, when he spoke to John, the stylist did not even deny it. He rationalized that the salon was costing him too much money and he was getting the clients to "chip in" on his salon space rental.

Evan told him that he would have to stop immediately and John agreed. "Are you going to report me?" John asked Evan. "It was only a couple hundred dollars, you know."

Case Questions

1. Explain John's rationalization from a utilitarian point of view.

2. How would Kant view this situation?

3. If you were Evan, what would you do? Which ethical theory (utilitarianism, Kantian ethics, Rawlsian justice, or Aristotelian virtue ethics) was most helpful in making your decision about what to do?

 # Case Study—Front Desk Politics

Three young women have been working at the Devil's Rock Inn, a popular conference and banquet spot located in a beautiful country-like setting. Molly is a front desk agent, Jane is a banquet salesperson, and Sue is in charge of the marketing and sales department.

In the past, whenever banquet information requests came to the front desk, Molly always forwarded them to Jane because Jane gets a full commission when she handles the requests directly. A month ago, Jane embarrassed Molly at an office event and Molly has been angry with her ever since. Now, she automatically forwards the requests to Sue in marketing and sales. Sue assigns one of her staff members to follow up. When the information finally gets to Jane, she receives only half the commission she would earn if the request had come to her first. She now has to split the commission with one of Sue's staff members.

Molly has two reasons for re-routing the requests. Not only is she still angry with Jane, but she also wants to get a job in Sue's department. She appreciates how Sue treats her employees and also knows she will make more money once she gets into marketing and sales.

Case Questions

1. Are there any ethical issues involved? If so, what are they? Explain your answer.

2. Is Molly treating Jane in an unethical manner? Or is this just a case of office politics?

3. If you were the assistant manager, overseeing all of these employees, would you see the situation as merely a practical question to solve without ethical consequences? Or would you find yourself involved with ethical issues? Explain your answer.

 ## Case Study—Always Read the Small Print

The management at the Dover Inn adds 15 percent to every hotel gift shop purchase when it is charged to a guest's room. The policy is noted only on the guest's final bill at check-out time. Most guests do not notice the charge and just pay their bill. The hotel profits by several hundred dollars a week from this covert policy.

Moreover, gift shop employees are instructed to encourage shoppers to charge their purchases to their guestrooms. It is suggested that salespeople ask, "For your convenience, would you like me to charge this to your room?"

Front desk agents are mandated to remove the additional fees if a guest complains. At check-out time, Mrs. Kramer noticed the additional charge on her bill. She very politely asked Ellen, the front desk agent, what the additional charge was for. Ellen, just as politely, explained the policy, showing Mrs. Kramer the small print.

Mrs. Kramer became incensed. She demanded that the charges be removed immediately. She also said that she was going to send a report of this to her three favorite Internet travel sites. She then insisted on seeing the general manager and told him that aside from the Internet sites, she was going to write a letter to all of the local newspapers in the region.

Case Questions

1. What ethical issues are involved with the Dover Inn's policy? What would you advise the general manager to do? Explain your answer.

2. What ethical issues are involved for all of the employees concerned? What would you advise the front desk employees? The shop employees? Explain your answers.

Case Study—The Safety Sheet

Rebecca, the front desk agent at the Goodfriend Inn, was told to hand out a safety sheet with each room key that she distributed. However, she found that the safety sheet (which details safety precautions in case of fire, hurricane, electrical failure, and more) was upsetting to most of the guests. She decided to stop handing out the sheet, except when a supervisor was around.

Case Questions

1. What are the ethical issues in this case? Explain your answer.
2. What would Kant say about this case? Explain your answer.
3. What would a utilitarian say about this case? Explain your answer.
4. What would you do if you were Rebecca? Why?

 # Case Study—Who Are You Anyway?

Peter is the morning shift front desk agent at Roger's Roadside Motel. The Roger's motel chain has grown rapidly in recent years and now, due to its excellent reputation for both great service and cleanliness, it has 62 sites around the United States.

Periodically, Peter pilfers guest credit card information. He uses two criteria for his selection process. He chooses someone he thinks would not notice additional charges on their credit card statement or he chooses someone he thinks would not know what to do if they did get overcharged on their bill.

Peter does not use the credit card information himself. He sells the information to Jack, a friend of his; who in turn sells it to Christopher, who sells it over the Internet for identity theft purposes. Their identity theft ring has been going on for well over two years.

Gerald, the general manger, recently got wind of the theft. He did not have specific proof until just a few days ago when he asked his friend, Gertie, to check into the hotel and stay a few days. He instructed Gertie to act as absentmindedly as she possibly could. Gertie had fun with the undercover work. When her credit card statement arrived at the end of the month, she found several minor charges totaling about $150. Each charge was so minor that she had trouble spotting them.

Gerald was in a quandary. He knew he had to fire Peter. He also knew he had to break up this identity theft ring. But he did not want to involve the local police. He was afraid that the bad publicity would be ruinous to the business; he was sure that guests would be afraid to come to the hotel. But he also believed that justice should be served.

Case Questions

1. What would you do if you were Gerald? Explain your answer.

2. What would a utilitarian say about the situation? Explain your answer.

3. What would Kant say about the situation? Explain your answer.

4. What would Aristotle say about the situation? Explain your answer.

 # Case Study—Blowing the Whistle

Pablo has been a front desk employee at Odell's Roadside Inn for four years. He has a lot of responsibility for a front desk agent and he is paid extra for it. This particular Odell's is one of 22 inns started by the Odell family in 1955.

Victor is the front desk manager. He has worked for the Odell's chain since he graduated from college in 1996. He enjoys his job very much. Recently, he bought a new convertible sports car, which he likes to talk about to anyone who will listen.

Four months ago, Pablo noticed something strange when he did the night audit. He knew that room 222 had been rented for that night because he had made the reservation himself. However, it showed up on the audit as vacant. Over the next month, Pablo watched for further inaccuracies, and he found a minimum of one per week. He realized that someone was pocketing cash at the owner's expense.

He called his friend Wade, who was also a front desk agent with night audit responsibilities for Odell's. Wade and Pablo had been friends for a long time and Pablo felt comfortable discussing the situation with Wade. They decided not to say anything but to keep watching. Wade was going to pay special attention at his hotel, too.

During the next month, they realized that there was a scam going on and that it probably affected other Odell properties as well. Neither one of them wanted to blow the whistle. Both of them liked their jobs and neither of them wanted to tattle.

Case Questions

1. What should Pablo and Wade do? Discuss at least two or three alternatives. Which one would you select?

2. Assume that Pablo spoke to a regional manager about what he knew and the very next day Victor fired him with no explanation. As far as Victor can see, nothing will be done. Now, what should Wade do? Explain your answer.

3. Analyze the situation in question two from a utilitarian point of view and from a Kantian "rights" point of view. What does each analysis tell you should be done and by whom? Explain your answer.

 # Case Study—Lady of the Night?

Ethan is the front desk agent at the Harbor Inn in Fort Lauderdale, Florida. He has worked the front desk for two years, while completing his college degree in hotel management. Ethan noticed that Adrienne Shaw, a guest that checked in a week ago, left the hotel several times each night and returned with a different man. He strongly suspects some type of prostitution.

Case Questions

1. What are the ethical issues involved in this case? Explain your answer.

2. Apply each of the ethical theories we have studied to this case. Explain each of your applications.

3. What would you do if you were Ethan? Explain your answer.

 Case Study—"But What Happened to My Room?" ──────

Liz Borden arrived at the Savoy Hotel at 9 P.M. on a very snowy night. She did not have a reservation, but did not expect to have trouble getting a room.

Paige Lewis was the front desk agent. She had been with the Savoy for six months and enjoyed her job very much. Her supervisor, Claire, was pleased with her work and told her so often.

Liz explained her situation to Paige, but the hotel was completely booked. Liz was very upset. She was especially upset at the thought of going out into the snow again searching for a room.

"You don't really think all of the guests will show tonight, do you? I mean, look at that snow out there. Surely people are stopping as soon as possible. And," she added in a conspiratorial tone, "you don't want me to have to go back out there. Just look at it!"

Indeed, it was snowing hard. Paige thought to herself, "There probably would be a guest or two who did not show. But, also, I know the policy of the Savoy: *Honor the reservations at all cost.*"

Just as Paige was about to say "no" once again, she noticed a $50 bill in Liz's hand. "This is yours if you manage to find me a room," Liz said. Paige found a room for Liz.

Just before midnight, a harried young woman with her small child came in from the snow. "I have a reservation," she said.

But her room was gone. There were no rooms left at the Savoy. When she was told that there had been some mistake and there were no rooms left, she said, "But what happened to my room?"

Case Questions

1. What are all of the ethical issues involved in this case? Explain your answer.

2. Apply each of the ethical theories we have studied to this case. Explain each of your applications.

3. If you were Claire's supervisor, and discovered what Paige had done, what would you do?

Applying Ethics to the Housekeeping Function

You get the best out of others when you give the best of yourself.—Harry Firestone

HOUSEKEEPING IS A CENTRAL FUNCTION to any lodging establishment. The decor could be beautiful, the food wonderful, the service outstanding, but if the room is not clean, the guest probably will not return and may well tell many of her friends about the bad experience.

Housekeeping is an area where many ethical issues may arise. It is an area that directly touches the customer, creating multiple ways that company-customer ethical issues might show up. It is also an area where the highest percentage of the cost lies in labor, making management-labor issues very important and likely causes of ethical conflict. Housekeeping may initially appear to be a peripheral aspect of a lodging establishment's business, but that can be a misleading impression. Virtually all aspects of housekeeping involve person-to-person contact, making it inherently an undertaking with important ethical dimensions.

Case Study—The Housekeeper's Friends

Ruth had been a housekeeper at the Highway 12 Motel for almost ten years. She considered herself a good employee and a good judge of character. Recently, she had helped two of her friends, Shirley and Roz, get hired at the motel. Ruth felt comfortable about assisting both of them because she had known them for many years.

When Eduardo, the motel manager, agreed to hire Ruth's friends he told her he expected her to train them. "I expect them to be as good a housekeeper as you are, Ruth." And Ruth knew he meant it. She had seen him fire many housekeepers over the years.

Roz jumped right into her tasks and it became obvious to Ruth that Roz was a born housekeeper. Ruth only had to show Roz how to do things once and she had it down pat. She even did extra niceties that Ruth did not discourage as long as she finished her rooms in the allotted amount of time. Shirley, however, was another story. Every time Ruth checked on her, Shirley was either on her cell phone or taking a break. The most shocking event occurred one morning. Ruth walked into room 144 and found Shirley curled up on the bed, reading a steamy novel.

Case Commentary: Utilitarianism

The actions of all the characters in this case could be analyzed from a utilitarian perspective. Most obviously, we could look at the behavior of Shirley and determine that her actions are definitely not leading to the greatest good for the greatest number of people. She is not maximizing benefits or social welfare as a whole. The consequences of her actions include rooms not cleaned for customers, work being paid for by the employer but not being performed, embarrassment for her friend Ruth, and a potential rupturing of their friendship. Furthermore, she is not even leading to desirable consequences for herself, because it is obvious that she will be fired shortly if she doesn't shape up.

Shirley's actions put Ruth in an ethical dilemma. What should she do? She has a responsibility to Eduardo and the motel to train Shirley, but Shirley is not learning or following through on the training. She has been Shirley's friend for quite a while, but if she covers for Shirley out of loyalty or works extra hard by doing both her own job and half of Shirley's, she is aiding and abetting Shirley's laziness and irresponsibility, permitting Shirley to not perform a full day's work for a full day's pay.

Any course of action Ruth takes is likely to lead to *some* negative consequences. If she simply turns Shirley in, she causes her friend to be fired and probably loses a longtime friend forever. If she tries to cover for Shirley and finish the work without Shirley pulling her own weight, Ruth exploits herself and other housekeepers who have to do some of Shirley's work. If Ruth undertakes some action between the two extremes of turning Shirley in or covering for her, she might produce the best overall balance of benefits over harms, but potential negative consequences might result, no matter what she does—she could lose her friendship, lose the confidence of her employer, etc.

A utilitarian analysis of this situation can probably most easily be done from a rule utilitarian perspective. As a general rule, how should one behave in a situation like this? What general rule, if followed, would most likely lead to the greatest net positive consequences? While the exact consequences of any course of action may not be fully knowable, the best advice would be to talk sternly to Shirley. Ruth should explain that Shirley is heading toward dismissal; that she is cheating both the customers and her employer; and that, although Ruth values her friendship, Ruth cannot and will not cover up Shirley's behavior. Shirley needs to change her attitude toward work quickly and become more attentive and conscientious. Ruth should stress that she is willing to show Shirley what to do and how if she'll try, but Shirley would be wise to simply resign if she is unwilling to try.

That course of action may not lead to positive consequences—for example, Shirley may continue to mess things up and get fired anyway, or she may become angry with Ruth and break off their friendship. But this approach seems to have a higher probability of leading to a positive outcome than either extreme (immediately turning Shirley in or covering up her behavior repeatedly). Therefore, it seems to be the best course of action to take from a utilitarian perspective.

Case Commentary: Kant's Categorical Imperative

By not keeping her explicit promise to the employer to work for her wages, and by not keeping at least an implicit promise to her friend Ruth to attempt to do her job,

Shirley is breaking Kant's categorical imperative. She can't make her deceitful behavior a universal rule that everyone should follow, and her behavior does not treat others as human beings. As usual for Kant, such deceptive and dishonest behavior is a violation of the humanity of others. Shirley is to be condemned for her actions.

How would Kant counsel Ruth to behave? The important question here is that Ruth behave honestly with everyone involved. What does that require? For one thing, attempting to cover up Shirley's misbehavior would not be allowed, since that involves deceit toward Eduardo and the motel management. For another, it requires being honest with Shirley also, and that probably means that Ruth should warn Shirley rather than simply turn her in. Thus, Kant's counsel to Ruth about what to do appears to closely parallel that of the rule utilitarian: honestly and firmly letting Shirley know where her destructive behavior is heading (toward dismissal) and treating her as a rational adult capable of living up to her responsibilities (i.e., of acting in an ethical manner). If she fails to change her ways and gets fired, it is not because Ruth has failed to live up to her duties to Shirley or to her employer.

Case Commentary: The Ethic of Justice

Shirley is not acting in a just manner because she is unfairly distributing the burdens of cleaning the rooms to her fellow housekeepers while she indulges herself. No one observing this set-up from behind the veil of ignorance would find it just, because each person would understand that he or she might end up being the one having to carry the load for Shirley.

If and when Shirley gets caught not doing her job conscientiously, the question of retributive justice will come up. What should be Shirley's punishment? From the case description, we know that Eduardo must be a fairly strict disciplinarian; it says that he has fired many housekeepers over the years. The important principle here is that the punishment fit the crime. The more severe her infraction, the more severe should be the punishment. Firing is just about the most severe punishment an employer can inflict on an employee (unless a law has been broken), so permanent dismissal should be reserved for only the most severe cases of misconduct or for repeated misconduct. That is why most discipline, unless the first instance is quite serious, is progressive in nature—it initially aims to reform the errant conduct and progressively becomes more severe, up to and including dismissal, if the employee continues to misbehave or fail to perform.

Case Commentary: Aristotle and the Ethics of Virtue

From the viewpoint of virtue ethics or character ethics, it is apparent that Shirley is not displaying a praiseworthy character. Several character flaws, or vices, are immediately apparent: laziness, dishonesty, injustice, and lack of prudence or wisdom. Beyond this, we can say little. There is not enough detail in the case for us to pass judgment on Eduardo's character or that of Ruth or Roz. We do know enough to know that Ruth and Roz have some positive character traits, including industriousness and (apparently) honesty. But we lack enough detail to really make a fuller assessment of their characters.

Case Study—The Housekeeper's Paycheck

The Bushman Resort and Spa is located an hour's drive northwest of Austin, Texas, along the Colorado River. Family-owned and operated for 30 years, the resort was built on property that had been in the Bushman family since 1858. In 1970, the family sold off 1,200 acres of land, along with several buildings that belonged to the original ranch. The total selling price was $14.2 million.

The cost of building the resort was approximately $6 million. Most costs were financed by a local savings and loan association owned by Mr. Jibber Chaney, a Bushman cousin on the maternal side of the family. William Bushman, the present CEO and owner of the Bushman Resort, is the great, great, great-grandson of the original William Bushman, who settled the property after giving up his journey to California to find gold in 1856.

The resort boasts 185 all-suite guestrooms on 450 acres of wilderness that winds its way along the Colorado River. The site offers guests total privacy. Prices are high, ranging from $300 to $1,200 per night, excluding the executive guest suites. These run $2,000 to $4,000 per night.

Offerings at the Bushman Resort include a full-service spa and health club, 14 tennis courts, horseback riding, two executive 18–hole golf courses, river rafting and other river activities, and four heated swimming pools (two outdoor, two indoor). There is also an onsite dinner theater and movie theater as well as seven restaurants, three of which are open 24 hours, seven days per week. In order to maintain the very high level of service that the clients have come to expect, there is a 1:1 ratio of guests to employees. At all times, there are as many employees on staff as there are guests.

Occupancy rates over the last two years have varied greatly, especially in summer. Whereas the 1980s saw summer occupancy rates ranging from 85 to 95 percent, summer occupancy rates have lately declined to 65 percent. In his office conservatory overlooking the main garden, Mr. Bushman examined the latest occupancy statistics. He was quite distressed about the most recent summer occupancy percentages and called in his general manager, Ms. Candy Leman, to discuss improvements.

"Our biggest cost is labor, as you well know, Candy," Mr. Bushman explained. "We are going to have to find some way to reduce our labor cost and yet maintain our high level of service. If we don't maintain our high service levels, we won't attract the right type of clientele."

Ms. Leman took the papers from Mr. Bushman and looked them over.

"How much do we pay our housekeepers?" Mr. Bushman inquired when she finished reading the report.

"$10 per hour," Candy responded.

Bushman was aghast. "Why, that's criminal! Why are we paying them so much above the minimum wage?"

"Because if they are paid well, they do a better job," Candy replied.

"Do they all have proper documentation? You know, green cards, citizenship, etc.?" He then lowered his voice and continued in a conspiratorial manner, "Do we have any undocumented workers who are earning money off the books?"

"No, not that I know of," Candy answered.

"Well, there's your answer then. We'll save lots of money that way. Start laying off the higher-paid housekeepers and look for employees who don't have proper papers. They'll work for next to nothing. Also, we can lay them off and rehire them as we see fit and they won't complain. So, if one week our occupancy is down, we'll just tell a few of them not to come in."

Candy was very quiet, so Bushman continued. "How many rooms does each housekeeper do per day? Eight?"

Candy nodded that he was correct.

"Well, those new workers will just have to work a bit more quickly. They'll each do 10. Or maybe even 12."

It was Candy's turn to look aghast. "I can't do that Mr. Bushman. I know these people. They do a good job. Some of them have worked for us for more than ten years."

Bushman thought it over silently for a few minutes. "You'll do it, or you'll be the first one to leave," he stated.

Case Questions

1. In your judgment, are Mr. Bushman's suggestions ethical? Why or why not?

2. If you were in Ms. Leman's shoes, what would you do? Explain your answer.

3. How would a utilitarian look at Mr. Bushman's suggestions?

4. Apply Rawls's ethic of justice to this case.

Case Study—Only Your Housekeeper Knows for Sure

Ms. Leslie Hunter had been a housekeeper for the Brightman Spa Resort for eight years. She had worked her way into housekeeping management two years ago and was quite proud of the fact. She had built an excellent staff. Morale was high; absentee and turnover rates were low.

Three months ago, Mr. Antonio Mitchell became the assistant manager for the resort. He was young and ambitious, and Ms. Hunter did not trust him. She knew that he cut corners and he had tried to pressure her to add additional duties to the housekeepers' workdays without additional pay. To date, she had refused.

This morning, Mr. Mitchell brought Ms. Hunter two cases of gallon jars of generic shampoo. He also brought her several thousand empty, recycled, individual-sized shampoo bottles. The labels on the bottles were *Haute Hair*, a well-known, very exclusive salon product that the hotel had been using for the past several years. Mr. Mitchell's instructions were simple: fill the *Haute Hair* bottles with generic shampoo. Assign each housekeeper 200 bottles to fill each shift until the job is finished.

Ms. Hunter was flabbergasted. She was in a total quandary. She was unwilling to do the job herself, and she was also unwilling to assign it to anyone else. To make matters worse, she had only recently found out that Mr. Mitchell was the son of one of the hotel owner's best friends.

Case Questions

1. List the benefits and harms done if Ms. Hunter follows Mr. Mitchell's instructions. Also, state who benefits and who is harmed.

2. From a utilitarian perspective, is there anything wrong with what Mr. Mitchell is requesting? Explain your answer.

3. What would Kant say about this situation? Explain your answer.

4. What would you do if you were Ms. Hunter? Explain your answer.

Case Study—The Clean Linens

Patty was a housekeeper at the Sommerset Hotel and Lodge on Lake Superior. It was a lovely family resort and she felt lucky to have the summer job before she returned to college in the fall.

On this particular day, Patty was in a hurry to finish her work. Both her mom and dad were out of town on business and she had to pick up her younger sister Penelope from ballet class. She had explained the situation to Mr. Gibson, her boss, who told her she could leave as soon as her work was done. "But do your usual good job. I'm counting on you," he warned.

Patty was getting nervous because time was of the essence. She didn't want her six-year-old sister to have to wait. She entered her last room, room number 12, and found it in good order. She was relieved to think she could be in and out in just a few minutes.

The room had two double beds and one had obviously not been slept in. She changed the linens only on the one that had been slept in, even though she knew she should change both. She gave the bathroom a good scrubbing, changed the towels, vacuumed the floors, dusted accordingly, and was done. She was on her way five minutes after she finished cleaning room number 12.

She arrived at Penelope's ballet class just as it was finishing. Penelope chatted all the way home and Patty was relieved to see this day come to an end. When her parents came home later that evening, she told them what a close call she had had. Everyone was relieved that the day had ended well.

The next day when Patty arrived at work, she was called to Mr. Gibson's office. Within two minutes of entering, she was fired. A couple had checked into room number 12. When they went to sleep that night, they were horrified by the dirty, stained sheets they found. Mr. Gibson did not care how or why it happened. It happened and it was her room, so she was fired.

Case Questions

1. What are the justice issues in this case? Is the retribution appropriate? Explain your answer.

2. From a utilitarian viewpoint, is Mr. Gibson's decision justified? Why or why not?

3. How would Kant view this situation? What are Patty's duties?

4. How would Aristotle view the situation? What would he say about Patty? What would he say about Mr. Gibson?

Part III

Other Hospitality Applications

13

Applying Ethics to Club Management

The reputation of a thousand years may be determined by the conduct of one hour. —Japanese proverb

MANY OF THE ISSUES that private club managers face are similar to the issues that managers face in all areas of hospitality. However, some aspects of the job are unique to club management. Most managers have only one boss, but club managers must also answer to what may seem like hundreds of bosses. The club manager reports not only to the board of directors, but to all of the members as well.

Private clubs are member organizations. When an equity club or a corporate club is founded, it is based on the interests of the members (social clubs, athletic clubs such as golf or tennis, professional clubs for journalists or lawyers, etc). By their nature, clubs can be exclusionary places. In one model, membership can be organized and controlled solely on the basis of a costly membership fee. Another method of control places membership decisions under the board of directors or the board of governors of a club. Applicants might need a sponsor, and then have to meet with the board of governors, who would have final approval on a membership. If there is an unspoken ban on certain types of applicants, an individual might meet all membership criteria, but still be denied membership without further explanation.

The cases below examine various aspects in club management. The first case is a financial issue. It is followed by cases on exclusionary practices, tipping in a no-tipping venue, and accepting gifts. Imagine yourself as a club manager facing these situations sometime in the future. What would you do?

Case Study—The Board of Directors

Fairview Country Club is a private club with 265 affluent members. Initiation fees begin at $100,000. The club has 60 years of history in the community. A board of directors consisting of ten club members and the general manager, Mr. Smith, manage the club. Mr. Smith has been employed for 25 years at Fairview Country Club and is now nearing retirement age. In the past few years, Fairview has fallen on hard times and has issued yearly assessments to its membership.

Recently, during one of his weekly department head meetings, Mr. Smith discussed the current financial condition of the club. He explained that the club was in dire need of improved cash flow and that expenses had to be slashed across the board. He then handed out the previous month's profit and loss statement.

Mr. West, the director of golf, briefly examined his profit and loss statement when he returned to his office. He was surprised to see several line items, expenses, and irregularities that should not have been there. He immediately called the controller, Ms. Nuñez, for copies of his department's profit and loss statements for the past six months. The controller hesitated at providing the copies, but after further questioning, provided the paperwork.

Mr. West carefully reviewed the reports. He soon realized that his department had not been given proper income credit. He also noted several irregular expenses that required further research and additional trips to the accounting department. The next morning, Ms. Nuñez notified Mr. West that she was instructed "by administration" that the club's financial statements were no longer available to employees and that information would be passed to department managers as deemed appropriate by the board of directors.

Concerned, Mr. West approached Mr. Patrick, the board member responsible for the golf department. After a long conversation about the situation, Mr. Patrick assured Mr. West that the situation would be resolved at the level of the board of directors. Mr. Patrick concluded his discussion with Mr. West by saying, "You were hired to run a program, not to analyze the club's financial statements." Both parties left with a clear understanding that Mr. Patrick was going to correct all of the irregularities.

In the following months, Mr. West began to feel that Mr. Smith, the general manager, was not happy with him. Knowing that his department was doing well financially, Mr. West tried several times to bring this to the attention of Mr. Smith. On one particular occasion, Mr. Smith responded in a shocking manner, leaving Mr. West with an unforgettable impression. Mr. Smith had said, "Not good! How is this club supposed to survive if your department is off budget?"

This left Mr. West extremely confused. His records showed a year-to-date increase in net revenues, up $66,000 from the previous year. Mr. West again approached Mr. Patrick and the two of them went over profit and loss statements in a private meeting the following weekend. As the statements were still for the board of directors only, Mr. Patrick insisted that this meeting be kept between the two of them.

The following week, the president of the club asked Mr. West to come to the general manager's office for a brief meeting before the monthly board meeting. As the door closed, Mr. West was surprised to find Mr. Smith sitting at his desk. Mr. West had been under the impression that the meeting was between the club president and himself.

The club president and Mr. Smith made it clear to Mr. West that if he wanted to keep his job, he would refrain from speaking about his budget's irregularities immediately. In addition, he was to quit his research into the club's financial status.

Two weeks later, Mr. West discovered that purchases from other departments had been attributed to his department and that revenue that his department generated had also been attributed to other departments. He knew the exact whereabouts of all of the money and reported it to Mr. Patrick. The next day he was fired for not following instructions.*

Case Commentary

This case potentially has many ethical questions and issues attached to it. We will not explore all of them here, but will focus on the most central issues to be considered. A preliminary question concerns the morality of the behavior of the country club president, board member Patrick, and country club manager Smith. Although we don't have definitive proof from the way the case is presented, circumstantial evidence indicates that all three are involved in unethical, secret manipulation of the country club's financial books. It appears as if they are covering for either secretly "skimming" money from the country club's treasury, or else secretly covering up inept management and/or stealing from the country club in some other department than the golf department. If these suppositions are true, there is no ethical debate: all three are guilty of immoral behavior.

There may be less clear-cut ethical issues facing Mr. West. In general, it appears that Mr. West attempted to behave in a straightforward and ethical manner throughout this episode. Certainly, he was not in any way involved in any financial manipulations of hidden stealing from the country club. Nevertheless, perplexing ethical issues may still face him in this situation.

For example, was Mr. West wrong to agree to meet in secret with Mr. Patrick? In general, it appears that he did no wrong in this instance, because he had no reason to suspect that Patrick was in on any wrongdoing; he saw the secrecy of the meeting merely as normal protocol under which only those with a need to know were consulted in the normal course of business.

A second question for Mr. West is the propriety of blowing the whistle by going once again to Mr. Patrick after he had been explicitly ordered by his boss not to discuss the financial irregularities with anyone. This, of course, was an act of insubordination and was the alleged cause of his dismissal. As a "loyal agent," it might be argued that he had a duty to obey his superior and refrain from any further investigation or conversation. Yet, this line of reasoning seems to be deeply ethically flawed. It would counsel Mr. West to relinquish all ethical responsibility to the country club members regarding the finances of his job—to look the other way when clear improprieties had been committed. This would directly contradict a Kantian ethical duty to not deceive (either by commission or omission) if that deception denies others what they need to act rationally as a human being—i.e., to deny others their humanity by degrading them to a means rather than an end.

It also would violate rule utilitarianism, since we would never conclude that such deceptive practices as a general rule would work out for the best of everyone. Likewise, it also most likely violates act utilitarianism if one considers all consequences over the long run. In a similar vein, it would allow injustice, since club members are likely being cheated without their knowledge.

---

*This case was authored by Eric Johnson, Golf Administrator, Sports Entertainment & Event Management Program at Johnson & Wales University, Florida Campus.

Therefore, it appears that Mr. West did the right thing by blowing the whistle and telling Mr. Patrick of the irregularities, even if it did result in his being fired. This is a heavy price to pay for doing the right thing, but sometimes that is the price of being morally right in an immoral situation.

Additional questions for Mr. West would include: Should he continue blowing the whistle by going to other club members and/or board members? Or should he just walk away from the situation, happy to be out of a moral cesspool? We could also ask if Mr. West should be compensated for his loss of job—perhaps he could sue under any whistleblower legislation that might cover his situation, or perhaps new management following an overthrow of the old, corrupt management should reimburse him and club members for their losses. And, of course, retributive justice issues also arise regarding the proper punishment for those responsible.

Some of these questions may not have clear-cut answers. For example, should he pursue this further or just walk away? Utilitarian considerations would involve a whole host of questions to which we do not presently have factual answers. We would need to know all sorts of things about his personal and family circumstances, as well as the state of the law and of likely results inside the country club should he pursue it further. From a Kantian perspective, Mr. West should continue pursuing the matter—this is his only way of living up to the categorical imperative to always treat others (especially country club members) as ends, not merely means to some other end.

Compensation and retribution likewise have ambiguities that may require more information than we have. But the general outlines of this case are clear: Smith, Patrick, and the club president acted immorally, and their character is deficient. In general, West behaved properly, and we can judge his character relatively favorably. Additional whistle-blower activities could very well be warranted, and compensation and retribution should be exacted for wrongs done.

Case Study—Are You a Member?

The Equine Club of Moreville is recognized as one of the finest equestrian clubs in the southeastern United States. It is a corporate club, managed strictly on a for-profit basis, and is owned and operated by the Devler Corporation. Approximately 30 miles away, the Belle Glade Country Club, an equity club, had been established as a country club specializing in golf and tennis. Some people had attempted to join the Equine Club but had been turned down. They became some of the founding members of the Belle Glade.

Jay Theriault had decided to join the Belle Glade because his wife, Andrea, and their daughters, Elsie and Lulu, were avid tennis players and the Equine Club had only mediocre tennis facilities. Even though Andrea also liked to ride, she wanted her daughters to enjoy the club experience. On the other hand, Jay didn't like tennis at all, but loved to ride and was hoping to work out an opportunity for himself.

On a perfect riding day in early autumn, Jay mentioned his desire to ride at the Equine Club to Luke, a friend and fellow lawyer at work. Jay knew that Luke was an Equine Club member and wanted to know if "outsiders" were allowed any access to club facilities. Luke said he would be happy to sponsor Jay and a few friends for riding any time they got a group together. They made a tentative date to meet at the club dining room for brunch the following Sunday, to be followed by a full day of riding. As soon as Jay told Luke how many friends he was bringing, Luke would arrange for the horses.

Jay was ecstatic. He immediately called his friends Perry and Seymour, a couple from his old neighborhood in Brooklyn Heights with whom he used to ride in Central Park in New York City. They were thrilled to have the opportunity. Later that afternoon, after speaking with Andrea, who also was looking forward to the riding opportunity, he called Luke and told him they would be a group of four joining him. Luke said his wife, Eleanor, would also ride.

Jay and company joined Eleanor and Luke at the table. Introductions were made; Eleanor seemed a bit aloof, but Luke was in too good a mood to notice. They all decided on the buffet brunch. Eleanor excused herself while everyone else went to get their food. A few minutes after everyone was seated and began eating, the maître d' came over to their table and asked who Perry and Seymour were. Luke explained they were guests; the maître d' answered that unfortunately there were too many reservations today and there was no room for guests. Luke asked to speak with the maître d' privately; Luke led him out to the hallway and started to chastise him. The maître d' stopped him and said he was operating on orders from the president of the Devler Corporation. He reminded Luke that his membership was solely at the discretion of the Devler Corporation.

Luke was livid. "Just tell me," he spat out in anger. "Is it because Seymour is Jewish or is it because they are a gay couple?" The maître d' answered, "Mr. Devler had a call from a very influential guest. I suspect by now he has had more than one call. I am not privy to the nature of his phone calls, but I was told that we need your table." And he walked away.

Case Questions

1. What are the ethical issues in this case?

2. Are there any legal issues in this case? If so, are there either retributive justice or compensatory justice issues in the case?

3. What would you do if you were Luke?

4. What would you do if you were Jay after Luke came back to the table and said that the group had to leave?

5. How would Kant view this situation?

6. How would a utilitarian view this situation?

 # Case Study—To Tip or Not to Tip; That Is the Question

Malcolm Ortiz was the assistant general manager at the Hollyhocks Country Club in Hollyhock, Michigan. He had been in this position at the club for five years. Previously, he had been the assistant general manager at a smaller club, the Estero, about 50 miles south. The Hollyhocks Country Club had been established over 100 years ago and it was considered a pillar of the community. It was very exclusive and very expensive.

Malcolm had visions of becoming the general manager sometime over the next five years. He knew that Gannon Sage, the present manager, was approaching his 63rd birthday and considering retirement. Malcolm also knew that Gannon was eyeing him for the position of general manager. One indication was that recently Gannon had passed several sticky problems on to Malcolm that he normally would have handled himself.

Today's problem involved tipping. The club had a "no tipping" policy that was strictly followed. It was a time-honored tradition that had existed since the club was established. There were two specific reasons that had been written into the original documentation. The first reason stated that since everyone paid a large membership fee, which included a food, beverage, tennis, and golf allowance, there should be no reason to have to spend more money. The other reason stated that everyone was paying equal amounts of money to belong to the club and no one member should be treated better than any other member. All members would be required to wait their turn to be seated in the dining room, to get prime golf or tennis times, and so forth.

In the last two years, this had become a difficult problem at the Hollyhocks. The staff had been complaining about the policy for as long as Malcolm had been at the club. Additionally, Malcolm knew that a few staff members were blatantly disregarding the policy and accepting tips. When Malcolm was privy to discussions on the topic, the typical argument was something like, "Sure, we get a decent salary, but there is no reason why it can't be augmented. We work hard and deserve the little extras that go along with the hard work. Why should I go the extra mile when I don't get anything out of it?"

In actuality, Malcolm agreed with the staff. He thought that tipping should be acceptable at Hollyhocks, which was one of the reasons he had been ignoring the problem. He also had figured that Mr. Sage would deal with it. But now, here it was in his lap.

To make the situation even worse for Malcolm, Sage was taking a different approach than he would take. Sage had handed him a list of the offending staff members and told Malcolm that he had to give warning letters to them. Malcolm would have preferred to bring it up at the next board of directors meeting to try to get a new policy on tipping instituted. His strategy would be to explain to the board members that if they wouldn't allow tipping, then they could expect to either lose some of their best employees, or they would have to raise wages.

Case Questions

1. Are there any ethical issues in this case, or are the issues entirely ones of good management? If some issues are ethical, what are they?

2. In a situation such as the one Malcolm faces, when he disagrees with the policy of his boss, should he just look the other way when his boss's policies are disobeyed? Explain your answer.

3. Is Gannon Sage's policy of "no tipping" ethically right, ethically wrong, or ethically neutral? Explain your answer.

4. Explain exactly what you would do if you were Malcolm. Then analyze any ethical issues that may arise from your proposed course of action, and show why your choice is ethically justified.

Case Study—Pair of Tickets

Joe is the assistant general manager of Club Green. Club Green built its reputation over the years as the best club in town. It was established in the early 1900s and is located directly on a beach with stunning views of the Atlantic Ocean and a state-of-the-art clubhouse where members socialize. The clubhouse overlooks Club Green's award-winning championship golf course. This newly renovated championship course is set on 150 acres, featuring lush green fairways bordered by native trees and its trademark sand traps.

Joe joined Club Green three years ago. Every one of the club members and the club associates knows Joe because of his great personality and his ability to listen to every request. He not only listens, he ensures that requests are handled.

Joe just finished his meeting with the new wine vendor. At the end of the meeting, the vendor produced a pair of tickets for Joe to the upcoming World Series game. Joe was shocked. The tickets are always impossible to find and very expensive if you do stumble upon them.

All day, Joe kept thinking about whether it would be appropriate to accept the tickets. He specifically considered the propriety of accepting gifts from vendors regardless of the amount involved. But just as Joe would decide he had to give the tickets back, he would remind himself that he doesn't have vendors like this one lined up outside his office with these types of offers every day. He went back and forth about the tickets for hours. Each time he would come to a decision, he would tell himself that he needed to stop thinking about the problem and get back to work.

Case Questions

1. Is it the cost of a gift that decides between right and wrong? Explain your answer.

2. How would a utilitarian view the gift-giving and acceptance? Explain your answer.

3. How would Kant view the gift-giving and acceptance? Explain your answer.

4. Would a justice ethicist think that gift-giving is acceptable under all circumstances? Explain your answer.

5. What would you do if you were Joe? Explain your answer.

This case was written by Samer Hassan, Ph.D., Associate Professor, Johnson & Wales University, Florida campus.

14

Applying Ethics to Cruise Line Management

Every now and then go away and have a little relaxation. To remain constantly at work will diminish your judgment. Go some distance away, because work will be in perspective and a lack of harmony is more readily seen. —Leonardo DaVinci

CRUISING IS A POPULAR ACTIVITY the world over. However, before cruising came into its own, steamship travel was for either the very rich or the very poor. The very rich were traveling to see new sights while enjoying every possible luxury onboard. The very poor were below in steerage, traveling toward a new life. Often, they were cramped too many to a bed in too small a room with too little to eat.

Out of steamship travel, cruising has developed into one of the world's most popular leisure activities. It has also become a very affordable activity. There are cruises for all ages, groups, and bank accounts. One can find family-friendly cruises, gay-friendly cruises, cruises for adventure-seekers, jazz enthusiasts, political thinkers, and more. In any of the situations above, a ship becomes a community unto itself while it is traveling the high seas.

A ship is a citizen within many different communities: its ports of call, its main harbor, and the waters in which it travels. Ships operate as floating cities— comparable in terms of complexity to a utility and public works department of a small shoreside community. Concurrent with the principal focus of entertaining guests, ships must operate in a safe and environmentally responsible manner, complying with the regulations of international maritime law, various federal laws, and the local regulations of the ports they visit.

A cruise ship can bring riches as well as misfortune to any place it sails. As you read the following case, imagine yourself a crew member on this ship and decide what you would do in this situation.

Case Study—Gray Water/Black Water Overflow

Super Cruise Line, Inc., owns five large cruise ships operating from Gulf of Mexico ports in the southern United States. Compliance with all relevant laws is mandated by the company's environmental management policies and procedures. The ships offer seven-day round trip voyages to Cozumel, Belize, and the Cayman Islands, entertaining guests with world-class performers, warm sunshine, plentiful food and drink, and activities ranging from mundane "sit by the pool exercise" to the exploration of the ancient Mayan ruins of the Yucatan Peninsula.

139

Two of the dominant waste streams are black water and gray water. Black water is the term used for the waste stream generated by the ship from toilets, urinals, and drainage from the ship's infirmaries (including wash basins and wash tubs located in the medical area). Gray water is the waste stream generated by the ship, for example, effluent from galley services (such as sinks, drains, dishwashers, etc.), laundry services, showers, baths, and washbasin drains. If gray water becomes mixed with black water, the entire mixture would then be classified as black water, which is regulated more strictly than gray water.

All passengers and crew members aboard a ship add to the two waste streams. Due to the nature of a ship's construction and the inability to hold this water for longer than 48–76 hours because of limited tank space, the waste requires continual management by ship officers. Black water is always treated to an acceptable level through a United States Coast Guard–approved Marine Sanitation Device (MSD) before being discharged overboard. At Super Cruise Line, Inc., gray water waste is held while in port and then discharged untreated into the sea. The company allows discharge of these wastes only outside of twelve nautical miles from land and marine sanctuaries, even though discharge is usually allowed by most port regulations while in port. In fact, most commercial ships routinely discharge in port.

While all waste is processed according to international law and the laws of the states where its ships visit, the company has instituted a policy that exceeds regulatory compliance requirements. It believes that protecting the marine environment protects the beautiful destinations in which its ships operate and its guests enjoy. It makes good business sense to preserve the environment.

Super Cruise Line, Inc., has entered into voluntary, formal agreement with Florida state regulators, agreeing not to discharge either gray or black water into any Florida waters.

However, one Saturday afternoon in December, in the Port of Tampa, there was an accidental release of both gray water and black water. The situation surrounding the release began as a typical busy turnaround day in port with disembarking guests passing through customs and immigration en route to their transportation home. At the same time, new guests were preparing to board for the next cruise. The ship's officers and crew were putting the ship in order for the next voyage. The hotel staff was washing linens and cleaning over a thousand cabins as the engineering staff loaded fuel and supplies for the coming voyage.

Edward Smythe, a young man of 29, was in charge of the engineering watch. He was a European but licensed as an engineer by the country of Liberia. His responsibilities included the operation of the engineering plant and the management of his assistants. Although young, he was an experienced engineer. However, his experience was mostly gained aboard commercial tank ships transporting gasoline between South Africa and Europe. This was his second voyage aboard a cruise ship and his first as the responsible person for the engineering plant. His immediate supervisor was the chief engineer, Dominick Dupree. The chief, as he is called, was responsible for the entire engineering department of the ship. He managed a staff of 75 operators and maintenance personnel.

The chief was 55 years old and well experienced aboard cruise ships. He had operated cruise ships for 30 years and had been employed by Super Cruise Line, Inc., for the past 19 years, the last five years as chief engineer.

The chief was second in command seven years ago when he witnessed an incident that would later result in a $7 million fine and seven years of probation for the company, because the previous chief engineer was found to have illegally dumped water mixed with oil into the sea for over two years. The previous chief's attitude was very cavalier, saying the ocean could "take it" and the machinery was more trouble to run than it was worth. Because of this criminal activity, he spent a year in prison.

Consequently, the current chief engineer had first-hand knowledge that it was not worth cutting corners when it came to obeying the law. Through the seven-year probationary period, he and his colleagues learned to go beyond compliance. This attitude was deeply instilled in him as the company went through a cultural change resulting in a real appreciation for the environment, followed by a mandate to protect it as best they could. Chief Dupree became committed; he promised never to allow himself or his staff to take shortcuts regarding the environmental aspects of the operation aboard his ship. This culture was the one that the new engineer, Edward Smythe, found himself in; it contrasted sharply with the culture in which he was trained—one in which corners were cut whenever possible in order to increase profits.

About 1:00 P.M. on that turnaround day, Edward Smythe was a busy man. He was responsible for loading fuel and potable water into the tanks of the ship. His staff was performing maintenance, and the hotel staff was busy cleaning the ship. During this period, large volumes of water were being sent to the holding tanks. This included black water from the toilets, gray water from the showers, laundry water from the washers, and water from the floors being scrubbed. Additionally, the galleys had generated large volumes of water from cooking and cleaning after the breakfast meal for 3,500 people. When cooking for lunch began, the wastewater load was already abnormally high.

Furthermore, during the previous week's cruise, the ship experienced a failure of the black water treatment equipment. Because of this, Chief Dupree ordered the holding of all black water for the three days that it would take to reactivate the system. Chief Dupree planned to hold the waste until the treatment system was repaired and then treat what was held before discharging any of it into the sea.

Unfortunately, the generation of the week's black water was 20 percent over the normal production. Although the chief calculated that he had sufficient holding capacity until the system was fixed and the effluent could be processed overboard on Sunday, he did not anticipate the extra load from the additional cleaning during the turnaround day on Saturday.

Smythe, fully aware of Chief Dupree's plan, became alarmed when he saw that, of the three tanks holding the excess black water, two were completely full and the third was rising quickly, soon to reach its maximum capacity. There were no extra tanks to put the rising black water into, except for one gray water tank. Although it was acceptable to use the gray water tank for this purpose, it was not normally done aboard company ships.

Smythe decided to open the proper valves, start the pump, and transfer half of the almost full black water tank to the gray water tank. This put both tanks at half capacity. During the operation, he became distracted when the electrical generator, a critical piece of machinery, indicated a malfunction in its cooling circuit. He changed focus and became involved with addressing the problem with the cooling circuit on the generator. He stopped the pump transferring black water to the gray water tanks, but he forgot to close the valves. For the next three hours, the open valves allowed water to flow freely into the tanks.

At 4:00 P.M., the bridge officer, Mr. Jamison, noticed some liquid spilling out of the vent on the port side of the ship. He called the engine control room and informed Smythe of the leakage. Smythe told Mr. Jamison that there was no pumping operation going on at the moment and not to bother him, as he was busy with other tasks. But bridge officer Jamison, having worked through the same environmental cultural transformation as Chief Dupree, immediately called the captain and chief engineer. Chief Dupree went straight to the engine space to investigate and discovered the open valves. He closed the valves without delay, and the flow overboard stopped. The time it took from the first sighting of the leakage to the cessation of the overflow was about 15 minutes.

Chief Dupree then went to the engine control room. Upon entering, he confronted Smythe who uttered, "It's not my fault." But Chief Dupree was less concerned with fault than with ensuring that proper immediate actions were taken. He tried to help Smythe understand that transparency is the key word in all environmental operations. Nevertheless, Smythe kept insisting that he was not at fault.

Before long, the chief had enough information from the ship's machinery automation systems to understand what had happened. He was able to identify when the valves had been opened and the times that the pumps were started and stopped. He also established that Smythe neglected to close the valves, and that the overflow of the gray water tank into the sea resulted from gravity flow of the waste waters into the tanks from above. After he completed his investigation, the chief left the control room to discuss the event with the captain.

Dupree briefed both the captain and the environmental officer. Every ship has an environmental officer to oversee environmental compliance who reports directly to the captain. Afterwards, the three contacted the shoreside environmental compliance department to report the violation via speaker telephone. The time was 4:30 P.M. It took 30 minutes from the time of the overflow sighting to the first report.

These officers were aware of the culture that existed prior to the environmental compliance plan and the probation days in the company's history. They knew that this type of reporting would never have happened so quickly then, if at all. Subsequent to a short discussion, everyone mobilized to report the events to the United States Coast Guard and the state environmental authorities.

First, they contacted the local United States Coast Guard Marine Safety Office and reported that approximately three cubic meters of gray water, mixed with untreated black water, had overflowed into the sea, and therefore the spillage was illegal. Secondly, they contacted the Florida authorities. All the details were fully and completely revealed to the authorities within 60 minutes of the event.

An investigation team was dispatched from the company's environmental management department. The team was scheduled to arrive at the next port of call, which was Cozumel, Mexico.*

Case Commentary: The Company

A utilitarian, a Kantian, and a justice ethicist would all give the company a positive ethical review. After committing some serious errors in the past, the company turned itself around and created a corporate culture that includes putting a very high value on protecting the environment. Moreover, it has backed this corporate culture with training.

From a utilitarian perspective, all of the company's recent actions are to be praised. The company is clearly promoting the greatest good for the greatest number by taking critical action to ensure that the environment is protected. In addition, it has taken its environmental obligations seriously enough to instill strict corporate practices and to train its personnel to adhere strictly to those practices. A utilitarian might also scrutinize the legalities of the situation. The cruise line has shown itself to be a good business recently because it has avoided getting into serious trouble; it has done everything possible to avoid lawsuits and bad publicity. The predominant view here might be that good ethics is good for business. All of this demonstrates ethical behavior from both an act utilitarian and a rule utilitarian perspective.

Kant would be concerned with the company's true motivation. Is it doing right because it is *good for the environment* or because it is *good for business?* If the former, praise is merited; if the latter, the behavior has no particular moral significance. Are the new practices and new corporate culture really a change of heart from previous negligent behavior? Are they indeed evidence of a new ethical perspective based on responsibility to others? Assuming that the new attitude is a genuine change of heart, Kant would laud the company for its strong adherence to an ethic of duty to others through its environmental practices. The rights of others are being respected by this company, which is not attempting to hide facts from others or to deceive them.

Likewise, both justice ethics and virtue ethics would praise the actions and the character of this company and its leadership. Justice is being served by ensuring that environmental pollution (an externality to the company's profit and loss statement if the company can get away with polluting while the taxpaying public picks up the tab) does not unjustly harm those least advantaged. Additionally, those corporate officers formulating and carrying out the company's strong environmental protection policies display strong, virtuous characters.

Despite all of its good intentions, the company has inadvertently committed another environmental infraction. Should the company be held responsible for the action of one of its employees, even if that employee had been trained regarding the protection of the environment?

---

*This case was authored by Robert C. Spicer, Environmental Compliance Officer, Carnival Cruise Lines and Roberta Schwartz, Assistant Professor, Johnson & Wales University, Florida Campus.

There are two justice questions at play here: compensation and retribution. First, let's look at compensation. The company should unquestionably pay for any necessary cleanup. The company may also incur some further expenses, perhaps to retrain Smythe or to train additional diligent personnel working in this area but, beyond that, no other compensatory costs are evident in this case.

Beyond compensation, is retribution warranted in this case? Should the company be heavily fined for this violation? No, because it has diligently attempted to work within the law and has shown itself to be reasonably responsible. In this particular instance, it is clear that they jumped into action to curtail the situation as quickly as possible once they discovered the error, and that they promptly and honestly reported the matter to authorities.

Beyond a fine, retribution could also involve some other category of penalty for the company. Examples might include an additional probationary period or other curtailments of its activities. But, again, there appears to be little basis for retribution in this case. The company acted responsibly and promptly when it learned of the leakage. It had worked very hard at training employees and endeavored to maintain an environmentally sensitive corporate culture. In fact, in this case, the worst that could possibly be said against the company is that it hired the wrong employee, Smythe. At most, any reprisal should be minor. For instance, the company might be told that the violation will be marked onto its record, or it might receive a written warning about the spillage.

Case Commentary: The Individuals

Chief Dupree, bridge officer Jamison, the environmental officer, and the captain are all to be commended for their swift and timely action. If they had not moved so quickly, the spill could have been much worse. They had been through similar circumstances; they put their training and knowledge into action and brought a potential disaster under control.

There is still the question of Mr. Smythe, the engineer who became distracted, thereby allowing the spillage to occur. The same two justice questions that we discussed earlier are at play again: the issues of compensation and retribution. First, let's look at retribution. Should Mr. Smythe be punished for allowing the spillage to occur? And if so, how severe should the punishment be?

Mr. Smythe should definitely face some type of retribution. He failed to close the proper valves; he allowed himself to become distracted in a key situation, which showed him to be unreliable; and he was dismissive to a crew member when the crew member tried to bring significant information to his attention. The ethical question becomes whether or not his carelessness was reckless and morally wrong. However, no great and lasting harm occurred, and the carelessness may be understandable, so one might not think that Smythe's behavior was unethical. Perhaps no major ethical question concerning Smythe is involved. A spillage occurred that could be cleaned up.

On the other hand, Smythe also was unwilling to accept the responsibility for his actions. He immediately claimed that the action was not his fault. Furthermore, he was unable to understand that fault was not the issue at hand; the danger to the environment was the fundamental matter.

Assuming that Smythe has engaged in morally problematic behavior, what is the wisest course of action by the company toward this employee? Possible courses of action range from severe punishment, such as discharge, to taking no action at all. Probably neither course of action is wise or warranted. A middle course, such as additional training and milder punishment (probation, suspension, etc.) may be the wisest course.

If we were to examine the overall situation strictly from a utilitarian perspective, we could measure the benefit against the harm. How much harm is going to occur from the spill? Will marine life be devastated for years or will the spill dissolve quickly and not have any lasting effect? If it is the latter, actual harms are not that many.

We might ask if firing Smythe would lead to better consequences for everyone involved. A utilitarian would say that he should not be let off the hook completely, because it could likely lead to other infractions, either by Smythe or others who see him get off the hook. Some type of penalty is warranted because that will lead to better long-term consequences. A rule utilitarian would insist on a universal way to treat all employees who commit environmental violations. However Smythe is to be treated for his infraction is the way all employees should be treated for similar infractions.

Kant would find Smythe's behavior to be ethically problematic. Smythe was not following the categorical imperative when he failed to treat others and their welfare as paramount (as an end in itself); his refusal to take responsibility for his own actions shows a further unwillingness to do his duty to other humans. He has shown himself to be morally irresponsible.

From a justice perspective, Rawls would find polluting our environment to be unjust to the many who depend, indirectly or directly, on that part of our environment. A brief step behind the veil of ignorance quickly reveals this. So, Smythe's actions have also led to an injustice, albeit a relatively minor one since the problem was discovered and corrected so quickly. The remaining justice question is what form of retribution Smythe should face, a matter discussed earlier.

Aristotle examines a person's character. He would find both Chief Dupree and bridge officer Jamison to be of fine moral character. They both showed courage and prudence (wisdom) through their immediate actions. Conversely, Smythe showed himself to be unethical in two ways. First, he evaded his responsibility by claiming that the leakage was not his fault. This demonstrated a lack of both courage and honesty. Second, he exhibited a distinct lack of prudence through his careless behavior. According to Aristotle, Smythe did not act in a reasonable fashion. He failed to exercise reason and lacks character.

 ## Case Study—The Ride to Paradise

West Coast Cruise Lines advertises for cruise business throughout the United States. On any given day of the week, cruise goers line up at Seattle-Tacoma International Airport awaiting their cruise escort, who assists them in beginning their journey to the paradise of their choice on one of West Coast's famous cruise ships.

The passengers are instructed to await their cruise escort at a predetermined location. On this particular day, Charles and Hilda Erskind arrive from Butte,

Montana. Without delay, they seek out Lawrence Gonneff, the company employee with whom they have been corresponding frequently regarding their cruise. When they find him, their first question is, "How do we get to the ship? We are so excited, we just can't wait to get there!"

Mr. Gonneff has tickets to the West Coast Paradise Van to sell to the Erskinds. The tickets cost $22 each. He tells them that the van is waiting right outside the luggage area of the airport. What Mr. Gonneff does not tell the Erskinds is that if they were to take a taxi to the cruise port, it would only cost $25 (including tip) for a total of $12.50 per person. Mr. Gonneff does not get a commission on taxi service; he gets commission only on the tickets he sells to the West Coast Paradise Van. He rationalizes his decision not to tell the Erskinds, or any of the other passengers, about the taxi service. He assumes that if they can afford a cruise, they can certainly afford the extra $19. Furthermore, the West Coast Paradise Van knows exactly where to go; a taxi driver might not. He has even heard horror stories of people being driven to the wrong port. So, he is really doing it for their benefit as well as his own. Besides, any of the passengers could have searched on the Internet for airport to cruise port transportation. If they didn't bother to do their research, why should he assist them now? He may as well make a few bucks, right?

Case Questions

1. Is Mr. Gonneff conforming to competitive business practices or is he ripping off the cruise passengers?

2. Has Mr. Gonneff made a sound business decision? Why or why not?

3. Would any of the ethical theories support his decision? If so, which ones? Explain your answer.

4. Would it change your evaluation if Mr. Gonneff told customers there was no other way to get to the port? Why or why not?

15

Applying Ethics to Sports Management

Sports do not build character. They reveal it.—Heywood Broun

THE PROFESSIONAL ATHLETE TODAY is a revered person. Occasionally, however, we hear or read about a successful athlete who has acted in an immoral or unethical manner. When one of these heroes has ethical lapses, the entire sports industry is affected.

The most frequent stories in the press recently have concerned steroid abuse, but there are numerous other ethical questions facing athletes, coaches, families, and the general public. These include coaches overlooking the minimum GPA requirements of star athletes, parents' interactions at children's youth league games that border on the absurd, non-disabled guests purchasing ADA seating because it offers a better view while ticket sellers look the other way or allow the practice for a fee, point shaving, questionable recruiting practices for college athletes, and many more issues.

The following cases address some of these problems. Place yourself in the positions of the different characters in each of the cases. How would you resolve the ethical dilemmas?

Case Study—Quarterback Sneak

Even though he was the star quarterback of Emerald High's football team, Phil was not particularly liked by many of his teammates. There were several reasons. One was that Phil had a natural athletic ability, so he didn't have to work very hard to accomplish a lot on the field. More important, however, was the fact that he was very much aware that the team needed him to win, and he was not afraid to use this fact to get what he wanted. As a senior with talent, strength, and size, he found it easy to intimidate most of his teammates, especially the underclassmen. Many times he would make them carry his equipment from the bus to the locker room when traveling for away games. He also demanded the front of the line at team meals and any time he needed to see the athletic trainer for a taping or ice down. Phil made it clear that if his teammates did not comply with his wishes, he would be sure they did not receive the ball during the next game.

What made matters worse was the fact that the coaches were basically forced to look the other way whenever Phil used his power to bully his teammates. For the coaches, it wasn't so much that Phil's athletic talent was superhuman, but rather that his parents were extremely wealthy. Phil was their only child and they wanted

147

the best for their son. As a result, they donated enough money to replace the entire football field with state-of-the-art Astroturf his freshman year, supplied the team with new uniforms each season, and promised each member of the coaching staff a new car if Phil was signed by a Division I school his senior year.

With the best season of his high school years under way, Phil really started to get out of control. Perhaps it was the attention of the scouts at each game, or maybe it was the fact that he realized this was his last season. In either event, he began to make requests of his teammates that would leave some wondering when enough was enough.

To begin with, he ordered James, one of the primary wide receivers on the team, to write his English essay. When James refused, Phil assured him that if he didn't do the assignment, he would not catch another ball all season. Reluctantly, James agreed, since he too had scouts watching his every move at each game.

Next, when Phil found out that Kyle, a first-string wide receiver, was taking Hillary to the upcoming homecoming dance, he demanded that Kyle not do so. Kyle didn't know it but Hillary had turned Phil down when he had asked her to the dance. At first Kyle blew him off, but then later reconsidered after Phil made sure Kyle seldom touched the ball during that Friday night's game.

The coaches were aware that Phil purposely disregarded the plays being called as he made his point to his teammates. Phil, never one to ignore the power he held, assured the coaches he was only acting in the best interest of the team, which is what a great quarterback does ... especially when the scouts are watching. After all, if the scouts were happy, he would be playing with a Division I school the following season and each coach would be driving a new Mercedes.*

Case Commentary

At the most obvious level, this case is about Phil. It requires very little ethical reflection to see that Phil's behavior is unacceptable and would not be condoned by any credible ethical theory or perspective. Certainly none of the theories we have studied in this book would find his behavior to be adequate. From a utilitarian perspective, he is far from promoting the greatest good for the greatest number. In numerous and obvious ways, he is sacrificing the greater good for his own selfish and egotistical desires—denying the team its best plays according to the coaches' judgment, forcing teammates to behave dishonestly or to slavishly follow his will instead of their own free will, etc. And from a deontological or Kantian perspective, Phil is not living up to his duty to others—bullying and coercing others is denying them their humanity, and is an obvious violation of Kant's categorical imperative. From a distributive justice perspective, the distribution of rewards and burdens he is forcing on others in this situation is also obviously unjust; he gets the glory and the rewards while others are forced to do tasks that properly belong to him. An Aristotelian perspective would also condemn Phil's character. He lacks many virtuous character traits, including honesty, generosity, justice, modesty, and trustworthiness among others.

---

* This case was written by Sherry Andre, Instructor, Johnson & Wales University, Florida campus.

So there is really very little to argue about regarding a judgment on Phil's actions or on his character. Both are to be condemned. But that does not exhaust the ethical questions that arise from this case. For our purposes, the actions (or lack of them) by the coaches, and the character of the coaches, are more interesting.

Analyzing the behavior and character of the coaches requires that we address the sometimes slippery notion of moral responsibility. Given that Phil's behavior is unethical, what responsibility do the coaches have to intervene and prevent it from happening?

Let's begin with the general obligations of the coaches according to the theories we have studied. From a utilitarian perspective, they have the duty to promote the greatest good for the greatest number. Does allowing Phil's behavior to continue unabated contribute to this goal? From a deontological or Kantian perspective, they have a duty to treat every other human being as a human being, meaning a person of intrinsic worth. From a justice perspective, they have the duty to promote a distribution of burdens (efforts) and rewards that is fair, and accepted as fair by those who would look at it from *all* points of view. Finally, from an Aristotelian or character ethics perspective, they have the duty to behave habitually in a manner exhibiting a good or virtuous character.

An important question is: can any of these requirements be met by the coaches if they do nothing and allow Phil's behavior to continue? On the face of it, the answer appears to be no, since Phil's behavior violates all of the requirements of ethical behavior or character under any of the theories.

There are three potential counter-arguments that would attempt to justify or condone inaction on the part of the coaches. First, it might be argued that the harms done by Phil's action are really quite minor, and that the positive consequences of letting him continue acting that way could be quite large. This would be an attempted utilitarian counter-argument. Second, it might be argued that the coaches have, or feel, an implied loyal agent duty to further the interests of their employer (the school), and thus they have to let Phil continue because that is most likely to lead to a problem-free football season and a winning team. Third, it might be argued that if the other players don't have the courage to stand up to Phil, then maybe they shouldn't be on the team and/or get what they deserve. Let us examine these three arguments in turn.

First, can it be true that the damaging consequences of allowing Phil's behavior to continue are really quite small, outweighed by the potential positive consequences? This argument appears to be based on a very selective reading of consequences. Phil's behavior is causing widespread negative consequences, many of them probably improperly ignored by this argument. The demoralization of the team, the overall decline in moral standards and respect for the coaches and the school for allowing this to continue, and the long-term impact on Phil himself and his likely future behavior are all probably being overlooked or minimized. In fact, an objective look at all of the consequences of Phil's behavior toward his teammates shows an overwhelming preponderance of negative outcomes, and thus it should be stopped. As the people in control of the team, the coaches have the responsibility to intervene, and any attempt to minimize the negative consequences of not intervening is really nothing more than a selective reading of consequences and a rationalization of an indefensible lack of action.

Second, do the coaches have a loyal agent duty, either explicit or implied, to not "rock the boat" since the team is winning and the school's interest in a winning football season is being served? As we demonstrated earlier in this book, the loyal agent argument is usually quite weak. In no case does it justify otherwise unethical behavior, especially when the agent (in this case, the coach) is in a position to intervene and do the right thing. It is questionable whether the school's best interests are being served by allowing Phil to continue this way (we would argue that it is not), but even if it was, that would not let the coaches off the hook for their own individual behaviors. This loyal agent argument is not a good one; it can't justify inaction by the coaches.

Third, is it true that the other players don't deserve to be protected from coercion and bullying if they don't feel strong enough to stand up for themselves as individuals? Some people may argue that position, but if they do, they would have to stand against all the ethical theories we have presented in this book. They would have to endorse a "might makes right" ethic that has been condemned by virtually every ethical tradition of substance in the world. The idea that one's humanity deserves to be respected only if he or she has the courage and power to force recognition of it absolutely contradicts Kant's assertion that all human beings are ends-unto-themselves, or utilitarianism's requirement that all interests be counted equally. In addition, the injustice of respecting people's rights only to the extent that they can force that respect is obvious under any common understanding of justice.

Thus, the coaches have a duty to intervene to curb Phil's behavior and to protect the rights and interests of Phil's teammates. All theories require this, and so would any attempt to live a life of integrity that exhibits a good moral character.

Case Study—Game Day

Jackie Ridley was a college senior. He had played on Denton University's Black Bears baseball team since his freshman year. In fact, he had a baseball scholarship that he had to work hard to maintain. His grade point average requirement was a 3.0 and he was not allowed more than three "C" grades per year. Consequently, he had very little time for either a social life or a part-time job.

The season would soon be coming to a close and Jackie knew that he had to face the outside world of work. He had a few decent job offers and was also considering graduate school. Whatever he chose, he knew it was time to move beyond Denton. He had played well while he was there, but the team had never had any true successes.

It was sad for Jackie to admit, but tonight's baseball game was barely a blip on his radar. The season was almost over and, as hard as the team had tried, they were not going to be in any of the post-season competitions.

Jackie decided to have a snack before he headed to the field. While he was preparing his food in the kitchen, his roommate and teammate Wilbur walked in. Jackie had played second base to Wilbur's shortstop for almost four years and they were good friends. So Jackie was very surprised when Wilbur didn't say hello; he just walked over to the refrigerator, took out the gallon jug of orange juice, and proceeded to finish it off in less than 20 seconds. Then he left the kitchen without acknowledging Jackie in any way.

Jackie became concerned and went after Wilbur. "Hey man, what's up?" he asked his friend. Wilbur didn't answer. Eventually Jackie gave up, grabbed his duffel bag with his uniform and equipment, and headed to Black Bear Field. Wilbur showed up shortly before the game and appeared to be in a better frame of mind.

During the game, Jackie inconspicuously kept his eye on Wilbur. Everything seemed to be fine until Wilbur threw a ball four feet over Jackie's head. The other team scored two runs on the error. The Black Bears never caught up after that. The game hadn't been an important one, but the error bothered Jackie for other reasons. He thought he knew why Wilbur was uncommunicative earlier and he was going to have a chat with him.

Case Questions

1. If you were Jackie, what would you do? Explain why.

2. Apply one of the ethical theories covered in this book to the question of what Jackie should do.

3. What are the different choices Jackie is facing?

4. Suppose Jackie has a chat with Wilbur and finds out that Wilbur intentionally threw the game for a $500 payment from a bookie. What should Jackie do in that case? Why? What would the ethical theories presented in this book counsel him to do?

 # Case Study—The Come On

Evan Berman is the human resources manager at the Athletics-to-Go Sports Arena located 30 miles south of Atlanta. He has held the position for four years. For the previous six years, he was the human resources director for a large event management firm in Hoboken, New Jersey.

The arena employs over 500 people and is open 364 days a year. Evan has worked very hard at getting to know all of the employees. He enjoys walking through the arena at various times of the day to say hello and to stop for a chat. He is personally involved in all training sessions for new employees, which usually last from three days to two weeks, depending on the positions being trained.

Jamie Lee is a new employee in the Athletics-to-Go Sports Arena box office. She is a recent college graduate and majored in sports management. This is her first post-college position. The only other job she had was waiting tables at the local college hangout. She sees the position in the box office as an opening into a career that she has always dreamed about. She aspires to a corporate-level post, but she knows it will take hard work and probably a graduate degree. That is another reason she is so content with her job at the Athletics-to-Go Sports Arena. After one full year of employment, the company pays for related schooling as an employee benefit.

Jamie will not complete her probationary period for another 45 days. This is causing her a great deal of consternation because she has a problem and feels she should speak with someone in human resources. She finally decided to tell Evan that the executive vice president, Mr. Bentley Wilder, has been making suggestive comments to her and has been touching her inappropriately, causing her to feel very uncomfortable.

Obviously embarrassed, Jamie repeated some of the graphic language Wilder had used, including a tasteless dirty joke that she had heard him tell at least three times in mixed company. Jamie told Evan that she politely asked Mr. Wilder to stop both the comments and the physical contact, but he just laughed it off and walked away. The unwanted behavior had been going on for three weeks. She didn't speak to Evan before because she did not want to come across as being overly sensitive. She added that she really enjoyed the job and was hoping to continue.

Evan asked Jamie if she would give him the afternoon to investigate the situation. Evan was a great deal more upset than he let on. For starters, Mr. Wilder is Evan's direct supervisor. Also, two other young women had approached Evan recently about Wilder's behavior. Evan had witnessed Wilder making inappropriate gestures and comments on many occasions. It seemed to Evan that Wilder thought he could do whatever he wanted. What was going to stop him? His family was the major shareholder in the publicly held Athletics-to-Go Sports Arena.

Case Questions

1. What are the ethical issues involved?

2. What should Evan do? Explain your answer.

3. Did Jamie do the right thing by going to Evan with her complaint? Explain your answer.

4. Should Jamie have waited until she finished her probationary period? Explain your answer.

Case Study—Manager Incentives

Charlie is the assistant manager at Jake's Sports Pub. He has held the position for a little over a year. One of his responsibilities is ordering the bar supplies for the establishment. While the bulk of his inventory is ordered electronically through the pub's primary supplier and shipped on regular intervals, he must also order some items directly from vendors and distributors. Many of the vendors and distributors visit the establishment only after Charlie calls them to place an order. On the other hand, some of the vendors like to visit the store more frequently in hopes of securing additional sales. At first, Charlie did not enjoy taking time out of his busy schedule to meet with the outside vendors. He felt like it was a waste of his time, and he really disliked when they would try to push him to buy products he didn't want or need. Even so, he wanted to be respectful, so he would often sit and listen to them. He was often surprised at how many of them would try to entice him to buy their products by offering him tickets to local events or suggesting they could throw in some type of merchandise, such as a polo shirt or even golf clubs, if he were to place an order with them. He had to admit sometimes the offers were tempting, but he was well aware of the company policy that did not allow employees to accept gifts from distributors for their own personal use. He also knew his storage area was extremely limited. It was very important that he limit his inventory strictly to the amount of product he needed. Therefore, when presented with such offers, he would always politely decline the offer and be sure to let the representative know about the company's policy regarding gifts, as well as his limited storage space.

As time went on, Charlie found he actually came to enjoy meeting with some of the vendors who stopped by. By listening to what they had to offer, he found he was able to improve his product line, which often led to positive customer feedback. He also took advantage of some of the sales promotions they offered, which helped to lower his costs. Lastly, he noticed over time that he had come to build a friendly relationship with a few of the vendors. Many times, the main discussion of the sales meeting focused more on sports than on sales. For example, one of his favorite vendors, Nick Winston from Alexander's Wine & Spirits, had attended the same college as Charlie. Both were still die-hard fans of the school's football team and spent a lot of time reminiscing about past games. Now that the season was in full swing, they both looked forward to discussing the previous week's game during Nick's sales appointments. The team was off to the best start in school history and, with a little luck, a lot of team effort, and two more wins, they would secure their first spot in a championship bowl game.

As luck would have it, Nick and Charlie's old college team finally qualified for a championship bowl game. Both of the men were ecstatic at their Tuesday morning sales meeting. Neither one could believe it. You would have thought the two men were still attending their old college!

Nick was even more excited than Charlie. He knew that his company held tickets for many of the championship bowl games, including the one his old team would be playing in. The primary purpose of the tickets was to offer them as incentives to clients who purchased large quantities of product in advance. As the vendor, Nick would then have the honor of attending on behalf of his company in an effort to network with his clients. While he still had to get at least one client to purchase a large enough quantity of product to qualify for the tickets, he knew Charlie would do it in a heartbeat. How could he possibly pass up the opportunity to see his former team play in their first-ever championship bowl game?

Case Questions

1. If you were Charlie, what would you do?

2. How would a utilitarian analyze the situation? Explain your answer.

3. How would Kant analyze this situation? Explain your answer.

4. If you were Charlie's boss and you found out that Charlie purchased unnecessary product in order to secure the tickets, what would you do? Explain your answer based on ethical theory.

This case was written by Sherry Andre, Instructor, Johnson & Wales University, Florida campus.

Case Study—Championship Game

"Bobby! Bobby, let's go, you're in!" yelled the head coach of Jasper High. It was the semi-final high school football championship game. The winning team tonight would be headed to the state championship game next week. It had been a tough game so far. Both teams were exhausted from the long season. Jasper High was currently trailing Westmont High 16-14 midway through the third quarter. The Westmont High players outsized those on the Jasper High team, but Jasper High had a stronger coaching staff and a more rounded team.

Bobby Ralston, a junior, was a second-string wide receiver. He had hoped he would get to play tonight. This game could be the end of the season or the chance of a lifetime if they were to advance to the state finals. To date, Bobby had started in only one game this year. On the other hand, his hard work and dedication this year had earned him a regular rotation in virtually every game thus far. He was considered a huge asset when either of the leading receivers needed to step out of the game. At this particular moment, Ernie, the primary receiver, had just been carried off the field with an ankle injury. It was still unclear how serious it was, but Bobby knew the drill and felt more prepared than ever. He was to go into the game and fake left, then cut right, and finally head for the end zone. There was a good chance the opposing team would underestimate his speed and ability and he would be left wide open to catch the pass. If the coverage on the leading receiver was too tight, he was to be ready for the ball.

Filled with anticipation, Bobby listened to the quarterback count. The ball was snapped and off he went. He was not about to let his team down. He ran faster than he had ever run before, and sure enough, as he looked back over his shoulder, he saw the ball was coming to him. He also knew he would have to hold on tight, as he could see not one, but two defenders closing in quickly.

Bobby jumped high into the air, and just as he did, he felt the leather of the ball on his fingers. This was the moment he had been waiting for. He clutched the ball with all the strength he had, knowing he was about to be sandwiched between two very large defenders that were running full force toward him. Slam! Crack! The only thing on his mind was "don't let go of the ball." And he didn't. After the hit, he just lay in the end zone looking up at the starry night sky, the ball clutched tightly to his chest. At first he couldn't move; everything seemed to be a blur. Clearly, he had just had the wind knocked out of him. Then he could hear the crowd going wild. He knew he had just scored a touchdown that would put Jasper High on top. In what seemed like an eternity, he finally was able to catch his breath. His teammates were surrounding him. Everyone was cheering. With their help, he stood up. Still a bit shaken, a couple of them helped walk him off the field and over to the team bench.

"Great catch, Bobby!" screamed the coach as Bobby sat down. "You OK? Didn't break anything did you? Looked like a hard hit."

Bobby just shook his head back and forth to acknowledge "no," although he could feel a sharp pain piercing through the center of his back. It was probably nothing. He just needed to catch his breath and he would be fine.

"Good. We're going to need you back in the game soon. Ernie most likely broke his ankle and won't be going back in tonight.

"I'm good, coach," Bobby responded. "Ready to go when you need me." This was his chance to prove himself. He had to show the coach he could be counted on.

"All right then. Next play, you're in."

With that, Bobby stood up. The pain in his back was excruciating. What could he have possibly done? Sure it was a hard hit, but he had been hit hard before and never felt anything like this. The coach was waving him over. As he took a couple of steps forward the pain worsened. The coach could see by the look on his face that he was in pain, but he also knew there were no athletic trainers or doctors present to medically assess the situation. More than likely, he was just shaken up. After all, it was a hard hit. "Shake it off, Bobby," he hollered. "Think about the championship game you're going to be playing in next week."

"The coach is right," Bobby thought. He couldn't let coach or his team down now. Still, he couldn't ignore the pain that kept shooting through his back. He decided to let the coach know about it. "Coach ... my back ... there's a sharp pain running through my back."

"Bobby, we need you now more than ever," the Coach replied. "Maybe you just pinched a nerve and need to run it out."

"I don't know, coach. It really hurts."

"This is it, Bobby. Season's over if we don't get a win here tonight. This is what you've been working for all season. This is what the team's been working for all season. But it's up to you, Bobby. What do you say? Can we count on you?"

Case Questions

1. What are the ethical issues in this case?

2. Carefully look at the ethical choices and responsibilities of Bobby—explain how you see them. Then do the same for the coach.

3. Analyze the case from a utilitarian perspective. List all benefits and harms you see following from different courses of action in this case.

4. What would you do if you were Bobby? The coach?

This case was written by Sherry Andre, Instructor, Johnson & Wales University, Florida campus.

16

Applying Ethics to Entertainment Management

Acting is all about honesty. If you can fake that, you've got it made.— George Burns

ENTERTAINMENT MANAGEMENT COULD POSSIBLY be one of the most difficult areas in hospitality management to negotiate. Imagine being an agent to five different stars, each of whom thinks he or she is truly the most important human being around.

Entertainment management deals with a world of possibilities and excitement. It is also known for its difficult and backstabbing ways. Because entertainment in our society is so intimately connected with money and fame, there seem to be many opportunities for unethical practices to occur.

Imagine yourself a few years out of school. During college, you worked as a promotional manager with some student music groups and actually landed them a few outside gigs. Even after you started your first post-college job, you continued to manage a few of these groups. In time, you have become successful enough to be the exclusive agent and manager for most of the quality acts in a certain musical genre locally.

Local musical venues are asking for bids on available gigs for the type of music you essentially have a monopoly on. You put in bids for each of your groups. Because you control the bids for all the groups, you are able to drive up the price of the bidding. You have accomplished two things: you have effectively driven out the competition and you have increased the price that the winning group will command. There is an unwritten industry rule known as a non-collusive agreement that says you should not collude to raise prices beyond a competitive level but, in practice, it is not easy to prove nor is it usually prosecuted as an illegal activity.

Do you think this is ethical? If you had the opportunity to drive up the wage that one of your clients would receive through collusive activities, would you take advantage of the situation? What if you felt that musicians are generally underpaid for the work that they do, and that owners of the live performance musical outlet venues make large profits with little contribution? What is the ethical way that prices should be set? Is the free market always just? Is collusion, either open or covert, ever justified? A number of complicated ethical issues may arise from situations like this, although the general understanding in a market economy is that collusion is unethical and is to be avoided. This is only one of many ethical issues one might face in the entertainment industry. See the following case for another example.

157

Case Study—To Buy or Not to Buy? ──────────

Ned Balsam and the Laughing Hurricane was becoming a regionally popular band. Until this point they had been performing the music of well-known top-ten performers. Their popularity had so increased that several agents had contacted them offering representation. Each agent, including Blake, the one they had finally selected, had encouraged the group to start performing some of their own music in addition to the popular tunes for which they were so well regarded. Ned had one good tune, *The Laughing Crying Hyena,* and it was always well received. Although he tried hard, he just had not been able to create another tune that had any appeal. But at band practice the following afternoon, the band's drummer, Bart Nagle, offered to help.

"I have a friend who would probably be willing to sell you a few tunes," Bart told Ned. "He's got 'em all over his house, on napkins, matchbox covers, you name it. He's a little dizzy, but he can write."

"I can't buy tunes; I've got to write them. But go ahead. Talk to your friend. If he's so dizzy, maybe he would let me lift a few tunes."

The next afternoon, Bart stopped to see Ned. "I spoke with Dooby. He said he would ghostwrite a few tunes for you, but he would want a percentage."

"Tell him I'll talk to our new agent and see what he says," Ned replied.

A few weeks later, and after several mild wrangling sessions, Dooby accepted 8 percent of total sales for the three songs he would ghostwrite for Ned. As part of the agreement his name would never be connected to the songs.

Case Commentary: Utilitarianism

At first glance, an act utilitarian might be able to rationalize the secretive nature of Ned's passing Dooby's work off as his own. More music would be developed and released. This would create satisfaction among fans. It would be useful to Ned's career and his popularity would be enhanced. His band would be happy. His agent would be happy.

Dooby would also gain. He would earn money, and since he agreed to the transaction voluntarily, he has been given the opportunity to calculate what was in his best interest. He freely chose to sell Ned tunes for an exchange of much needed cash. Therefore, it is possible that an act utilitarian could say that everyone had gained and there was no real loss. But that is not the only way an act utilitarian could view the situation, because one could easily foresee other consequences that, over the long run, may lead to all sorts of negative consequences. Remember that utilitarianism requires that we measure the positives and negatives of *all* the consequences, both long-term and short-term, that we can reasonably foresee following from an action. And different people might reasonably disagree about what are likely to be the foreseeable consequences of deceptively claiming someone else's work as one's own while secretly paying them. Many act utilitarians might foresee important negative consequences over the long run. Thus, there is much to argue about in this case, if viewed from within the act utilitarian perspective.

From the point of view of rule utilitarianism, the whole arrangement is even more problematic ethically. Can we make it a rule that deceptive authorship claims should be allowed in circumstances like this, because such a rule will lead to the greatest good for the greatest number? As a general rule, it looks even more doubtful that this is an acceptable practice.

This could be a complicated issue from a utilitarian point of view, depending on a variety of factual issues that may be difficult to determine easily. If fans found out that Ned was not writing his own music, they could become cynical and resentful. When heroes are shown to be dishonest, the public is harmed. It can lead people to think these practices are now acceptable, leading to an overall degeneration of moral standards in society. It can also lead to the cynical view that anyone can be bought. Such an attitude, if widespread, cannot be considered morally beneficial in its consequences.

In addition, it could encourage exploitative situations where the rich and powerful always gain the upper hand in business deals negotiated with less advantaged people, because they can buy whatever is necessary in order to negotiate a better deal. In general, when deceptive practices are routinely accepted, it leads to a decline in moral behavior. On the other hand, some utilitarians may consider this and other unattributed forms of ghostwriting just another form of little white lies that actually provide the most benefit for the majority, with minimal negative consequences. Therefore, depending on what one thinks the consequences would be, a utilitarian could come down on either or both sides of the issue.

Case Commentary: Kant's Categorical Imperative

Kant would see ghostwriting as a form of deception. Anything that is deliberately hidden or consciously left unidentified would be considered a violation of the categorical imperative. From Kant's viewpoint, this behavior violates both formulations of the categorical imperative. It violates the first formulation because making false authorship a universal rule would undermine the very basis of having authorship, and thus would be self-contradictory and immoral, as is any form of cheating.

The unethical nature of this deal from a deontological or Kantian perspective is even clearer from the second formulation of the categorical imperative. By not being honest with the public and with his fans, Ned is not treating each and every person as having unconditional worth or as being an end unto himself or herself. Ned's fans are human beings, and as such they deserve to be treated as autonomous, rational creatures, not things to be used or manipulated with false information. They are being denied their autonomous rational, moral self-worth, and instead are used to accomplish Ned's goal. When Ned withholds the true authorship of the songs he performs, he is not treating his fans as people of independent moral worth. He is using them.

Kant would find universalizing deception to be immoral. He would say it is wrong to falsify authorship. He would condemn the monetary transactions involved in the case: earning money falsely for work that is not one's own and accepting money for hidden authorship.

Case Commentary: The Ethic of Justice

Although this is not primarily a case about distributive justice, there is perhaps a secondary issue of justice in this case. If one were to stand behind the veil of ignorance, would he or she consider the distribution of money in this case to be acceptable? What would people find to be acceptable if they were in the original position? The answer is not entirely clear because Dooby is receiving some payment for his work, albeit secretly and not in full. It is likely—but not certain— secret authorship that does not fully compensate the songwriter for his work would not be considered acceptable because those in the original position would believe Dooby is not getting a fair share of income, and they realize that they may end up being the person in Dooby's shoes. The lack of certainty arises because Dooby is making more money than he had been previously.

The real question from a distributional justice perspective is: Would some alternative arrangement (for example, giving Dooby a larger percentage or giving him open credit and therefore greater name recognition so he could promote his songs more widely) be fairer to all concerned? How would people in the original position feel that fame and fortune should be distributed when unknown songwriters like Dooby team up with better known performers like Ned and his band? The way one answers that question will decide the distributional justice issues contained in this case. From an overall ethics perspective, the distributional justice questions are probably secondary to questions about deception and credit.

In the event that Ned's deception is discovered, retributive justice questions could arise. What should be the penalty Ned pays if he is caught and this is judged wrong? This is not a legal question under the U.S. legal system, because the deal between Dooby and Ned was agreed upon by both sides. Any retribution may come from Ned's adoring public. If word got out that he was passing Dooby's work off as his own, record sales and attendance at his concerts may drop, although this is far from certain given the degree to which bad behavior by celebrities is often accepted and even glorified.

Case Commentary: Aristotle and the Ethics of Virtue

The character of any person who passes the work of another off as his own would be questionable from the point of view of character ethics or virtue ethics. The most important virtue missing in this case is honesty; put another way, the most important vice is dishonesty. Other potential virtues to consider in this case are courage, justice, and prudence.

Ned and those around him all acted in a dishonest manner. Ned did not have the courage to admit that he could not write any new music. Ned was not giving his fans what they deserved and none of them (Ned, Dooby, Blake, or Bart) had the prudence or wisdom to know that fooling the public was inappropriate. None of the actions showed good character. Aristotle would say that their actions were immoral because they were lacking in character.

 ## Case Study—To Buy or Not to Buy? (Part II)

One year later, two of the three songs that Dooby had ghostwritten for Ned Balsam were sailing high on the popular music charts. Ned had become a nationally known figure and Dooby wanted a piece of the action. He managed to get in the door of Ned's agent after weeks of phoning and demanded more money. He threatened to expose Ned's inability to write, at a time when Ned had become famous for his songwriting ability.

Case Questions

1. What does this case illustrate about the types of consequences that could occur when secret deals are made? Be complete and list both the positives and negatives.

2. What would you do if you were Ned? Explain your answer.

3. What would you do if you were Dooby? Explain your answer.

4. What would you do if you were Blake? Explain your answer.

5. In order to exhibit a good (virtuous) character, what should Ned do?

6. What is a fair distribution of money from the songs? Explain your answer from a justice ethics point of view.

 Case Study—The First Job

Malcolm Garcia was the promotional agent for the very famous country and western group The Buckskins. He was planning to book a show in Phoenix at The Saloon, one of the largest music venues in the area. He called his old friend Cooly Hatcher, the Saloon's manager, to make arrangements but found out from Lionel Masters, Cooly's new assistant, that he was unavailable. Cooly was on his honeymoon with his new bride and was unreachable. He had left Lionel in charge and Lionel felt that he could handle just about any situation that would come up.

Malcolm explained to Lionel that he wanted to book The Saloon for a Buckskins concert. Lionel was very excited about writing the contract on his own and they made an appointment to work out the arrangements for the following day.

After ten minutes of small talk, Malcolm realized that Lionel was a real novice at contract writing. By the time Malcolm and Lionel had banged out the contract, Malcolm had managed to include many policies and procedures that he knew Cooly would never agree to. Malcolm was quite pleased and thought, *"If Cooly catches the sneaky stuff, I'll let him change it. But if he doesn't, it will serve him right for leaving a rookie in charge."*

Case Questions

1. Is Malcolm acting in an ethical manner? Explain your answer.

2. Apply a utilitarian analysis to this case.

3. Apply a deontological or Kantian analysis to this case.

4. Apply an Aristotelian analysis to Malcolm's character in this case.

 Case Study—The Big Name

Dennis Oldgren managed the Flying Leapers, one of the most popular teen groups around. He also managed Ella Darvis, Macy Quinn, Rose Sebastian, and countless other less known singers and singing groups. He was searching out ways to get some of his smaller talents more exposure when he came across The Darbyshire Inn, a newly opened hotel in Lansing, Michigan. It had an attached entertainment facility that could hold up to 2,000 people and it was being co-managed by two recent college graduates. Dennis had found out about the new facility when he met the proud managers, Elmer Hodge and Dwight Ferris, at the restaurant show in Chicago.

Dennis stopped in to chat with Elmer and Dwight a few weeks after the restaurant show. He had a portfolio and brochures detailing all of the performers that he managed. Together, the three agreed on a booking for the following April. The show headliner would be the Flying Leapers. The show openers would include Ella Darvis, Macy Quinn, and Rose Sebastian.

Dennis told them he would have his office prepare a contract and get it back to Dwight and Elmer within the week. In fact, Dennis did not send the contract for almost a month. Elmer and Dwight received the new contract and looked it over. They decided that it looked fine and did not feel there was any reason to ask for advice from the hotel general manager. They signed the new contract and sent it back.

The concert was sold out and the Darbyshire was filled with hundreds of pre-teen girls and their moms. But the audience wasn't too happy when it became apparent after three hours of show-openers that the Flying Leapers were not going to appear. Girls started storming the box office and demanding their money back. While Dwight tried to calm the crowds, Elmer found the contract to get Dennis's phone number. While he was waiting for Dennis to come to the phone, Elmer read over the contract to see about responsibility in the event of a no-show, and he realized that a no-show clause was not included. He knew that they had been had and his biggest worry now was who was going to be responsible for all the money that would have to be refunded. He also thought that what Dennis had done was not illegal, so taking legal action against Dennis was not a possibility.

Case Questions

1. Assuming that Dennis's actions are legal, are they ethical? Explain your answer.

2. Would an act utilitarian analysis differ from a rule utilitarian analysis of this case? Why or why not?

3. Are there any compensatory justice issues in this case? Explain your answer.

4. What are the harms and what are the benefits of this situation?

 ## Case Study—Crowd Control

Lance Holder represented the G-Man 5, a rap group with a very large, unruly following. The crowd was always largely 16- to 20-year-old males, typically African-American. Past concerts by the G-Man 5 had been accompanied by some minor acts of vandalism and fights, both during and after the concerts.

Laramie Souza was the facility manager at the Beach Arena. He was excited about the opportunity to have the G-Man 5 as the show headliner for the upcoming Caribbean Days Festival. But he also felt that any venue that booked the group should insist on extra money to pay for security and city law enforcement.

When Holder and Souza sat down to discuss concert particulars, Souza explained that he would require extra funds for security purposes. Holder was livid and claimed that he was discriminating against his group for being African-American. But Souza was insistent, stating that it was his responsibility to keep all attendees safe. He said, "It is my decision to charge the G-Man 5 for extra security. I am doing it because I am responsible for the crowd. I do not take unnecessary risks. I will do what I need to do to avoid potential problems. And there are always potential problems with the kind of crowd the G-Man 5 brings. Take it or leave it."

Case Questions

1. What facts would you need to know to determine if Souza is being discriminatory? Explain your answer.

2. From a utilitarian perspective, state as precisely as you can the facts that would lead you to conclude that Souza is ethically right in this dispute. What set of facts would lead you to conclude that Holder is ethically right?

3. Is this an easy case to apply Kant's categorical imperative to? Why or why not? Can you think of a set of facts or circumstances here that might lead Kant to conclude that this is not even an ethical issue, merely a practical disagreement? Can you construct a set of facts that would lead to Kant condemning Souza as unethical, or condemning Holder as unethical? Does deontological or Kantian ethics apply to this case?

4. Do we know enough to be able to make judgments about the character of either Souza or Holder? Try to add details to this case that would make Souza praiseworthy from a character ethics perspective. What virtues would he be exhibiting under this scenario? Try the same thing for Holder—add details that make him praiseworthy and show the virtues he is exhibiting.

17

Applying Ethics to Event Management

*Creativity can solve almost any problem. The creative act, the defeat of habit
by originality, overcomes everything.* —George Lois

THE ACADEMY AWARDS is an event. A 75th birthday party for grandpa's family is also an event. Strict policies, procedures, and contracts should be the groundwork to build upon in any event management venue. When getting involved in large events, as opposed to the small family parties, there are many more issues that can become complicated from a moral standpoint. Issues such as familiarization trips, business meals, freebies, perks, and confidentiality are just a few.

Creativity is probably the single most important attribute an event manager can have. But creativity on policies and procedures will lead you down the wrong path. A good event manager will ensure that policies and procedures are in place and adhered to and that he or she abides by them to the letter as well. There is nothing more demoralizing to a group of employees than the "Do as I say, not as I do" rule. If employees see you putting aside table flowers for yourself instead of giving them to the host family, they will follow suit. If employees see you fudging due dates for certain customers but being hard-nosed with others, they will begin to make their own rules, and follow them, as well.

Honesty and integrity play a large role in the event management industry. The following is an example of what happens when the rules aren't quite followed.

Case Study—The Résumé Upgrade

Earline Moberly is a hospitality college graduate from Kolsen College in Kansas City, Missouri. She majored in event management and has been working in the event industry since her freshman year of college. She has worked for three different event management companies in three different jobs. Each new job was a promotion and Earline has a lot to offer.

Earline has been out of school for over a year and feels that she is ready to go out on her own. She knows everything there is to know about event management and now she wants to have the money to go along with the knowledge she has acquired.

Earline understood early on, from her events management classes, that a good résumé is only as good as the professional portfolio or brochure one has to back it up. Luckily for Earline, she had been taking photos of all of the events she had attended over the years. She put together an excellent résumé and included a beautiful portfolio filled with pictures of the many events she had worked at.

In July, when she was ready, Earline gave notice at her job. She planned to move to San Francisco in September to live with her older sister Georgia, who had an extra room in her house, while she established her event management company. The new company was called *Balloons and More*.

Georgia's friend Winona worked in the human resources department at the local cable television company. Winona told her manager Rowena about "the hip new event management company" and suggested that Rowena consider *Balloons and More* for the office holiday party in December.

In preparation for the interview with Rowena, Earline decided that she would only offer the brochure and not make it obvious that she was just starting out. She had a beautiful brochure and, she thought to herself, everyone knows that a picture is worth a thousand words.

On the day of the interview, Earline dressed in her new black suit, placed several copies of her brochure in her new black leather briefcase, and felt ready to go. She arrived at the interview ten minutes early, stopped in the ladies room to freshen up, and then showed up, right on time, at reception.

Rowena was a gracious interviewer and Earline immediately felt comfortable. Everything was going quite well until Rowena said, "What beautiful work your company has done over the years. You must be quite proud of yourself."

Earline was speechless. Rowena believed that *Balloons and More* had accomplished all the work represented by the brochure. Even though she knew she had to disavow the idea, she didn't. She made a split-second decision to allow Rowena to think that *Balloons and More* had accomplished all the work represented in the brochure. What could it hurt, after all?

After she finished looking over the brochure, Rowena immediately started discussing terms and conditions for the event. She told Earline that a contract would be offered within the next few weeks to one of the five event management companies she had interviewed.

A few weeks later, Earline received a call offering her the office holiday party. She was told to expect a contract in the mail within the week. The contract came and she carefully studied the details to make sure everything had been included. She was very happy with the terms and returned the signed contract the next day.

Several months later, the holiday party was a huge success. Earline was having a wonderful time networking and handing out her business card. But imagine her surprise when she saw Vern Gillyard, a fellow graduate from Kolsen College. They had been in two liberal arts classes together in their senior year. Vern had been a business student, majoring in accounting. Earline was afraid to speak with him because she worried that he would give her away as a recent college graduate. She left the room and stayed backstage for the remainder of the event.

Case Commentary: Utilitarianism

The question Earline might have asked herself at the time of the original misunderstanding regarding her résumé is will there be more harms or benefits if I do not clarify my company's history? The major harm, of course, would come from getting caught. Her reputation would suffer terribly; she might not even recover from such a situation. This one act of untruthfulness could destroy her new company.

If Earline had been thinking as a rule utilitarian, she would know that she could not make it a rule to be deceptive. A rule condoning deceptiveness would lead to a breakdown in trust among individuals.

Case Commentary: Kant's Categorical Imperative

Kant would look at the motive of Earline's actions. Originally, she used the photographs to show that she has experience working at a variety of events. However, once the misunderstanding occurred, her motive changed. By hiding the truth, her motive became one of deception. In addition, her duty at the time of the deception was to explain that she had only worked the events, not been fully responsible for them.

The categorical imperative would not condone deception in any form. The first formulation states that we must be able to make a universal rule, a rule that everyone must follow, out of our actions. Earline could not make a universal rule out of misrepresentation.

The second formulation states that we must not use other people for our own gain. Earline is using both her sister Georgia and Georgia's friend Winona. If the truth were revealed, it could interfere with Georgia's friendship with Winona. Furthermore, by not being truthful to Rowena, Earline is allowing Rowena to think that she has hired someone with many years of experience and ownership.

Case Commentary: The Ethic of Justice

If Earline's dishonesty was discovered, she might face some type of retribution, although it is doubtful. However, if someone became ill from eating the food and then it was discovered that Earline was not all she claimed to be, she might be open to a lawsuit.

Case Commentary: Aristotle and the Ethics of Virtue

It should be obvious that Earline's deceit shows her character to be deficient from a virtue ethics or character ethics perspective. Deceitfulness is a vice, not a virtue. Dishonesty is likewise a vice; the opposite of the virtue of honesty. The way that one act of dishonesty can begin to build a dishonest character is beautifully illustrated in this case: now she finds herself hiding out of sight at the event to cover for the earlier dishonesty. She is entangling herself more and more into a life of deceit, all originated by her initial moment of weakness when she didn't clarify the misunderstanding. Aristotle and other character ethics thinkers would point out that you have to habitually behave in an ethical manner if you wish to build up a good character. Instead, Earline is developing exactly the wrong habits, and therefore a dishonest and ethically deficient character.

Case Study—Sally's New Bicycle

Pamela Rumstedt was the event planner for the Cheshire Wolves, the minor league baseball team in Cheshire, Ohio. Since Cheshire was geographically far from any towns or cities with major league teams, the Wolves enjoyed good attendance on a regular basis.

Tonight was Pamela's biggest night of the year. Once each year, the Wolves put on an extravaganza as a fund-raiser for one of the local non-profit organizations. This year's lucky recipient was to be the Cheshire Society for the Prevention of Cruelty to Animals (CSPCA). Pamela had begun working on the event only one month after the completion of last year's event, which had been for the local Habitat for Humanity.

One of Pamela's biggest responsibilities for the fund-raiser was acquiring items for the silent auction, and this year she had done a superb job. The list of prizes seemed to be endless. Items ranged from a Caribbean cruise to autographed baseball bats and everything in between. All in all, there were almost 100 auction items.

As Pamela was setting up the items in their viewing spots, she noticed a brand new Iron Horse Warrior mountain bike that she knew her daughter, Sally, would love. Sally had been pining away for a new bike ever since her best friend, Callie, had gotten one. And this one was even red, Sally's favorite color! Pamela couldn't decide if she should bid on the bike; Wolves employees were allowed and even encouraged to bid on merchandise. "Why should I?" she thought. "This is such an athletic crowd that someone will surely outbid me anyway." Pamela moved on and continued her work. A short while later, she saw her assistant, Audrey, setting out notes on the table in front of each item. The notes contained descriptions of the items as well as the required opening bid. Pamela was pleased to see that Audrey was on schedule with all of her assigned tasks. Pamela had recently given Audrey more responsibilities and she appeared to be handling the new duties well.

Several hours later, the evening had gone quite well. Almost every item had been spoken for and distributed. But Pamela was surprised to see that there were no takers for the Iron Horse mountain bike. She went over to give it a second look and that's when she noticed the card. The line next to the opening bid request was filled in with the amount of $500. Anyone interested in the bike would know that $500 was more than the retail price. "Oh well, we'll just have to give it back," she thought to herself. But the more she pondered the situation, the more she wanted the bike for Sally. Finally, she decided that it would be acceptable for her to pay $100 into the fund and take the bike home to her daughter. The CSPCA would make $100 more than the evening's present take, the bike store already donated the bike, she was giving her donation and her daughter would be thrilled. What could be wrong?

Case Questions

1. What would you do if you were Pamela? Explain your answer.

2. How would a utilitarian view this situation? Explain your answer.

3. How would Kant view this situation? Explain your answer.

 **Case Study—Wedding Worries**

When Michelle Mahoney and Dray Drexel got engaged a year and a half ago, her parents quickly convinced her to use a wedding planner. Michelle was the youngest of five and her parents fully understood the work involved with planning a wedding, not to mention they only wanted the best for their little girl. As such, they hired Alison, a senior wedding planner, from Wedding Works. Working with Alison had been a pleasure. She truly understood the business and knew how to work with a limited budget. Her contacts in the industry enabled her to negotiate great prices for many of the expenses associated with the wedding, such as the photographer, flowers, and entertainment. Alison also saved the Mahoneys money by booking the rehearsal dinner at the same hotel, the Looking Glass, where the out-of-town guests would be staying.

With less than three months until the big day, Michelle was finally beginning to feel like everything was on track for a perfect wedding...that is, until she received a phone call from Alison. Apparently, the Looking Glass had failed to realize in advance that the weekend Michelle and Dray had selected for their wedding was the same weekend that the Super Bowl was to be played in town. Millions of people were expected to be in the area for the big weekend. As such, local hotel rooms were in high demand. The limited supply allowed for room rates to double and triple, with many hotels also being able to implement a mandatory minimum stay of three to five nights. After realizing the potential profit available for the weekend, the Looking Glass notified Alison that the 15 rooms she had reserved a year ago for her clients' wedding party would be cancelled. They neglected to give her a reason, only stating that unforeseen circumstances had led to their decision. However, they did assure her that her client would still be able to hold the rehearsal dinner at the hotel. Needless to say, Alison quickly attempted to secure rooms at other local hotels. Unfortunately, the best she was able to find was a room rate that was nearly double the rate of that originally reserved.

Case Question

1. What are the ethical issues?

This case was written by Sherry Andre, Instructor, Johnson & Wales University, Florida campus.

 Case Study—The Ploy

Minnie Atlas had been working at non-profit organizations since she graduated from college three years ago. She had done a great deal of fund-raising in those three years. Because of her background, as well as her fund-raising ability, she was now the executive director of the Boontown Homeless Shelter.

Minnie's first big challenge was the annual fund-raising event. This year, the board had decided on a western theme and rodeo. The group had produced a similar event four years ago and it had been their most successful fund-raiser ever.

The western theme had been selected several months before Minnie's arrival on the job. Some work had been done on the event but, in general, the group had been waiting for the new director to take over.

This was a problem for Minnie. Even though she had overseen fund-raising events in the past, she had never done anything with a western motif. In fact, her ideas of western went no further than cowboys and Indians. And she was sure no one was interested in that. She had been born and raised in New York City and taking the position in Boontown, Pennsylvania, had been a big step.

Minnie pondered her problem. Her professors in college had told her to seek the experts whenever she didn't know what to do. They had meant books, of course. But right now, Minnie had no time for books.

Instead, she hit upon the idea of "hiring" an event coordinator for the job. She looked up three large events organizations in nearby towns and started calling. Only one, Lucky Days, had time to see her within the week. Minnie spoke with Mabel Crossly and they set a date for the following Tuesday.

Mabel knew that the Boontown Homeless Shelter had no money to spend on an event coordinator. She was even surprised that there was a new executive director. When Mabel told her boss, Pete, that she had a meeting set with the new executive director of the Boontown Homeless Shelter, he told her to cancel the meeting. "It's a waste of your time and my money," he said.

"Let me just give her an hour. I don't have much on my plate these days anyway."

Finally, Pete relented, but he knew that there was no business forthcoming from the Boontown Homeless Shelter. Mabel knew it, too, but she was curious about Minnie.

The meeting on Tuesday went quite well. The women got along and Mabel spent the promised hour laying out all sorts of possibilities for the fund-raising event. At the end of the hour, she told Minnie that she had another appointment and she was looking forward to hearing from her.

At the end of the meeting, Mabel had the feeling that she would never hear from Minnie again. She also thought she might see some of her ideas at the Boontown Homeless Shelter fund-raising event.

Minnie's next stop was the local hospitality college. She had contacted Marvin Delaney, department chair, asking if she could stop in for a chat about the upcoming fund-raising event. Marvin liked the idea because he thought it was a good opportunity for his students to complete their community service hours.

Minnie laid out all of Mabel's ideas as if they were her own. Marvin loved the ideas and brought in one of his event management professors, Leslie Hyde, who thought she could use some of the ideas for her class project.

Two months later, the Boontown event had been a success and Minnie was a local heroine. The hospitality students had done a wonderful job and Leslie Hyde's voluntary assistance had been invaluable. Mabel spent a few hours at the event seeing all of her personal ideas put to work. She wasn't sure how she felt about it, except for the fact that she certainly felt ripped off.

Case Questions

1. Were Minnie's actions ethical? Explain your answer.

2. How would a utilitarian view Minnie's actions? Explain your answer.

3. How would Kant view Minnie's actions? Explain your answer.

18

Applying Ethics to Meeting Management

Great ability develops and reveals itself increasingly with every new assignment. —Baltasar Gracian

MEETINGS, WHICH ALSO INCLUDE conventions and expositions, come in all types and sizes. A meeting consists of two or more people coming together for a common purpose. It can be thousands of teachers from across the country coming together to discuss education today or two retirees planning the next local chapter get-together of the American Association of Retired Persons.

The planning of a meeting can be arduous and complicated. Because there are so many different types of people, facilities, locations, etc., there are many opportunities for ethical dilemmas to arise. For example, a meeting planner may have two meetings booked in the same day, one in the morning and one in the evening. She might negotiate the contract for both event groups separately, but negotiate only one contract with the venue. Suppose she charges both groups for the event space for the entire day, even though she will be charged for the space only once. This is not illegal, but is it ethical? Read the case below and see what you think.

Case Study—A Day at the Bon Visage

Jasmine Stringer is an independent meeting planner in northwest Indiana near Lake Michigan. She has been working on her own for the past two years. Her previous experience included three years with the Royalty Corporation, where she spent some of her time as a meeting planner.

Jasmine felt like she got really lucky today. She just landed a second contract for a January 15th meeting, this one for the state humane society's annual statewide meeting to be held from 8:30 A.M. until 12:30 P.M. Jasmine already had an afternoon meeting set for the same day beginning at 1 P.M. with a regional educators group. Both organizations asked Jasmine to make suggestions about the meeting location.

Jasmine decided to call her friend Pierce first. He was the catering manager at the Bon Visage Hotel on Delancy Beach. It was one of the few places that stayed open on Lake Michigan through the winter, but it did not do too much business, as people tended not to have meetings and events in the area at that time of the year. Jasmine also knew that the Bon Visage had a beautiful view of the lake and would be an ideal location if it didn't snow. But snow wouldn't be her problem, anyway.

She also thought she could reserve it for a good price. Jasmine charged her clients actual costs plus her fee.

Jasmine met with Pierce the following day and agreed to rent the Snowflake Room for January 15th from 8 A.M. until 6 P.M. She explained to Pierce that she would need two different set-ups but did not mention the two different groups. The room rental was $700 for a half day but would only be $1,000 for the full day.

Independently over the next week, she brought representatives to the Bon Visage to view the Snowflake Room. Both groups were very happy with the room and Jasmine told them she would put together a contract and get it out within the week.

Jasmine prepared the contract. She decided to charge each group $700 for the half day, ensuring herself an extra $400 profit. She knew it was pretty unlikely that either group would find out. She also knew that what she was doing was perfectly legal.

Case Commentary

If Jasmine looks at the situation from a utilitarian perspective, she may initially conclude that no real harm is being done to anyone by her decision to charge the two groups $1,400 even though the Snowflake Room is costing her only $1,000. After all, if she had not had two events the same day, the best she could have done for each group was to get the room for half a day at $700. Therefore, the accidental fact that she also had another booking the same day doesn't change anything for the client—it just makes this Jasmine's lucky day because she is able to cash in with an extra $400. Both clients were charged the normal price for booking half a day.

Is this persuasive reasoning? One alternative is for Jasmine to explain to the two groups that she fortunately was able to book two events at the same place in one day, thus lowering the cost of room rental from $700 to $500 for a half day. Each of the groups saves $200, and Jasmine gets only her normal payment for arranging and managing the meetings. If we try to compare benefits and harms, can we put a greater or lesser value on the $400 cumulative savings for the two groups compared to the $400 windfall profit to Jasmine? If she indulges in the natural human tendency to give greater value to one's own benefit, Jasmine might find the net benefit to all concerned to be greatest if she just takes the money and lets no one know—no one's the wiser, and she is richer.

However, that is a very selective reading of the total benefits and harms in this situation. Remember that utilitarianism requires that all benefits and harms must be counted equally. If we look at the overall costs and benefits to everyone, it is apparent that these two meetings cost more than necessary. This type of economic inefficiency is harmful to the organizations involved. They can do less of their customary work because some of their resources are unnecessarily taken so that the meeting planner can make a larger profit through deception. Seen in this way, the total harms outweigh the benefits, and Jasmine is morally obligated to inform the groups of the real cost of their half day in the Snowflake Room.

The utilitarian case against Jasmine's deception is even clearer by adopting a rule utilitarian perspective. Will the greatest good come from adopting a rule that allows deceptive overpricing? The answer is obviously no.

Note that the situation would be different if Jasmine's fee arrangement with the two groups was not one of "costs plus a meeting planner fee." If it were simply a business arrangement in which Jasmine presents a package for a certain fee and competes with other meeting planners on that basis, she would be able to set her profit margin at whatever level she chooses. However, the competition from other planners under these circumstances would normally prevent her from overcharging as she is attempting to do in this situation. The main point is that the arrangements should attempt to provide the greatest good for the greatest number, and competitive bidding needs to be on an open and clear basis for this to be accomplished. If a planner misrepresents costs to a client, this is not being achieved.

From a Kantian perspective, Jasmine's actions are deceptive, and as with all forms of deception that deny other human beings an opportunity to behave as rational beings, it denies them their humanity and is a violation of the categorical imperative. If Jasmine is itemizing a bill and puts down a charge for the room that is higher than the charge actually being incurred, she is lying. As should be obvious at this point in the book, Kant would condemn such behavior.

Our analysis of this case may be controversial, because a situation such as the one described above is relatively common, and some do what we are claiming is unethical from both a utilitarian and a deontological or Kantian perspective. Yet, we believe our analysis is a correct application of these ethical theories. The reader is encouraged to think hard about such practices, apply the theories learned in this book to them, and see what conclusion should be reached. If you disagree with our analysis, be sure you can articulate why a different interpretation is correct.

Case Study—Traveling with Exotique

The Exotique Destination Management Company recently purchased 50 three-day incentive travel packages to St. Lucia for $115 each (excluding airfare). Exotique had been aggressively marketing St. Lucia as a meeting venue, and Frank Yardley, manager for Exotique, felt this would be a good investment.

Frank had his team create a brochure geared toward meeting planners who had been receiving the marketing information from Exotique on St. Lucia. He also had them prepare brochures for a local travel fair that was being held the following week.

Within the month, Exotique had sold every incentive travel package to St. Lucia. Moreover, the prices that the travel packages had brought ranged from $225 to $325. Frank felt that he had made a good investment.

Case Questions

1. Is there anything unethical in what Exotique is doing, or is it just normal business practice of buying things as cheaply as possible and selling them as expensively as possible?

2. Are there any circumstances under which a company buying a product and reselling it at a profit might violate ethical rules? What would they be, if any? Why do you think so?

Case Study—Star Power

Randall Grisham was hired by the office of Senator Jake McGowery to plan the senator's annual meeting with the leaders of the statewide Soldiers Home organization. Soldiers Home meets annually with both of the state's senators to offer advice and to seek assistance for members.

Randall had been working as a meeting planner for several years, but this was the first time that he had gotten such a high-powered contract. He was very excited and was determined to do an excellent job. He put together the contract.

Because he knew there would be many high-powered political people at the event, he included a strict confidentiality clause. The confidentiality clause was written to ensure the privacy of those attending and included the following items:

- The event planner will not take anything of value from the event. "Souvenirs" associated with a celebrity were specifically mentioned.

- The guest list will not be made public by the event planner and is to be shared with no one other than the event assistant.

- No videos will be taken at the event.

- The event planner will be allowed to take pictures of the setting for the event before the event itself, but the confidentiality of those attending the event is not to be compromised.

- Staff members are not allowed to ask for autographs.

Since the Soldiers Home annual meeting was happening so close to election time, Randall thought that many famous entertainment people would be present as well. He knew that Senator McGowery would have his own photographer there, but Randall was hoping he could take a few of his own photos.

The day of the event went quite well. Randall managed to take a few photos of some of the well-known actors and politicians on hand. He even managed to get a photo of himself with the senator. The local newspaper published a notice of the event the following day that mentioned some of the celebrities in attendance, but it did not publish a picture of the event itself.

The following year, Randall decided to update his portfolio. He used several of the photos from the Soldiers Home event. The brochure was entitled "The Best in the Business." The cover of the brochure had a large picture of Randall with Senator McGowery.

Case Questions

1. What are the ethical issues, if any, in this case? Explain your answer.

2. How would Kant view this situation? Explain your answer.

3. Attempt a utilitarian argument to justify Randall's actions. Does it hold up under scrutiny? Explain your final conclusion.

4. From what you know so far, do a character analysis of Randall utilizing the virtues and vices.

Case Study—Who's Responsible?

Olga Darling was elected Vice President of the Chesterville Women's Club. In that capacity, she was in charge of the upcoming annual meeting and given a strict budget. Since she had run a household for 40 years on a very tight budget, she was sure she could manage.

Her first step was to meet with Sally Woodson, the daughter of Eleanor Woodson. Sally was a recent graduate of the local community college. Sally had worked part-time at the Chesterville Convention Center for several years and offered to help with the meeting arrangements.

After visiting several venues, Mrs. Darling settled on Sabrina's Restaurant in downtown Chesterville. The complete price came within the allotted budget, and Mrs. Darling was satisfied. They were allowed a choice of two entrées with soup or salad, dessert, and a bottomless cup of coffee. But, best of all, Sabrina had a party room for the luncheon, so the event would be quite private.

Sally and Mrs. Darling sat together with Sabrina to discuss details and Sabrina said she would have a contract to them within the next few days. When Mrs. Darling received the contract, she and Sally went over it carefully before she signed and returned it.

The day of the meeting arrived. More than 40 women attended, which was a record number for the Chesterville Women's Club. The meal went well. The food was delicious and the service was quite good. But the meeting dragged on and on. With so many women in attendance, coupled with a bottomless cup of coffee, Mrs. Darling thought it would never end. Finally, when waitresses started pulling the cloths off the tables and no one was being offered any more coffee, the women got the hint and wound up the meeting.

Olga stayed behind to settle with Sabrina. She had her checkbook in hand because she wanted to get home after such a long day. Sabrina asked her to sit and handed her the bill, which was $120 more than she expected.

Olga was shocked. She took out her contract and showed Sabrina the total amount that was on the original contract.

Sabrina said, "You were in my party room much too long. I have a large group coming in tonight for an engagement party. I had to call in two extra waitresses to do a fast cleanup and reset, and I am not going to eat that cost. You told me the meeting and the luncheon would last no more than three hours."

"But it never did before," Olga moaned. "I can't pay this money. We will be over budget."

"You have to pay it even if it comes out of your own pocket."

Olga was adamant. "There is nothing written in the contract that says we had to be out by a certain time. I don't think I have to pay you anything except for what is on the original bill."

Case Questions

1. What are the ethical issues in this case?

2. Should Olga pay the extra money? Explain your answer.

3. How do justice ethics play into this case?

4. Would a rule utilitarian think differently about this case than an act utilitarian?

5. What would Aristotle say about this case?

6. What would Kant say about this case?

Part IV

International Applications

19

Ethical Issues for
International Managers

Other nations of different habits are not enemies: they are godsends. Men require of their neighbours something sufficiently akin to be understood, something sufficiently different to provoke attention, and something great enough to command admiration. We must not expect, however, all the virtues.—Alfred North Whitehead

Managing in a culture outside your own presents myriad challenges. If it is coupled with managing a workforce in a language other than your mother tongue, the challenges multiply. You may even find yourself facing these challenges while also navigating your way through a foreign society. Many large lodging and hospitality companies now operate all over the world, so those working within this industry frequently find themselves facing challenges of this nature.

Even when you speak the language of your host country competently, it is not always easy to function well in a foreign environment. Cultural differences between societies assert themselves constantly in the workplace. Understanding typical leadership issues such as status at the workplace, customary work breaks, the functioning of the grapevine, and the like are all important. Things like hand gestures, when to take off your shoes, handshaking, time management, and many others may be very important in your host country.

Along with the differences in manners and ways of reading a particular type of behavior, ethical issues that are closely tied to different cultural customs easily arise. Since ethics relates to deeply held beliefs about right and wrong, potential ethical clashes between different cultural practices are a serious matter. Other cultural differences may concern practical preferences that can be easily changed, but ethical beliefs are core values that ultimately matter much more. Ethical dilemmas that arise from clashing business cultures are among the most difficult to resolve in today's hospitality world.

Case Study—Bakshish

Tyler Osborne had been working for the American View hotel chain for 14 years. He began his career as a high school student, working part-time at the front desk in Wichita, Kansas. When he went to college in Boston, he continued his employment with the chain at one of their Boston properties. He did whatever job he was asked to do and eventually worked his way into the human resources management office. Upon graduation, he started in the manager trainee program. After six years with the company, he became the general manager of one of their medium-sized properties in Atlanta, Georgia.

After Atlanta, Tyler's career took off. He developed a reputation for opening new properties for American View. He always met his budget and he always opened on time. He had even opened several new properties in Europe and was now about to face his biggest challenge to date: the company was sending him to the Middle East to open the first American View property there. The company had hopes of many more to come.

The big day finally arrived. Tyler was picked up at the airport and driven to the soon-to-be-opened American View property by his new assistant, Isaiah. Isaiah was fluent in French, Arabic, Turkish, Hebrew, and English, all of which would be needed in the new location. He had been living in the vicinity for ten years and was also familiar with the local business customs. Isaiah explained that he had set up meetings with vendors over the next several days and that he would be available for any necessary translation.

Tyler asked to look over the schedule and was surprised to see only three meetings set per day over a two-week period. He would never get this place opened on time if they operated at that rate. "You need to re-schedule some of these meetings, Isaiah," Tyler explained. "If I am to get this place opened in a timely manner, I'll need to work a lot harder than that."

"With all due respect, Mr. Osborne, please trust me on this. The first meetings will be long and always involve eating and drinking. You must establish a personal relationship with a vendor if you are going to expect good service."

Tyler was upset, but he didn't want to alienate his new assistant. After all, Isaiah was his lifeline to the community, both professionally and personally. "OK, Isaiah, I'll go with you on this, but we're going to be working some long hours, you and I, so I don't want to hear any complaints."

One week later, Tyler felt like pulling his hair out. He was going crazy. He was willing to put in 22 hours a day and no one else was willing to even work, or to do what Tyler considered work, anyway. Each and every meeting had gone on for hours. The meals had been lavish, but there was no budget for meals for meetings. No one seemed to understand the budget process. No one seemed to understand that there was a timeline.

He had finally narrowed down the drink vendor and was meeting with him again in just a few minutes. Isaiah knocked on the door and asked Tyler to accompany him to the conference room. Tyler had wanted to meet in his office, hoping to avoid all the hoopla, but Isaiah had insisted. Sweets and coffee were laid out on the table, and Mr. Avla, the vendor, was patiently waiting.

Tyler tried to push the meeting along and get to the contract, but Isaiah and Avla kept moving at their own pace. Finally, the time came, and Avla produced the contract. Tyler made a comment about the acceptable times of day for deliveries and Mr. Avla smiled. Tyler tried again to obtain a commitment from Avla, but only received a smile in return.

Tyler looked at Isaiah, who said something to Avla that Tyler did not understand. Heated words followed, as Avla and Isaiah discussed Tyler's comment and presumably other things as well that Tyler could not understand. But one word he did understand from their conversation was "Bakshish."

Tyler had had enough. He stood up angrily and said, "This is an American company with American ideals and I will not succumb to bribery as a way of life. If you can't deliver according to our deal, then the deal is off. I'll leave it to the two of you to figure out." Then he left the room.

Case Commentary

"Bakshish" is a term used to describe the practice of passing money under the table to someone to get something accomplished. It is a common practice in some countries, and is widely accepted (at least in an "underground fashion") in many cultures. In fact, in some places, it is seen merely as a tip. Clearly, the major underlying ethical issue involved in this case is bribery as a way of doing business. If bribery is widely practiced in a society, even if not officially accepted in that society, is it OK to go along with the practice in the interest of getting things done?

Approaching the issue first from a utilitarian perspective, which stance leads to the greatest good for the greatest number: engaging in bribery to get things done or refusing to engage in the practice? If the practice is widespread and it is extremely difficult to accomplish anything without giving out bribes, it might appear at first that utilitarianism counsels going along with the practice. After all, if that's the way things are done in this culture, it is important to be able to get things done—that's how the organization achieves its own goal of profit-making and is able to house guests and serve them effectively. If refusing to go along with bribery means that you can't get things done, you appear to be doing a disservice to everyone by refusing. Look at the comparative consequences of going along with bribery versus not going along: operating at an acceptable level in the local culture versus not being able to operate effectively, and thus harming both your employing organization and the potential customers. The former produces more beneficial consequences and, hence, is the course of action one should follow.

However, as is so often the case when applying a utilitarian analysis, it is important not to look at consequences selectively. We must look at all the consequences of alternative courses of action. One way to keep a sharper focus on all consequences is to use the rule utilitarian approach: which set of rules, if consistently practiced, would lead to the greatest good for the greatest number?

Let us apply a rule utilitarian analysis to this case. Which general rule, if consistently practiced, would lead to the greatest good: the rule that bribery for private gain is acceptable in business practices, or the rule that bribery is forbidden and all business dealings must be aboveboard and transparent to all concerned? There may be a lot to argue about in attempting to answer this question, but if we examine all the evidence impartially, we will almost certainly arrive at the conclusion that, from a human welfare perspective, a bribery-free society is preferable to a society rife with bribery. While a country's degree of corruption is not a perfect gauge of its provision of human welfare, it is safe to say that those societies most free from bribery and other forms of corruption are generally the societies most successful in meeting the needs of their citizens. Conversely, those societies most enmeshed in corruption tend to be societies where the general welfare is sacrificed in favor of the interests of a few powerful private interests and individuals. Therefore, from a rule utilitarian perspective, bribery is to be condemned, and it should not be practiced. Even an act utilitarian argument probably leads to the same conclusion, although it may take a much longer chain of reasoning to arrive at this result. Changing focus to the general rule clarifies matters and makes the central issues (and evidence) clearer.

From a deontological or Kantian perspective, the deception involved in bribery immediately indicates that it is unacceptable. To give or take bribes as a price of doing business involves deceiving other human beings, thereby denying them their full humanity. This is a violation of the second formulation of the categorical imperative. Bribery also cannot be made into a universal practice, because doing so would undermine the very practice of doing business, which relies on transparency and straightforward dealings. Making bribery universal would be self-contradictory. Therefore, it is also a clear violation of the first formulation of the categorical imperative. Kant would condemn bribery in all instances as a violation of our duty to our fellow human beings.

There are also distributive justice issues buried in this case. Bribery involves a redistribution of money (resources) to the private individuals engaging in it, away from the general public and the business organizations engaged in serving the public. Would individuals in the original position behind the veil of ignorance condone this type of redistribution of resources? Because of the harms done to everyone except the beneficiary of the bribe, people would not accept bribery as a distributional mechanism. Bribery leads to injustice, as the bribe recipient unjustly enriches himself or herself at the expense of others. It is also to be condemned on the basis of justice ethics.

Finally, we can look at the character of the person engaging in bribery. Viewed from within the tradition of character ethics, such a person is lacking in character. Their character would be lacking in honesty and justice, at minimum.

Despite our analysis showing that bribery is wrong, some might argue that you cannot really impose morality on others. We should respect the different values of others and not consider our own moral values any higher than those of other cultures. There are several replies to this argument. First, it is telling that even other cultures where bribery is widespread consider it wrong—as evidenced by the fact that it is not official policy, but is practiced under the table. While it may be more tolerated in some societies than others, it is very hard to find a culture where it is openly condoned. This alone should show that the practice is morally suspect universally, not simply in the narrow confines of a particular culture such as our own.

Second, if we pursue the "everything is relative" argument to its logical conclusion, we lose all distinctions between right and wrong, and lose any basis for making ethical judgments. A serious argument that bribery is OK as long as it is practiced within certain cultural settings can be made, but it requires a rejection of all of the ethical theories we have covered in this book. If one is willing to reject utilitarianism, deontological or Kantian ethics, justice ethics, and character ethics, what ethical theory or basis for judgment can be put in their place? The reader who is inclined to push ethical relativism to the point where bribery becomes OK in some cultures is challenged to come up with a basis for differentiating right from wrong. If you cannot find any, you have chosen to abandon morality or ethics entirely.

Case Study—VI-Spain: Managing a Culturally Diverse Workforce*

Can human resources development improve organizational ethics in a company? The challenges that human resources faces are the simultaneous needs to be ethical and efficient, and to truly understand responsibility, loyalty, and passion—the essential traits of a good employee. This requires everyday ethics, including caring for workers, which carries over to caring for clients. This case is an example of human resources' challenge to make sure that every employee is universally represented with values and expected behavior.

Viajes Internacional (VI) is the Spanish branch of a worldwide tourism and travel company. It is the result of the merger of several previously independent companies. In May of 2002, the Spanish branch of the British company Edwards Tourism & Travel merged with Turismo Francesa, the Spanish affiliate of a French tourism company. Soon after, German VI service representatives were also integrated into the same branch. The newly-merged company had service representatives from three distinct national cultures: Spanish, British, and German.

Because the previously independent tourism companies experienced rapid changes in ownership and operations, the newly merged company faced operational difficulties. Previous policies were not the same in all branches and were not consistently followed in the merged company. Many employees distrusted the management team; they doubted that the new managers would be able to control a company that moved more than five million (mostly vacation) clients per year in Spain.

VI-Spain's Mission. VI-Spain is the first incoming agency from the VI group, and its main objective is offering services for tour operators in Spain. It provides a wide portfolio of excursions for clients. Its mission is as diverse as its multicultural identity. With an extensive network of more than 1,500 employees from many different nationalities, VI-Spain attempts to guarantee excellent service and top quality. Their headquarters is located in Madrid.

The VI group has become the top tourism conglomerate in Europe. The idea behind the VI group is creating vacations from a single source by combining many separate services into one product. With the mission of "putting a smile onto people's faces," the VI group aims to control all stages of the value chain.

Currently, the VI group comprises around 3,000 European travel agencies, 84 tour operators, more than 100 airplanes, 37 incoming agencies, and approximately

*Written by Katharine D'Amico, Esade University, Barcelona, Spain, with special thanks to Mr. Josep Antón Grasses and Ms. Beatriz Olvera of TUI-Spain for their kind collaboration, and their help and support with the case. The case is based on an ongoing international merger that actually occurred. The company and employee names have been changed. The case is divided into three portions and will be studied in this and the next chapter.

290 hotels on the European continent. The VI group has integrated several companies from different nationalities. Its initiatives include strategies for continual improvement (customer service, guides, excursions, etc.), opening up its network to new resorts in China and Eastern Europe, consolidating tour operators, creating online business, and expanding its hotel segment.

Mr. Jorge Fernandez became communications and human resources manager at VI-Spain's headquarters shortly after the merger. His team was given the mandate to stabilize the company on all levels. Team members started with a "collision plan" in order to orient themselves with a minimal risk of loss. The challenge became the integration of the distinct cultural entities within the company, each of which represented different philosophies of the business, different nationalities, and different corporate cultures. A strategic human resources goal was to create a cohesive team of employees who are highly competitive and dedicated.

Who Works at VI-Spain? At VI-Spain, staff members come from defined nationalities, each of which has a unique set of behavioral standards. These include beliefs about professional self-image, corporate culture, and impressions of other cultures. Spanish employees make up approximately half of the workforce; British former employees of Edwards Tourism & Travel consist of between 200 and 500 employees depending on peak or off-season; and the German contingent totals another 150 to 250 employees.

Positions include tourist service positions (representatives, call center agents, bus drivers); those whose main activity is to sell (commercials, operators); those in backend process related positions; people who innovate (product managers, tour operators); those who set frameworks (business roles); those who back up and support (office personnel); those who enable (information technology); and those who maintain (technicians).

The Problem. Mr. Fernandez states: "We are facing different groups within a company that have different ways of perceiving business. An example of this is the sale of excursions at the destination. While for one of these groups, the sale of excursions represents an opportunity for generating income, at the same time improving customer satisfaction, for the other group, the sale is perceived as a risk of 'bothering the client' and therefore affecting service quality."

Challenges for Management. Restructuring is significant not only from the financial standpoint. From both a management and an ethical viewpoint, the groups have distinct personalities and come not only from different nationalities but also with distinct ways of doing business. The merging of culturally distinct groups subject to one company mission is also the merging of differing corporate and human cultures. The integration process will be turbulent.

Case Questions

1.   What ethical issues might arise in the situation described?

2.   Have you ever been in a situation where cultural mores differed, causing ethical problems in the workplace? Describe the situation. What did you do?

Case Study—VI-Spain (Part II): The Cultural Model: A New Initiative Outlining Behaviors ———————————————————

The merging of culturally distinct groups affected human resources. Mr. Fernandez and Ms. Vizcaya, human resources training and development manager, decided to design *one common cultural model* taking into consideration the multiplicity of the groups in an effort to achieve quality in terms of product, customer service, and workforce. An external consultant was hired to assist in defining key competencies. Agreement was reached and a document was drafted. The following seven key competencies were proposed:

- Focus on results

- Focus on the client

- Leadership

- Teamwork

- Communication

- Innovation and focus on change

- Identification with the business project and responsibility

Mr. Fernandez explained: "First we defined a single cultural model for all of VI-Spain. In this model, the values for organizational members are outlined. It was drawn from the demands of a strategy; it recapitulates the behaviors necessary to reach our goals. Leaders understand that the changes we are making require a strategic reformulating. This requires innovative, proactive ways of behaving along with active leadership."

The work of bringing the cultural model into line began. The objective was to implement HR policies that are focused on the company's objectives and that could be highlighted by competencies in the model. Later that year, the key competencies were presented to all VI-Spain's employees. The first step was to explain the significance of a sole cultural model. Its key competencies focused on the following:

- Work with key people in each destination to facilitate communication and leadership

- Evaluation of output related to the competencies

- Rewards based on performance appraisal

- Evidence of good practice

- Messages via data transmission

- Incentives and mention of good practice

The three main cultural groups agreed on the need for new initiatives. However, their different corporate cultures resulted in varied reactions to the key competencies.

Spanish. Personnel from the original VI-Spain office had come from a successful, profitable business. Over the years, this office had managed many clients sent by tour operators. This was evident in the 1970s and 80s, but the incoming agencies linked to tour operators had changed and new technologies had overtaken the market, favoring a totally different business model.

The problem for the Spanish group was credibility. Employees with seniority were accustomed to a relaxed business culture that placed emphasis on personal relationships. Rules and regulations were a last resort when facing challenges. Uncertainty avoidance was ranked highest for the Spanish, reflecting their concerns about rules, regulations, and job security. No great importance was placed on time or punctuality; deadlines for objectives were not considered serious. Employees who had worked through the transition devalued the new proposal, stating that they had seen "too many" changes in management, in the form of five different executive boards since 1997. This group favored simple language and equated the new initiative with past failed policies.

British. The British group, Edwards Tourism & Travel, was only partially integrated into VI-Spain. Their self-image as professionals was very high, due to both the management style at Edwards and the internal promotion of the brand name, making this tour operator extremely successful. The style of management they were used to was market-oriented and focused on the client.

The main problem for the British group was communication. The British were strongly individualistic, and ranked uncertainty avoidance quite low. Punctuality was important, and precedent was used when faced with problems or challenges. They saw the need for the new initiative. Edwards Tourism & Travel employees saw the merger as a negative change; they had a strong corporate cultural identity and did not take favorably to the idea of being "swallowed." In addition, employee perception was that it was "too fast" as people changed from being their own agents to, in some cases, completely new positions from one week to the next. The cultural model was received in much the same way. This group found it important for managers to be able to follow through with policy. Presenting new ideas once was not enough for clear transmission and integration. Edwards employees were comfortable in their positions and were reticent to change. Together with a proud corporate identity, they stressed consistency in communication and felt they had not seen any indication of this.

German. The German VI group had reported to the German headquarters until the merger. Employee contracts were managed by a Swiss office, and their corporate and individual culture could be classified as Germanic. Specifically, this group placed importance on individuality and its uncertainty avoidance ranking was high. The Germans were serious in the workplace and thoroughly examined details when presented with any problem or challenge. They did not like surprises, and sudden changes were unwelcome. Punctuality was extremely important. This group valued specific written regulations that are explained and that permit little flexibility with regard to achieving objectives. This group agreed that one cultural model along with key competencies was needed.

The main problem for the German group was mistrust. Employees from this group stated that if initiatives were not clearly outlined, it was seen as inefficient and therefore uncertain. When group members could not see what was expected of them in the form of a clear guidebook that included alternatives in cases of doubt, uncertainty ensued. They felt the initiative was positive but lacking. The reaction of this group was similar when dealing with contracts in Spain. When they were made to wait during the process, uncertainty levels ran high, often to the point of feeling they were being misled.

Conflict. Edya, a member of the German group, completed her portion of a booking for a group of 500 and sent the materials on to Enrique, a member of the Spanish group, to complete his portion of the booking. Enrique did not know Edya, so he put her paperwork at the bottom of his pile. He knew he would complete the work from her before the deadline, but he also knew he wanted to first complete other work for people with whom he had developed a close personal relationship.

Edya was used to very prompt completions of her work once she sent it on, so she became quite upset when, two days later, she had not received the completed package from Enrique. Enrique got his work done on time and returned it to Edya on the fourth day, just one day before a deadline would have elapsed causing the entire deal to fall through. This caused Edya to have to break her strict routine and strict rotation of work to turn in the final paperwork from Enrique on time. This irritated her immensely. She heard from others in the company that Enrique had first handled other work that came to him later than hers, while hers waited. As a result, her routine was disrupted, although the work did get done.

Edya was very angry and went around the office telling everyone that Enrique was lazy and worthless. She also began to intentionally delay sending things to Enrique until the last moment, thereby making his life tough as he scrambled to get work done on time. Seeing what she was doing to him and hearing through the grapevine what she said about him, Enrique retaliated by intentionally sending Edya work only at the last possible moment, sometimes giving her less than an hour to get final paperwork in to avoid loss of a sale.

Hiram, the office manager, received notice that there appeared to be a "war" going on between Edya and Enrique. Concerned, he investigated and found out all the facts about how this started and where it had escalated to. He pondered what he should do.

Case Questions

1. Analyze the above situation from a utilitarian perspective. Consider each person's point of view (Edya's, Enrique's, and Hiram's).

2. Analyze the situation from a Kantian perspective. Consider each person's point of view.

3. How would Aristotle view each person's character? Explain your answer.

20

Managing a Culturally Diverse Workforce

The crucial differences which distinguish human societies and human beings are not biological. They are cultural. —Ruth Benedict

Managing a culturally diverse workforce will certainly have its trials and tribulations, ethically and otherwise. To be successful as a manager, especially when supervising areas that tend to employ diverse groups of employees, one needs to be sensitive to the employees' backgrounds. In certain instances, this might mean that a manager will have to know which employees need time off on certain days, what foods may be inappropriate, which days would not be good for an office party, etc. A good manager would not want to place an employee in a situation that would compromise the employee's ethics.

It is a challenge to supervise a diverse workforce, but it can be an enriching experience for everyone if it is managed correctly. Cultural diversity can enhance a workplace if it is celebrated, as opposed to shunned or ignored. Often when immigrants arrive at a new location, they feel the need to make vital decisions: Should we try to hide our background? Should we bring up our children (in the United States, for example) as Americans? Should we discard or ignore the old ways and embrace the ways of our new country? If the culturally diverse employees feel that their cultures are welcome, people will feel more comfortable with each other. People will not be afraid to speak up about issues that might compromise their personal ethics.

It has become the feeling today, at least in many large cities, that multiculturalism should be maintained and valued because many cultures and races have made substantial contributions to our history. However, many people remain opposed to the idea of cultural diversity awareness, mostly out of fear. At the same time, others often support it but have no clear idea of how it should be done.

The following cases offer examples of situations that students easily could find themselves in these days. The first case puts a vegetarian in a sticky situation; it pits his ethics against his kind heart. What would you do in his situation?

Case Study—"When in Rome…"

As part of his graduate studies in architecture, Kenny would be traveling to four countries: Germany, France, Poland, and Spain. He would be analyzing structural and aesthetic elements of post–World War II construction. Kenny would be housed by a family in each country he visited. This would enable a closer study of the structures' designs and functionality. This living arrangement would be great exposure to different cultures' ways of living and interacting within a family context. Kenny's dream was to build themed restaurants around the world, with each building based on the post–World War II architecture of the food's country of origin.

Needless to say, Kenny was very excited. Finally, he would be able to touch what he had up to now only read in textbooks, heard from professors, or seen on television. Kenny was ready to go.

During his years at the university, Kenny had become a vegetarian. He became a vegetarian for ethical reasons. He felt that it was unnecessary to eat animal flesh and that one could maintain a healthy lifestyle by eating balanced meals, especially by understanding how to complement protein foods. Whenever friends and family invited him to dinner, they were sure to have a vegetarian meal to accommodate his dietary preference. He did not sway from his vegetarian regimen. His study abroad would be no different, or so he thought.

In Poland, the host family prepared an elaborate and time-consuming meal for the night before Kenny was to leave for his next destination. Up until that point, Kenny had eaten most of his meals at the university, sharing only an occasional meal with his hosts. It had been easy for him to pick and choose from the fare and, to date, Kenny had not had trouble following his vegetarian diet. Most meals had consisted of potatoes of some type, sour cream, vegetables, and hearty bread. If meat was on a platter, it was always accompanied by cheese and Kenny would take something from the platter and pass it on.

The host family was of modest means but, for this occasion, they prepared what was for them a holiday meal. Only the best was served. The women of the house had been working on the meal all day. No one had been allowed into the kitchen.

Unfortunately for Kenny, the main course was lamb—a very expensive meat in Poland. The host family, with much pride and anticipation, served Kenny his plate. As the plate was placed before Kenny, the family waited and watched for Kenny to take his first bite. They had shown their most sincere and meaningful expression of hospitality in this meal.

What was Kenny to do? He knew that had he passed on the lamb, even with the kindest and greatest expression of appreciation, even if he had given a detailed explanation of vegetarianism and why it was important to him, he would have greatly offended the host family. It would have been an affront to the family as well as to their culture and tradition. So, he ate all that was on his plate including the lamb. The family felt honored. Kenny learned, "When in Rome..."*

Case Commentary

From a utilitarian perspective, Kenny finds himself in a real dilemma. It seems no matter what he does, he will be causing some harm. Eating the meat means

---

*This case study was written by Rachel Diaz, Associate Professor, Johnson & Wales University, Florida campus.

violating his own ethical code, and thus doing damage to himself in terms of his conscience and his psyche. Not eating the meat means offending his host family, causing them great distress, and creating perhaps a negative attitude toward other visitors and/or Americans.

Of course, Kenny would not have found himself in this dilemma if he had been more aware from the beginning of a potential conflict over this issue. He could have promptly let his host family know of his dietary restrictions right from the start. All of this would have been avoided. So we might say from a utilitarian perspective that Kenny failed to follow the proper course of action earlier than this moment of decision. He should have been more aware of possible complications because of his unusual dietary needs. He should have let his host family know of any special accommodations or preferences he had of which they would not ordinarily be expected to be aware. By doing so, he would maximize human happiness or human benefits and minimize unhappiness or harms.

That is quite likely correct, but in the case above, he failed to do so, and thus finds himself in a lose-lose situation. If he's stuck in such a situation, what should he do from a utilitarian perspective? The only answer is that he has to try to calculate all the harms and benefits that are likely to follow from either course of action: to eat or not eat the meat. Then, he must follow the course of action that will likely maximize the benefits (happiness) and minimize the harms (unhappiness).

To do such a calculation, he must ask himself how much he will harm his own conscience or psyche by eating the meat. Is his meat-free preference a deeply held value, or one that he feels only somewhat strongly about? How bad will he feel after eating the meat? Will there likely be longer-term consequences, such as him feeling really bad or depressed over a longer period of time? Or, will he just shrug it off as a one-time exception and go back to his vegetarian diet with little long-term remorse? He must equally ask himself how badly the host family is likely to take it if he refuses to eat the meat. Will they just be mildly puzzled and slightly put-off, or will they take deep offense? How upset will they be, and how is this likely to affect their future behavior, especially behavior toward guests from abroad or from the United States? The answers to these and similar questions must be weighed, and Kenny's ethical duty is to follow the course of action most likely to maximize human welfare and happiness on balance. And he must consider the welfare and happiness of others as equally important to his own. In the case above, it appears he decided that the damage to himself from eating the meat was not so great that it outweighed the damage he would do by offending his host family.

From a deontological or Kantian perspective, the consequences of his actions are not the decisive factor in making a moral decision. Instead, we must look at his motive to see if he is acting from a sense of moral duty. What is his duty according to the categorical imperative? Remember that the categorical imperative requires (1) that he be able to logically make the rule he follows by making an action into a universal one and (2) that he never degrade other human beings by using them. In this case, it is not clear that he would be violating the categorical imperative by following either course of action (eating the meat or not eating it). The members of his host family are not being used if he either eats the meat or explains why he can't eat it. In the latter case, they may be offended, but they have not been used or degraded to a status less than human—certainly no intentional deception or dishonesty is involved. If he eats the meat, he is not degrading himself or denying his own humanity, because he is exercising his own rational judgment in making the decision.

The only way Kant's categorical imperative might enter into this case is if we considered Kenny's earlier failure to inform the family about his vegetarianism a form of deception or trickery. In that case, Kenny would have acted unethically earlier by intentionally withholding this information from them. But there is no evidence that Kenny withheld this information intentionally and thus no intentional deception is involved.

Still, we might ask, was Kenny's obliviousness to the family's "need to know" before his final meal excusable simply because Kenny tends to be unaware? Perhaps, as a rational person, Kenny should have been more aware. Although it is a bit of a stretch to extend the categorical imperative this far, we *might* say that the Kantian duty to always treat others as humans and not simply as things extended to Kenny's duty to let the family know about his vegetarianism in advance of his final meal with them. Thus, if he acted unethically at all, he did so earlier by not letting the family know his dietary requirements. This conclusion is similar to the one we reached using the utilitarian approach.

There are no distributive justice issues involved in this case, but there are questions of character. From an Aristotelian or virtue ethics perspective, it appears that Kenny has many virtues in his character: he is good-hearted, caring, benevolent, sincere, etc. However, he seems to have a flaw, or vice, in his character. We might call this insensitivity, meaning he is a bit too oblivious or thoughtless about possible misunderstandings that could arise from his unique dietary requirements. His insensitivity or thoughtlessness also begins to bleed over to another vice: imprudence or lack of wisdom. We might say, "How stupid of him not to think about that in advance!" While we don't mean that he is stupid in general, we do mean that he lacks a certain amount of prudence or wisdom by not foreseeing something that a prudent person should have foreseen. Aristotle would advise Kenny to work on this aspect of his moral character.

 ## Case Study—Team Player

As part of a team-building effort, NMI Food Distributors planned an informal party at the end of the workday on Friday. For the past three months, the employees had been required to attend a series of workshops titled "Effective Communication in the Workplace." This three-part series consisted of conflict resolution, along with both oral and written communication. Once the workshops were completed, each department was to develop departmental strategies for improving communication. Wednesday was the deadline for each department to submit its strategies. Therefore, Friday was the perfect day to celebrate the completion of the workshops and the development of the departmental strategies.

Laila was the team leader for the purchasing department. She had been with the company for five years. Her leadership enabled the team to clearly and concisely identify and establish the department's communication strategies. It was because of this that the department was able to submit its initiatives before the deadline. The team members were excited to be the first to complete this task.

Laila was a native of Lebanon and a practicing Muslim. None of her co-workers knew where she was from, much less of her faith. She did not have what was considered a "Middle-Eastern accent," her name was not considered "foreign," nor had she ever worn a head covering. As far as her co-workers knew, she was "American."

On Thursday, everyone was talking about the Friday party. Employees mentioned the food that would be served and the last minute preparations that were still being worked out. Everyone was looking forward to this party. Others spoke of the hopes of some form of incentive for a job well done. The great work of the purchasing department, spearheaded by Laila, was sure to be recognized. If an incentive was given, the purchasing department would get it. Soon the excitement of being the possible recipients of the company's accolades was the entire buzz in the department.

However, Laila would not be attending the party. She was observing Ramadan, a 40 day fast that is part of the Muslim faith. She had not had food or drink from sunup to sunset for the past three weeks, as was the custom. At sunset, she would need to be home for evening prayers and her first meal of the day.

Her team members assumed she would be at the party. After all, she was the team leader. If the department was to receive any special recognition, it would be given to her. Laila, in speaking to her administrative assistant, said she would be unable to attend the party. Quickly, all the team members found out. "Why not?" everyone asked. Once they found out why, some said with disdain, "What's that?" Others said, "Come on, can't she just stay for a little while?" Another said, "Can't she just be a team player?" They could not believe she was a Muslim. "She looks just like one of us," someone was heard saying.

Case Questions

1. Is there an ethical duty to be accepting or tolerant of different religious beliefs or practices? Why or why not? Carefully explain any qualifications you might give to a simple "yes" or "no" answer.

2. What should Laila do? Why?

3. What should the company do about the internal situation within the purchasing department that has been exposed by this situation? Explain your answer carefully, and show why it is the ethical thing to do.

This case study was written by Rachel Diaz, Associate Professor, Johnson & Wales University, Florida campus.

 # Case Study—Let's Eat

The Hotel Management Students Association (HMSA) at Midwestern University organized a campus activity to introduce incoming students to the organization. Being students themselves, they knew, "If you feed them, they will come." They advertised the event with signs saying, "Come and learn more about us. Free lunch provided."

The organization purchased food from a nearby Cuban restaurant that had recently opened. It was the first of its kind in the area. Oscar Rivera, the restaurant owner, suggested serving gazpacho soup, Cuban bread, white rice, black beans, roasted pork, yuca (cassava), and sweet fried plantains with *tres leches* cake for dessert. Mr. Rivera gave the students a good price because he thought it was a good opportunity for him to become known at the university. The students thought it was a fun way of introducing prospective members to something different.

The students set up the luncheon buffet-style. The officers of the organization served the food while the potential recruits and other members walked by with their plates. The students ambled down the food line. Some asked, "What is this?" Others said, "No thanks." Then one student asked, "What's that?" referring to the roasted pork. Teresa, the organization's president, who was serving, said, "It's pork." The student said with repulsion, "Uh, I don't eat swine." Teresa looked over at the other officer and under her breath said, "You're welcome."

Later another student asked, "What's that?" referring to the yuca (cassava). Teresa explained. "It's a root. It's boiled and then sautéed in *mojo*, a garlic, olive oil, and sour orange juice sauce." The student replied, "A root? I think that's what we feed pigs in my country." Peter, the organization's vice president, really became agitated when, while serving the gazpacho, one of the potential club recruits said, "Yikes. That looks like something you might find in the toilet after a heavy night of drinking."

In the end, most of the potential recruits ate white rice, bread, and cake. The officers and other members ate heartily and wrapped up the leftovers for another day.

Case Questions

1. Are there any ethical issues involved in this case? Why or why not?

2. From what you have read in the case, are you able to make any "character judgments" about anyone in the case? If you are, please state what character virtues or vices you find, judging from the behavior of different individuals.

This case study was written by Rachel Diaz, Associate Professor, Johnson & Wales University, Florida campus.

 # Case Study—VI-Spain (Part III): Cultural Implications* ——

Integrating distinct cultural workgroups was a daily challenge. For example, a lack of language skills caused sectarianism among employees. Since clients were traditionally managed in a clear, personal cultural framework, openness to other cultural models was minimal. VI-Spain tried to enhance language skills. It covered teacher costs, offered classes during working hours, and offered financial incentives. However, classes were often empty, and the employees habitually arrived late or not at all. The lack of language skills further increased the cultural gap and the isolation of the groups.

---

*Written by Katharine D'Amico, Esade University, Barcelona, Spain, with special thanks to Mr. Josep Antón Grasses and Ms. Beatriz Olvera of TUI-Spain for their kind collaboration, and their help and support with the case. This case is a continuation of a case started in the previous chapter.

Culture had an impact on personal and professional relationships, on accepted values, and on corporate culture. An example of the impact the diverse cultures had on the VI-Spain management was seen in the e-mail system. The British employees had a system distinct from the others. Instead of using the new accepted e-mail system that all the other employees used, they continued to use their own e-mail system, causing confusion. It also led to missed information that would have been shared if everyone had been on the same system.

The impact of culture manifested itself in interesting ways, at times bordering on parody. In some areas of the VI offices in Spain, where employees from the three groups worked together, they had three different microwave ovens in the staff room, one for use by each group.

Management's Perspective. Mr. George Hedrick, regional manager, offered views that represented both his own perspective as manager and the viewpoint of the British group. In Hedrick's view, a problem still existed with understanding and absorbing management's initiatives to communicate the company's goals. His challenge had become moving the groups toward becoming future-oriented and open to change.

He noted how the Spanish group expected that the most senior employees should not have to embrace change. The German group demanded common group decisions and consensus before accepting new ideas. The British group in his view tended toward neither of these two extremes. He expressed the need for individual responsibility in adapting to modern-day client demands. A further challenge was day-to-day priorities inevitably pushing back items related to reaching agreement on the competencies as well as their implementation.

Human Resources' Reaction. Ms. Vizcaya of human resources discussed additional management initiatives, such as movement toward encouraging leadership in managers and a cultural model by consensus. In the latter, executive managers had the opportunity to identify two behaviors related to each competency and rate on a scale of one to six whether they were carrying it out. This in turn led to a personal development plan.

Communication breakdown occurred because different working languages were being used in developing work plans. Internal communication needed to be strengthened. Measurable indicators for the seven competencies were needed. A plan was developed with a class at Esade University in order to list specific indicators. The results were innovative ideas on employee recognition. None of the ideas put forth by students was financial.

Hadley Iverson had been working for Edwards, the British group, for more than ten years. He was used to the e-mail system and did not like using the new system at all. Even though he checked the VI-Spain e-mail periodically, he continued to transact all VI-Spain work on the Edwards system.

Hadley was assigned to work with Alejandro Barea of the Spanish group on a very important project. Greta, from the German group, was also assigned to the project.

The first time the group met, Ms. Vizcaya and Mr. Hedrick joined them. The two managers pointed out that this was a good opportunity to show that the cultural model was working. They told them the name of the project was *Alliance*.

They each offered suggestions, such as keeping each other informed and carrying out assignments in a timely manner. After an hour, they left the *Alliance* members to work on their own.

After another hour, they ended the meeting. Each had assignments he or she was to take back to his or her respective group to work on. They agreed that it was important to keep each other informed.

Hadley called his group together. He gave each person a task, telling everyone to "reply to all" on e-mails. "Can we use our own system?" one of the group members asked. Hadley agreed, as it was what he preferred anyway.

Alejandro went back to his group and started to work on the project. He had no intention of dividing tasks among the others in his group. He knew nothing would get done that way and he felt it was not anyone's business how he accomplished his work. This was the way he had always done it and he wasn't changing anything at this point. He had been working for the company for 20 years and intended to keep on working in exactly the same manner as he always had.

Greta was excited about the project. She couldn't wait to discuss it with her group. She knew they would have wonderful ideas and she would bring a valuable piece back to the next meeting, which was being held the following week. She spent the rest of the afternoon preparing for the discussion and told her group that they would meet first thing in the morning.

Greta's group assembled at 9 the next morning. Unfortunately, Herman was missing; he was out sick with a bad cold. Greta felt that Herman's input was very important, so she put off the meeting until the next day. She called both Hadley and Alejandro to let them know. Neither of them was available, so she left messages.

Since the *Alliance* members were to meet the following week, each person was supposed to send a draft of his or her group's assignment to the others. Hadley sent one, but since he sent it from the Edwards system, it got caught in the junk mail for both Alejandro and Greta.

Greta did not have anything to offer because Herman had not come back to work, and she did not want to work on something as important as this project without the consensus of the entire group.

Alejandro sent out his assignment to the others. But it was quite apparent that he had done it on his own as there was nothing included that he had not already mentioned at the previous meeting.

Nasty e-mails started to fly. Before too long, a minor war had broken out between the three *Alliance* members.

Case Questions

1. Are the differences between these three Alliance members ethical issues, or are they merely cultural differences and cultural misunderstandings that have no ethical content to them?

2. Is Hadley's decision to use the Edwards e-mail system ethical? Why or why not?

3. Is Alejandro's decision to work on his own and not include the other members of his group an ethical decision? Why or why not?

4. Is Greta's choice to wait for Herman's return in order to achieve consensus within her group an ethical decision? Why or why not?

Part V

Leadership Applications

21

Ethics and the Human Resources Management Function

Respect a man, he will do the more. —James Howell

Human resources management encompasses a wide range of topics as it deals with how people in the workplace treat one another. This chapter focuses on ethical issues relating to four areas: compensation, diversity, employee treatment, and working conditions.

Human resources management is, simply put, the administration and supervision of the people in the workplace. Human beings would like to be treated with consideration, respect, and dignity. They would like to be treated fairly. The human resources department in a hospitality organization is given both the responsibility and oversight regarding treatment of employees. It has the important task of balancing efficiency with equity. If the department can succeed in attaining this equilibrium, management will most likely enjoy a smoothly run operation. Employees who are well treated tend to be loyal to an organization. Loyalty ensures low turnover, which can provide stability to any company.

Many of the theorists we have studied discuss equitable treatment of people. Kantian moral philosophy focuses on respect for the rights of human beings. John Rawls's concept of justice concerns fair and just treatment. Aristotle's virtue ethics looks at moral character in one's dealings with others. And utilitarianism looks for a balance in achieving the greatest good for the greatest number of people.

The case below, "Salary Disclosure," is followed by ethical analyses in relation to utilitarianism, Kant's categorical imperative, Rawls's justice ethics, and Aristotle's ethics of virtue. The chapter closes with a series of case studies and questions about the cases that challenge you to analyze ethical issues that arise in human resources management.

 ## Case Study—Salary Disclosure

The Jensen Hotel has an unwritten policy that forbids employees to discuss their salaries with one another. It recently came to the attention of Dan Maloney, the front desk manager, that George and Barbara, two front desk agents, had compared salaries.

Barbara and George have worked at the Jensen Hotel for about a year. By all accounts, the quantity and quality of their work has been essentially the same. However, Barbara found that she earns less than George, even though she does the same work and they were hired at about the same time. Barbara approached Dan, wanting him to intercede on her behalf with Mr. Grey, the hotel manager. She told him that she would like her salary adjusted to George's level.

Dan explained to Barbara that even though she was doing the same job, she did not have the same experience as George, who had been in the hotel industry for more than five years, while Barbara had only recently graduated from college. He also told her that George had a family to support, while she did not.

The foremost issue in this case is possibly a policy of discriminatory compensation. Therefore, the principal human resources issue we have to consider is fairness. Is it fair to pay two people different salaries for doing the same work? This is both a legal and an ethical question. Many forms of discrimination that are considered unfair have been made illegal in the employment relationship. Beyond the legal ramifications, ethical and practical considerations show that it is unwise for a business enterprise to engage in human resources practices that are considered unfair.

Case Commentary: Utilitarianism

Utilitarianism claims that an action is moral if it maximizes benefits and minimizes harms. In this case, one of the potential benefits to the hotel might be a budgetary savings achieved by paying Barbara less than George, even though they do equivalent work. However, this type of thinking might do more harm than good. Many other consequences become apparent when we look more closely at the matter.

Many criteria can be used in deciding compensation: equality, effort, productivity, skills, need, etc. In the United States, most employers claim to adhere to the principle of "equal pay for equal work." In our case, since equal pay is not being given, a crucial question is whether there is equal work. Is Barbara performing as well as George? In other cases, this might be an issue, but in our case everybody agrees that George and Barbara are roughly equivalent in performance. Consequently, by not paying the same for similar quantity and quality of work, Maloney and Grey are breaching a widely accepted principle of society. Violating acknowledged principles of fairness and justice usually leads to other consequences, many of them negative for all concerned.

Unequal pay for equal work could demoralize the workforce, which in turn could lead to instability and turnover. The costs of turnover in a front desk position could be as high as $10,000 if we consider the expenses of training a new person, which involves pay for both the trainer and the trainee, in addition to human resources management's time in selecting the new staff member. Furthermore, consider the cost of the lower productivity that would result from a new hire. A new trainee will not work at the same level or speed as an experienced employee. Co-workers and supervisors would have to assist the new hire and, therefore, the cost of their additional work would have to be calculated, as well.

What is the balance of benefits to harms? If not paying people equally for equal work leads to a demoralized workforce, the harm will surely outweigh the benefit. If Mr. Maloney and Mr. Grey consider salaries from a utilitarian perspective, they might well conclude that any savings from Barbara's lower salary are far outweighed by the harm of violating a widely held principle of justice.

Additionally, Mr. Maloney, on behalf of the hotel, had prohibited the front desk employees from discussing their salaries, thinking that this would prevent awareness of salary discrepancies and any resulting discontent. However, the policy is illegal according to the National Labor Relations Act. Section 8 of the NLRA specifically states:

> It shall be an unfair labor practice for an employer … to interfere with, restrain, or coerce employees in the exercise of the rights guaranteed in section 7 (one of which is 'to engage in other concerted activities').[1]

Employees are unable to engage in concerted activities if they cannot talk to each other. Therefore, any type of dialogue between employees about wages or other terms and conditions of employment cannot be barred from discussion as long as it does not interfere with their work. The "no salary discussion" policy of Mr. Grey and Mr. Maloney is illegal and cannot be enforced. If it is unethical to break the law, the unethical behavior belongs to Maloney and Grey, not to Barbara and George when they compared salaries.

In summation, it appears that paying employees equally for equal performance is the ethical thing to do, according to a utilitarian perspective. In addition, prohibiting employees from discussing salaries is illegal and, therefore, is likely to lead to more harm than good.

Case Commentary: Kant's Categorical Imperative

Kant would ask if the rule or principle that is being used to determine compensation can be turned into a universal principle without becoming self-contradictory. "Equal pay for equal work" could easily be universalized, but what principle is being used by Mr. Maloney and Mr. Grey? If there is no principle, and they are simply arbitrarily assigning Barbara a lower pay because they think they can get away with it, their actions cannot be ethically justified. On the other hand, if they are employing a universal principle such as "those with a larger family will be paid more," or "greater experience will be progressively rewarded with higher pay," they may be able to come up with an *ethically* defensible justification for their action, even if that action may be practically indefensible or unworkable within the context of the United States legal system. The moral key for Kant would be that universal rules respecting the humanity and autonomy of all be followed. In this case, it is not clear that these kinds of universal rules are applied; but if they are, no moral offense has occurred.

Kant would also want to know if the rule prohibiting employees from speaking to each other about salaries violates the equal liberty of all to live and act as autonomous, rational human beings. If the rule treats adult human beings as children unable to reason for themselves, or if it degrades their humanity because they are being used, Kant would find the rule to be a violation of the second formulation of the categorical imperative (always treat humans as an end, never as a mere means).

On the face of it, Kant would probably consider the order to conceal salaries degrading. Kant's categorical imperative states that human beings have a clear interest in freedom from fraud and freedom to think, associate, and speak as they choose.[2] These rights can only be prohibited if we are willing to prohibit everyone from these rights. Consequently, we can infer that Kant would declare that the supervisors were not giving full autonomy to the employees. Based on Kant's categorical imperative, we see that the supervisors are taking away the employees' decision-making power. It is perfectly acceptable for George to decide not to discuss his salary with Barbara. However, in that case, it is George's decision. He has the choice to act in a free and autonomous manner. Kant's main objective is to assure that people are being treated like human beings and not as things. Anything that threatens our special moral status as human beings contradicts the Kantian perspective.

Case Commentary: The Ethic of Justice

John Rawls would ask all of the players in the case to step behind the veil of ignorance. What salary arrangement would Mr. Grey suggest if he did not know where he was to wind up in the situation? Would he be the front desk agent who is being paid less? Would he be the general manager or one of the other staff members in the scenario? The same goes for Dan Maloney, the front desk manager. It even would hold true for George, the higher-paid front desk employee. None of them would wish to be the lower-paid front desk agent. Therefore, if they would not want to see themselves in that situation, ethically speaking, they should not want to see someone else in those circumstances either.

Rawls proposes that economic inequality is acceptable only if it is to the greatest benefit for the least advantaged person in the situation. In our case, Barbara is the least advantaged person. Rawls would only consider the lower salary acceptable if it could be proven that she was receiving a higher salary because of this inequality than she would end up with if she were paid the same as George (e.g., if the equal pay were so harmful that the hotel had to lay her off and alternative jobs paid less than her current one).

Rawls's principle of equal liberty includes, among other rights, the right to freedom of speech. While management is allowed to restrict certain kinds of speech (disruptive, slanderous, inflammatory, etc.) among its employees, it cannot allocate those restrictions in an unjust manner (for example, only to lower-level employees). Subsequently, any such restrictions would have to be carefully justified under Rawls's principles of justice.

Being fair and just with your employees would be the basis of Rawlsian philosophy in the workplace. If you want to treat your employees fairly, place yourself behind the veil of ignorance. With all other things being equal, if you would not want to be in their position, then you are not treating them in a just manner.

Case Commentary: Aristotle and the Ethics of Virtue

Virtue ethics scrutinizes the character of the persons involved in a situation. We evaluate the morality of people's character as well as their actions. Of Aristotle's four cardinal virtues (courage, temperance, justice, and prudence or wisdom), one is especially relevant here: justice. If we pay an employee a just rate, he or she will receive exactly what they deserve. The salary will be based on job merit and requirements. Virtue ethics would never allow us to base an employee's pay on how little we could get away with paying the employee.

It is critical for managers to understand how employees view them and their influence on decisions. It is also vital that managers understand that if they promote honest communication, they will create a comfortable environment fostering honesty in the workplace.

Case Study—Discriminating Forces

Lenore Beck is the president of LB Consultants, Inc., located in Miami Beach, Florida. The company specializes in all aspects of the hospitality industry: food and beverage management, housekeeping, event management, and more. The company does most of its consulting in southeast Florida. However, in the last several years, the company has gained an excellent reputation in the Caribbean.

Lenore established her company ten years ago after she retired as regional director of human resources management for the Celebrity Hotel Group. Before that, she spent 22 years working at various hotel jobs, starting as a restaurant server in the hotel's main dining room while she was in college and graduating to a front desk position in her junior year. She was promoted to front desk manager three years later. Five years after that, she became the assistant director of human resources and, eventually, the director of human resources. She held that position until she was promoted to the post of regional director.

Lenore is well-known and well-liked in the industry. She is acknowledged as fair, impartial, and considerate. Eleven of the 15 consultants Lenore employs have been working for her for more than seven years; two of her consultants have been with her since she created the firm.

Recently, Lenore was contacted about a consulting job for the Windbreaker Resort, located on the very small and exclusive island of Elura in the Caribbean. Jim Wiley, the assistant general manager of the resort, spoke to her on behalf of the resort's food and beverage manager, Jack Mallory. Mr. Mallory employs Chef Ronald, an excellent chef known throughout the Caribbean for his culinary skills. However, he has not shown himself to be executive chef material. While creative in the kitchen, his purchasing and supervisory skills leave much to be desired. He often orders too much food, causing a lot of waste; or, he does not order enough food, creating dissatisfied guests. The kitchen always seems either overstaffed or understaffed, leaving the employees either unproductive or overly stressed.

Mr. Mallory had endured the situation for almost nine months, hoping that Chef Ronald would improve—until the incident with the Browns. The Browns, who have been guests at the hotel on and off for ten years, ordered 90 filet mignon dinners for their 25th wedding anniversary party at the resort. On the day of the dinner, only two hours before the function, Chef Ronald realized that he had only 50 filet mignons. Even after a mad scramble, he was unable to obtain the other 40. He hoped to solve the problem by offering guests a wide selection including: grilled salmon, shrimp Creole, shrimp scampi, chicken Kiev, lobster tails, broiled chicken, prime rib, or filet mignon. That night, there still were not enough filet mignons and the Browns were furious. They had reserved the party six months in advance and had paid in full the week before.

This is when Mr. Mallory asked Mr. Wiley for assistance and Mr. Wiley suggested Lenore's consulting firm. "I know each and every one of her consultants and they do an excellent job," Wiley stated. Mr. Mallory agreed and that is how Mr. Wiley came to be sitting in Lenore's office just one week after the "Brown fiasco."

Mr. Wiley told Lenore, "I am interested in finding a consultant who will be knowledgeable in all aspects of food and beverage management. We are especially in need in the areas of purchasing and supervision." Wiley then gave Lenore a shortened version of the fiasco.

Lenore replied, "I have just the person for you: Dave Maverick. He was the executive chef at the downtown Harris Hotel for ten years before he came on board with us. As you know, the Harris Hotel has one of the busiest dining rooms throughout the year. Maverick did an outstanding job and I know for a fact that the Harris Hotel was very sorry to lose him. He has been with me now for seven years. He does a fantastic job!"

Mr. Wiley sat quietly for a moment. He knew that Lenore was right; Maverick would do an excellent job. But he was hesitant anyway.

"This is between you and me, Lenore. I can't have Maverick. Elura is a very backwards island and there is no respect for black men there. The chef would never even agree to work with Maverick."

Lenore was furious. She argued a bit with Wiley, but he would not budge. Finally, she agreed to send Jordan Hopkins, a blond-haired, blue-eyed man whose family probably came over on the Mayflower. But she was angry. And mostly, she was angry with herself.

Case Questions

1. What are the ethical issues? Explain your answer.

2. What should Lenore do? Explain your answer.

3. Should cultural factors influence an ethical decision? Explain your answer based on the theories we have been studying.

 # Case Study—Is This Sexual Harassment?

Carl Bloom had been the assistant manager at the Pearson Hotel for three years. He is 60 years old and has been connected to the hotel industry for most of his adult life. He has held many jobs over the years, including high-level administrative positions.

This summer, the Pearson Hotel hosted 15 college interns from Northcoast University. The interns worked for six weeks, each week doing a different job. It was Carl's job to oversee the organization of the intern schedule. It was also his responsibility to collect evaluations from the interns' supervisors and administer grades for Northcoast University. He had complete oversight for the grading process.

The interns had weekends free and were allowed to travel. Carl had become particularly friendly with one of the interns, Christopher Blake. Christopher was a bit older than the rest of the interns. He had turned 35 during their stay at the Pearson. The difference in the maturity level between Christopher and the rest of the students was obvious. Carl sought Christopher's company on a regular basis.

Even though hotel regulations stated that there was to be no fraternizing between interns and hotel staff, Carl asked Christopher to join him in Carson City for a concert. He told Christopher that he had tickets for a JB Lincoln concert, a very popular local rock group, and that they could share a hotel room.

Both Carl and Christopher were aware of the strict hotel regulations. Carl told Christopher that nobody needed to know. If anybody asked, Carl would say that he was going to Carson City with a friend and Christopher could say he was going to Gemstone, a town 30 miles south of Carson City, to visit relatives.

Carl mentioned his plans to his co-worker Alice, the dining room manager. Alice became upset. She was angry with Carl for putting her in the situation of knowing that he was breaking the company's rules. She was also concerned because she was quite aware that Carl and Christopher were of the same sexual orientation. Carl told her there was nothing to worry about.

Alice stewed about the situation overnight. She finally decided to bring it to the attention of Margaret, her supervisor. When she spoke with Margaret, she also shared some of Carl's history that she was sure Margaret was unaware of. Alice told Margaret that Carl had once been her boss but had been asked to leave his position because he was sexually harassing one of the busboys. The employee brought a suit against the hotel and the hotel asked Carl to leave quietly, promising that the matter would not be made public.

Shortly thereafter, Alice had bumped into Carl at an educator's meeting where she had been asked to speak about hotel internships. Carl had become a teacher of hotel management in one of the local high schools. A few months later, Alice had read an article about Carl in the newspaper stating that two male students brought a harassment charge against Carl, but that the charges were dropped. Carl "resigned" his position shortly afterwards. A few months later, Carl secured the position with Pearson and had been there ever since.

Margaret was flabbergasted. She immediately called Jane Hunt, director of human resources for the Pearson. Jane was out of town but she told Margaret to wait out the situation, promising that she would speak with Carl after the weekend.

Margaret was stunned. She wondered how the company would feel if she went off for a weekend with a male student, sharing a hotel room. She felt that Carl was abusing his power as a supervisor. Margaret did not know if the student felt pressured to go because, in addition to everything else, Carl was to administer the student's grade for a full semester's worth of credit. Margaret just didn't know what to do.

Case Questions

1. What are the ethical issues involved here? Explain your answer.
2. Considering the fact that Carl is to grade Christopher on his work, is it ethical for them to spend social time together? Explain your answer.

3. Did Jane Hunt act in an ethical manner? Explain your answer.

4. What would you have done if you were Margaret? Explain your answer.

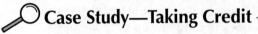

Case Study—Taking Credit

Kaye Goodman is the restaurant manager of Fortune Eatery in Hollywood, Florida. Kaye has been in the restaurant industry for more than 30 years. She has worked in managerial positions for several large chain operations around the country. She was recruited five years ago to take over the Hollywood restaurant because it was underperforming in a very competitive market. Since she arrived, sales at the restaurant have increased significantly each year and turnover has been reduced to almost zero. Whenever Fortune Eatery's national director, Dudley Cash, visited, he was astonished at the difference not only in the revenue, but in the restaurant's ambience as well. The atmosphere was cordial and the staff was always friendly and helpful.

Kaye had wanted to add regional food items to the menu for quite some time. Although she was promised a certain amount of autonomy when she accepted the job, Kaye found it very difficult to maneuver through Fortune Eatery's bureaucracy. Fortune Eatery is a national restaurant chain with 250 units across the country. Corporate offices are in Denver, Colorado. Purchasing is centralized at the Denver offices and coordinated through purchasing directors in each state. The chain has regional as well as state operations directors who support the units in their areas.

Lorna Chandler is Fortune Eatery's operations director for the state of Florida. Lorna is a young, ambitious woman who wants to climb the corporate ladder of Fortune Eatery. While in college, she worked part-time at corporate headquarters and at their flagship restaurant in Denver. Later, she opened the company's first restaurant in Florida and eventually became the operations director for all ten units in the state. Lorna works closely with Dolly Crassly, Fortune Eatery's director of purchasing for the Florida units. Their offices are located in a building adjacent to the restaurant managed by Kaye Goodman.

Kaye and her assistant manager, Stan Hensley, took the initiative to conduct a very thorough marketing study on what they refer to as menu item #99—a Caribbean barbeque sandwich accompanied by a specially formulated jicama slaw. This was in keeping with Kaye's desire to introduce regional foods at her restaurant. Their marketing study and other paperwork went back and forth between corporate and the restaurant until finally Kaye was told by the national sales director, Barbie Droop, to hold off on the item for at least a year because they wanted to try it in Denver first. Kaye tried to explain to Ms. Droop that the sandwich probably would not be successful in Denver; the target was the Florida market. However, Ms. Droop made it abundantly clear to Kaye that the corporate office would handle the matter.

Six months later, there was no progress with menu item #99. The Denver office was not doing a thing. Kaye went to Lorna and explained that she was worried another Florida restaurant would soon offer something similar. Lorna admired Kaye's entrepreneurial spirit and respected her savvy in regard to culinary and marketing issues. Lorna suggested that they talk with Dan Mason, Fortune Eatery's regional director of operations. Mr. Mason was due to visit the Florida office the next day.

After Mr. Mason heard from both Kaye and Lorna, he felt sure that they had to move on the item as soon as possible. He suggested that they roll it out the next quarter, but keep everything quiet in the meantime. Mr. Mason finished the meeting by stating, "This region knows what this region wants; the heck with them at corporate!" Kaye was excited and began putting everything in motion.

Three weeks before the scheduled rollout, Kaye left for a conference on food service management in Philadelphia. While she was gone, Doris Yenterley, Fortune Eatery's corporate vice president of purchasing, called Dolly Crassly, the Florida director of purchasing, and asked, "What's going on, Dolly? Why are you ordering all these weird spices? I've never even heard of some of them." Dolly had no idea what Doris was talking about, but she told her she would get to the bottom of it immediately.

When she hung up, Dolly went across to Lorna's office and asked her about the strange purchases. Lorna shrugged her shoulders and said, "I haven't a clue. Kaye's out of town, but let's call her assistant manager, Stan." Lorna put Stan on the speakerphone so Dolly could hear. Stan started to explain, "It's for new menu item #99." He started to say something directly to Lorna, but she cut him off. Lorna told Dolly that she knew "absolutely nothing" about menu item #99.

When Kaye returned from the conference she found a complete upheaval regarding menu item #99. She tried explaining to Dolly and others that she was told to keep quiet about the development and the rollout, but no one believed her. She went to see Lorna who replied, "If anyone ever asks me if I had previous knowledge of what you intended to do, I will emphatically tell them that I didn't know a thing."

Kaye was stupefied. She had no choice but to continue on with her plans to roll out the new menu item. The corporate office took over the glamour of opening day festivities, while Kaye and Stan were left with the grunt work. When the day came, it was a great success. Menu item #99 was very well received. The next day, the local section of the newspaper had a front page story. The headline read, "The Fortune Eatery Corporation does it again!" The picture below the article showed Lorna Chandler in the front center postion, flanked on one side by Dan Mason, Dudley Cash, and Doris Yenterley and on the other side by Barbie Droop and Dolly Crassly.

Case Questions

1. What are the ethical issues? Explain your answer.

2. Was Kaye treated in an ethical manner? Explain your answer.

3. What would you do if you were Kaye? Explain your answer.

4. What would you have done if you were Lorna? Explain your answer.

5. Apply each of the ethical theories we have studied to this case. Explain each of your applications.

Case Study—The Union

The Ramsey Hotel employs 250 people. Recently, Sloan Harris, the front desk manager, heard some of the employees talking about forming a union. He immediately went to see Hubert Morley, the general manager. Morley immediately called his friend Gilbert Johnson, a prominent labor lawyer. "What you need is a union avoidance consultant," Johnson informed him. "I know the best firm. It's Ralston & Ralston and they will do a great job keeping out the union."

Morley called Edsel Ralston, the senior partner at Ralston & Ralston. Edsel Ralston told him he could have partner Derrick Ralston at Morley's office first thing in the morning. "We'll handle this for you. But you'll have to let us take over the human resources department for the next month or so," Ralston said.

The next morning a meeting was set up with Derrick Ralston, general manager Morley, human resources manager Ethan Wright, and Nick Remus, the assistant manager at the Ramsey Hotel.

By the time the meeting with Derrick Ralston ended, Morley was less worried. Ralston had outlined a plan to set up an anti-union campaign. All employees would be required to attend, on company time, a series of strongly worded anti-union presentations depicting unions as nothing more than corrupt thugs, communists, and greedy "union bosses" trying to take money from the workers. The presentations would claim that unions are a direct assault on the right of workers to speak for themselves. The hotel employees would also be required to view a series of anti-union films. Morley particularly liked the film that depicted the union president being arrested on evening television news for stealing union dues.

Additionally, Ralston planned to set up one-on-one meetings with each employee. Managers would explain in no uncertain terms that a union would not be tolerated at the Ramsey Hotel. Ralston assured the assembled team that management would know exactly how each worker felt by the end of that one-on-one meeting. "We can pinpoint the troublemakers after that," he explained. He noted that this would "make employees think twice" about ever signing a union card.

Finally, he noted that he would have to take all supervisors off to a series of trainings on how to exert pressure on the employees and defeat the union. "They're our first line of defense," he stated.

"But that will take many, many hours. In addition to paying you $350 per hour, I'll lose a lot of employee hours having all this done. I'm going to be spending a fortune on this anti-union stuff if I let you do all of this," Morley complained to Ralston.

Ralston retorted, "These are proven tactics to keep the union out. You either pay now—once—or you pay later. And you keep paying later if the union gets in, I can guarantee you that!"

Assistant manager Nick Remus had been listening quietly to Ralston's plan. He finally spoke up, "You know, I come from a union family. I don't think there is anything wrong with allowing the employees to decide for themselves, without us interfering. A union is just a collective voice of the workers—it doesn't have to be our bitter enemy. Why don't we just let the employees decide for themselves if they want a union?"

General manager Morley responded, "No way! I won't have it! This is *our* hotel, and we're going to run it as we see fit, not by letting some union dictate to us what we will and won't do!"

Case Questions

1. Union supporters would depict Ralston's plan as "union busting" that uses management's powerful position at the workplace to intimidate and coerce workers into not exercising their democratic right to have a collective voice at work. Evaluate this argument: right or wrong? Explain your answer.

2. Many managers and all anti-union consultants would depict unions as undemocratic, corrupt institutions that harm companies and generally harm employees also. Thus, resisting them is a morally correct thing to do. Evaluate this argument: right or wrong? Explain your answer.

3. Make a utilitarian analysis of who is right or wrong: general manager Morley or assistant manager Remus.

4. If unions generally redistribute income and benefits to workers from owners and higher managers, at least to a small degree (and studies show that they generally do), evaluate this case from a distributive ethics perspective. Is this a good thing or a bad thing? Use the original position and the veil of ignorance to argue your case, whatever answer you give.

Case Study—Stars Are Difficult to Come By

As the food and beverage director of a 400-room hotel on Atlantic Beach in North Carolina, Mr. Mason knew the value of a star employee. Jenny, his "star" server, had worked for the hotel for the last four years. She started in the pantry and then became a line cook. When she became pregnant, management moved her to the front of the house where she worked as a hostess.

After she had her baby, she returned as a server, and loved it. The flexible schedule was important to her and she appreciated the extra tip money. The guests were very fond of her and frequently requested her services. Management thought highly of her; she was excellent in up-selling and she was truly a Jack of all trades. In an emergency, she could fill in for almost any position in the restaurant, kitchen, or banquets. She was even capable of managing the restaurant when necessary.

Mr. Mason had recently asked Jenny to become an assistant manager. The hotel's general manager, Mr. Roberts, discouraged the promotion. He reminded Mr. Mason that Jenny already had one written and two verbal warnings for tardiness and absenteeism. Nonetheless, he allowed Mr. Mason to go ahead and make the offer. Jenny turned down the assistant manager position. She did not want to take on the additional responsibility and was not ready to give up the money she made as a waitress.

A few weeks later, on a busy Friday afternoon, Jenny called in at 3 P.M. (her shift started at 4 P.M.), saying that she didn't have a babysitter and couldn't come to work. That same night, Mr. Roberts saw her at a local concert with her friends.

On Monday morning, a written suspension and discharge notice for Jenny was on Mr. Mason's desk ready for his signature. Mr. Mason called Mr. Roberts and convinced him to give the "star" another chance. He pleaded his case by stressing how difficult it was to find someone as versatile and well-liked as Jenny. However, Mr. Mason also understood that he was skirting his own ethical creed. Other associates were fired for lesser infractions. Later that day, Mr. Mason had a long talk with Jenny and made her understand this was her last chance.

Case Questions

1. How would a rule utilitarian view this situation? Explain your answer.

2. How would John Rawls approach this situation? Explain your answer.

3. What would you have done if you were Mr. Mason? Why?

This case was authored by Jude Ferreira, Assistant Professor of Hospitality Management, Johnson & Wales University, Florida Campus.

Case Study—Blue Vest Pizza and Customer Satisfaction

At the Corporate Office. "The logic is simple," said Tom, the new director of guest service relations for Blue Vest Pizza, Inc., "If we increase our customer satisfaction, we will increase sales. More customers are going to visit our restaurants because of our quality service. And if we increase sales, we will increase profits."

"But how can our restaurants demonstrate that they have increased customer service?" asked Lori, the company's skeptical but loyal director of operations.

"We embark on a full-blown measurement initiative," Tom replied. "I'm proposing a three-pronged approach. First, we fully stock our restaurants with comment cards. We make sure that every server presents a card and pen to each table at the same time the check is presented. It will also be the responsibility of each server to collect his or her comment cards and turn them into the store management.

"Second, because each store has the name and phone number of our take-out and delivery customers, we can access that database to contact a sample of each store's customers. We can hire an outside marketing service and have it call 20 customers per store who have recently dined there. We can ask questions pertaining to the speed and quality of service, the quality of the food, and whether or not they plan on returning to their local Blue Vest Pizza within the next two to three weeks. From that data we can draw correlations between our service quality and customer loyalty.

"And finally, and perhaps most importantly," Tom continued, "We can base our managers' quarterly bonuses on their customer service levels. Managers who can provide exceptional quality service and build customer loyalty will receive the bigger bonuses. Managers who fail to do so will receive little or no bonus."

"That's brilliant!" said Joe, the CEO for Blue Vest Pizza. "Now all our managers will want to work hard to ensure good customer service. Their bonuses will depend on it."

"Correct," said Tom. "And, both sales and profits will be increasing at the same time. It cannot miss."

"Hmm...I'm not too sure of this," said Lori. "I'll approve the initiative, but I'm going to be very surprised if it works."

At a Local Blue Vest Pizza. "This new customer service initiative sucks," complained Hal, the manager of the Berkley Ville Blue Vest Pizza. "Does the corporate office even know what goes on in their restaurants? How can I concentrate on all phases of my business if I'm in a constant worry about giving one customer bad service? Besides, I have a very high volume store. I can't always guarantee that every single customer is going to receive the best service. Even worse, I might lose my bonus. I was counting on that money to pay for my vacation this year."

"I'm with you," said Sarah, the Blue Vest Pizza manager in East Salamone, who was on the other end of the telephone. "But I've been studying the initiative closely. I think there's a way we can all get around it."

"How is that possible?" Hal asked.

"Look at the distribution and collection procedures for the comment cards. Do you think that servers in their right minds would want to hand a comment card to a table they just had a problem with?"

"Of course not," Hal said.

"Then why give one to them?" Sarah said in a sneaky yet playful voice. "We can shred the bad comment cards. Or, we can just fill out the cards ourselves, making them up so they have nothing but glowing things to say. We would certainly want to put in a bad card from time to time, just to show that we're not perfect. But for the most part, we can go through all the cards and make sure 99 percent of them are good."

"It's unethical," Hal said. "Besides, how can we get past this new initiative where our customers are called at random?"

"We have to remember that they will only call the people whose phone numbers are in our store database. We can get into our database from time to time and change some of the phone numbers. For example, instead of leaving in the customer's number, we can switch it out with the phone numbers of our friends. That way there's a better chance that they will call people who will cover for us."

"That sure is sneaky," said Hal, "but it will be fun switching out some of the numbers. I know a lot of people who would be willing to help me out."

"Something else we can do," continued Sarah, "is not answer the phone when we are really busy. The way I see it, if I can't guarantee the customer good service, why bother to go after their business?"

"That happens to me all the time," Hal said. "Since my restaurant is so busy, the phone rings like crazy on Friday and Saturday nights. I'll have my regular restaurant customers to take care of. They are my first priority. Besides, most nights one of my employees calls in sick or doesn't show up. When I'm a person or two short, this carryout and delivery business is just a nuisance. Since my bonus will no longer be based on sales, it really doesn't matter to me whether they buy from my restaurant or my competitors!"

"Absolutely," said Sarah. "With the new system in place, we're all better off concentrating on our dine-in customers anyway. Taking the phones off the hook on a busy night from time to time is the realistic thing to do."

"Thanks, Sarah. I feel much better now. As far as I'm concerned, my bonus is the most important part of my job. If I ever stopped receiving it, I would look for another job. It's as simple as that."

At the Corporate Office—One Year Later. "I simply do not understand this," a surprised Joe, the CEO for Blue Vest Pizza, began. "Our records show that our customer satisfaction and loyalty levels are at an all time high, yet this has been our worst year for sales growth. How do you account for this, Tom?"

"I'm just as much in the dark as you are about this, sir," the embarrassed director of guest service relations replied. "This has all been very confusing and counter to the logic behind customer service fundamentals. Some of our restaurants with the highest customer satisfaction levels are showing negative sales growth, while some restaurants with high sales growth actually have poor customer service ratings. How can this be?"

"Our system of implementation and accountability was all wrong," said Lori, the director of operations. "The majority of our managers are good people and want to do the right thing, but we created a system that pitted their ideals and ethics against their checkbooks. We were bound to fail. It's time to re-examine the initiative."

Case Questions

1. How was the customer service evaluation system implemented by Blue Vest Pizza flawed? Explain your answer through the lens of either a utilitarian or a Kantian thinker.

2. How can a corporation ensure the ethical nature of a customer service evaluation system, such as the one being implemented at Blue Vest Pizza? Explain your answer.

3. If you were a manager in this company, what would you have done?

4. Do you believe that these types of situations are common or uncommon in the restaurant industry? Why do you feel that way?

This case was authored by Alan Seidman, DBA, Professor of Hospitality Management, Johnson & Wales University, Florida Campus.

 Case Study—But Can She Do the Job?

Michele Danforth had been a part of the hotel industry her entire life. She grew up in a hotel owned jointly by her parents and grandparents and worked in the family hotel all through high school. When she went to college, she worked over 20 hours a week at various hotels near the school.

After Michele received her bachelor's degree in hospitality management, she decided that she wanted to work in New York City. She had several decent offers at graduation and accepted a management trainee position at the Belle Grande on

New York City's trendy Upper East Side. She chose to go with the Belle Grande chain for several reasons. The most important reason was because it was a small but rapidly growing chain. She thought she would make it into the corporate level much sooner than she would with other hotel companies.

Two years later, Michele applied for a corporate level position. She felt she was ready and she had excellent reviews from her supervisors. However, she was passed over and the job was given to a young man who had graduated in the class after hers at the same university where she had studied.

Michele was mystified. She spoke with Margaret in the human resources office. Michele asked her how many women worked at the corporate level. Margaret told her she was not allowed to give out that information.

Case Questions

1. Are there any ethical issues involved? If so, what are they? Explain your answer.

2. Is Margaret treating Michele in an unethical manner? Or is she just doing her job? Explain your answer.

Endnotes

1. *National Labor Relations Act* (1935), sections 7–8.

2. Manuel G. Velasquez, *Business Ethics: Concepts and Cases*, 5th ed. (Upper Saddle River, N.J.: Prentice Hall, 2002), p. 101.

22

Ethics in Financial Management

Never spend your money before you have it.—Thomas Jefferson

Financial Management could be the most ethically challenged area within hospitality management, as it would be in any business. Many people say that there is no such thing as business ethics, or that business ethics is an oxymoron. What they are referring to most often is money and the enormous greed that has overtaken many individuals, businesses, and corporations in recent times, whether by cheating on taxes or by cheating millions of people out of pensions. Ethical financial management in any business will be a major concern.

Aside from being morally upstanding, ethical financial management makes good legal sense, as well. There are many ways to cut corners, and we will cover a few of them in the following case studies, but staying within the law when managing one's finances, whether personal or business, can often coincide with the right or ethical thing to do.

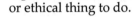 Case Study—Doing the Tax Shuffle

Matilda and Nat Amoson had owned and operated a family restaurant, Amoson's Café, in Miami, Florida, for 20 years. As a general rule, they hired only a few employees because, between the two of them, they could handle most of the work. This way, they were also able to pay themselves good salaries.

Five years ago, they noticed that business during the summer season was steadily declining. They decided to close for the summer to go to Dillsboro, North Carolina, a small town in the mountains of western North Carolina where Matilda's sister Enid lived. They stayed with Enid over the summer; Nat worked as a counterman at a local delicatessen and Matilda helped Enid with her garden.

The following year, the Amosons did the same thing. At the end of the summer, though, Nat became interested in a business opportunity. The Ice Cream Cart, a tiny store that sold only ice cream, was for sale. It was on a good corner, just outside one of the many local attractions in Dillsboro. It was open only from May through October, just long enough for tourists to enjoy the autumn leaves.

After looking over the numbers and working out a calendar with Enid, the Amosons decided to buy the Ice Cream Cart. Then they decided to purchase a small cabin, as well. Their house in Miami had been paid off long ago and they wanted their own place in North Carolina; they felt they had imposed long enough

215

on Enid. Before they returned to Miami, they had bought the Ice Cream Cart and a two-bedroom cabin just a mile from Enid.

The next year was a good one for the Amosons. They closed their Miami restaurant in early May while Enid opened the Ice Cream Cart for them on May 1st. The business did well over the summer and they looked forward to returning the following year.

One day in March while Nat was working on his taxes, Matilda started talking about packing for the mountains. It got Nat thinking about his two businesses and the difference in the local taxes in each place. He started playing with the numbers and realized that if he claimed some of the Amoson's Café paper goods were purchased for the Ice Cream Cart, he could save some tax money. Then he started to experiment with moving profits from one business to the other and moving employees from one business to the other. His best "game" involved salaries. He swapped the salary that he paid himself at Amoson's with the salary he paid himself at the Ice Cream Cart. By the time he was finished, he had figured out a way to save almost $10,000 in taxes.

Nat wasn't sure what to do. One thing he did know—he was sorely tempted. He considered himself an honorable guy, but he could sure use that $10,000. And it's not like he wasn't paying taxes. He was still paying plenty to the government.

Case Commentary

Nat is sorely tempted to save himself some money by creatively moving accounts back and forth between two states. Two questions immediately arise: Is it legal and is it ethical? First, is it legal? The answer is no. Although the odds of Nat being caught may be very low, it is against the law to shift incomes or business earnings to places other than the state in which they were earned to avoid state taxes.

Second, is it ethical? While the law and ethics are not identical, the fact that it would be illegal immediately makes it highly suspect that tax-dodging of this nature could be ethical. Only in exceptional cases can disobedience to the law be justified. Those exceptions have to appeal to some higher ethical principle (like racial equality, opposition to genocide, etc.), not a totally self-serving one such as having more money.

Nevertheless, it is worthwhile to briefly apply ethical theories to this case. From a utilitarian perspective, can dishonest tax avoidance such as Nat is contemplating be justified? Nat may go through more or less elaborate rationalizations to convince himself that it is okay. After all, he could always use the money. State governments often waste money. It will mean so much more to him than it will to the state, which is so huge that nobody will ever notice the difference, anyway. It would really just be a small harm to the state and a big gain for Nat. On top of that, wasn't everybody doing it in one form or another? Certainly, it seemed like the "big boys" at the top of the corporate ladder were avoiding taxes, so why can't Nat? Ideas such as these may tempt Nat to think that it would probably be okay, after all.

Unfortunately, such rationalizations follow the human tendency to selectively read the evidence, usually in a manner favoring oneself. If one steps back and looks dispassionately at all the evidence, it becomes apparent that cheating on taxes causes far more harm than good. It deprives the government of money needed for the general welfare; it unjustly shifts the tax burden onto others who are too honest to cheat; it forces the government to raise taxes higher to make up for the lost revenue; it lowers one's general ethical standards and may "bleed over" into other affairs; it undermines democracy by substituting individual judgment for the democratic will of the majority; it leads to cynicism and a lawless attitude among others to the extent it is known; and it is against the law and will lead to dire consequences if one is caught. Putting these together, the harms far outweigh any possible justification Nat might make.

The harms become even clearer when we elevate the question to a rule utilitarian one: will a universal rule allowing cheating on taxes lead to the greatest good for the greatest number of people? The answer is obvious, and it is no. To the extent that an individual opposes government taxes, at least in a democracy, their obligation is to convince the majority to lower or abolish taxes altogether, not to individually cheat or pay less than one's fair share.

From a deontological or Kantian perspective, there is no possible way to justify cheating on one's taxes. Such cheating involves intentional deception and dishonesty, and hence violates both formulations of the categorical imperative. It dehumanizes others (because of the trickery) and fails the test of following a rule that could be made universal. A universal rule allowing cheating would be self-contradictory since cheating, by definition, is breaking the rules. Kant would not hesitate to condemn cheating on one's taxes.

There are also distributive justice issues in this case. Cheating on taxes involves redistributing resources from the general coffers (the public treasury) to one's own pocket. If this is to be justified, it must be something that appears fair to everyone concerned. That doesn't happen when you cheat individually on your taxes. People in the original position behind the veil of ignorance would condemn cheating because they may end up being cheated; if they felt that more of society's money belonged in individual pockets instead of the public treasury, they would opt for that *as a matter of law and general public policy*. On distributive justice grounds, cheating on one's taxes is to be condemned.

If the perpetrator is caught, there are also questions of compensatory and retributive justice involved. A tried and convicted tax cheat owes the public compensation for what has been taken and deserves to be punished for the wrong that was committed.

Finally, from a character ethics perspective, one who cheats fails the elementary character test of honesty. Dishonesty is an important character flaw or vice. So is greed, which is usually present in cases of tax cheating. Aristotle would have no qualms in noting that a tax cheater is lacking in character.

Thus, every ethical tradition would condemn cheating on one's taxes. Nonetheless, it is well known that cheating on one's taxes in the United States is widespread; many people do not consider it to be a serious violation of ethical standards. Partly this is due to negative feelings about government and partly it is due to a growing consumerist, "me first" attitude that critics would characterize as greed. Whatever the reasons for the tolerance and even justification of tax cheating, we cannot find any support for it within any of the lasting and important ethical traditions of the Western world.

Case Study—The Partnership

Dale and Lenny had been friends since childhood. When they graduated from college, they decided to go into business together by opening up a small restaurant. Their division of labor would be simple and mirror their individual strengths. Dale would be in charge of the back of the house and Lenny would be in charge of the front of the house. They planned to share equally in the profits as they felt that they had equal responsibilities. They found a perfect location in their old neighborhood and sealed the deal with a handshake, which is how they always did everything. Within two months, they were in business.

The restaurant was very successful and everything went quite well for the first year. However, by the middle of the second year, Dale began to feel that he was being taken advantage of. He ran everything in the kitchen and was so exhausted at the end of every work day that he could hardly stand up. Lenny, on the other hand, seldom even showed up at the restaurant, instead letting the head cashier and hostess take on most of his responsibilities. Lenny would usually arrive toward the end of the evening, gather all the money from the cash register, and handle the deposits and books. He appeared to be working, at most, ten hours a week compared to Dale's 54 hours.

Lenny would always scrupulously divide the profit and split it evenly between the two owners. But Dale felt that he was contributing much more than half to the success of the restaurant and he wanted to have a financial management system that reflected that fact in the division of profits.

Dale decided he wanted to formalize the situation. He wanted to write a contract specifying exactly what each person's responsibilities were and then re-examine the division of profits based on the amount of work each person was doing. He also wanted to set benchmarks so that they could measure each other's performance. When he approached Lenny with these ideas, Lenny expressed displeasure. He became very angry at Dale's insinuation that he was not carrying his half of the work load.

There was an escalation of emotion on both sides, and soon the two friends were calling each other nasty names. For weeks, the two would hardly talk to each other and the tension began to spread to the rest of the staff. The restaurant was becoming a nerve-wracking place to work, even affecting the level of service to the customers.

Case Questions

1. Who do you blame for the problems overwhelming the restaurant? Who is behaving unethically?

2. What would a utilitarian counsel Dale to do? What would a utilitarian counsel Lenny to do?

3. Is the core issue here one of distributive justice? Devise a just distribution of work and rewards for both Dale and Lenny using Rawls's veil of ignorance.

4. From what you know of each of them from the case study, do a rudimentary analysis of the characters of both Dale and Lenny.

Case Study—Westward Ho!

The Westward Ho restaurant chain had been very successful for eight years. The CFO, Everett Lansing, had gotten in on the ground floor when Marshall Beals first came up with the idea of a restaurant chain based on Southwestern cuisine. It had been such a success that, after two years, they took the company public and made a lot of money for themselves.

However, now the Southwestern craze was over and the chain was not showing a profit for the year. Lansing had spent many sleepless nights worrying about the shareholders. He knew he had to figure out a way to keep the shareholders happy. Without mentioning anything to CEO Beals or other members of the board of directors, he decided to set up an off-the-books partnership with a dummy corporation he created called Westerly Café, Inc. He shifted most of the debt from the Westward Ho books to Westerly Café, making it appear as if Westward Ho was still as successful as it had been eight years earlier. Not only did Westward Ho no longer show any important debt to stockholders or the public, but Westerly Café was also set up to give a large consulting fee to Lansing's brother (who had done no real consulting) as part of the deal. With Wall Street and the shareholders happy, his brother well taken care of, and all around good will toward him from within the company, Lansing thought to himself, "Maybe now is a good time to retire, take that 'golden parachute' of $12 million in severance money I'll have coming, and be off doing something else, if and when things look worse for this company."

Case Questions

1. Is Lansing's behavior ethical or unethical? How would Kant answer that question? How would a utilitarian?

2. Suppose you are CEO Beals and a whistleblower brings to your attention what Lansing is doing. What would/should you do?

3. Discuss the fairness or justice issues involved in this case.

4. Do a character analysis of Lansing using the language of virtues and vices.

Case Study—The Race Is On

Maurice Charmer was the CEO of the very popular Racy Resorts chain of adult resorts. There were over 200 Racy Resorts nationwide. It was a publicly held company. Stocks had risen steadily for the first few years, but now they just seemed to be standing still.

Maurice was close friends with Aldo Packer, a business writer for the influential *World Daily* newspaper. Maurice invited Aldo for lunch one day to discuss his situation and to seek assistance.

"It's like this," Maurice said, "Too much funny stuff has been going on at a few of the resorts and I know some reporter is going to blow this up very soon. I know we should be more watchful, but everyone is an adult, after all. Anyway, I've been getting a lot of phone calls and it's making me nervous."

"I don't know who it is if that's why you asked me here," Aldo answered.

"No, that's not it. I just need a good column, something flattering about the resorts so maybe the shares will bounce up some. Maybe I can take the shock of a bad write-up after that."

"I could write a good column. I could write a great column. I've got shares myself, so it wouldn't hurt me," Aldo suggested.

One week later, Aldo's very complimentary column appeared in the powerful *World Daily*. Stocks bounced up in price. Maurice called Aldo on the phone. "What do you think? Maybe it's a good time to sell."

Case Questions

1. Discuss the ethics of what Maurice and Aldo are doing from a utilitarian perspective. Can it be justified? Apply rule utilitarianism to help clarify the analysis.

2. Apply a Kantian perspective to their actions. Are they living up to or violating the categorical imperative? Why?

3. Suppose you're a shareholder in the Racy Resorts hotel chain. Do you see any justice or injustice issues here? Explain.

4. Describe in ethical terms the character of Maurice. Do the same for Aldo.

Case Study—The Consultant's Fee

Frankie DeMilco was the controller for the Short Stop Bar & Grill, Inc., a chain of successful sports bars. The first Short Stop had opened on Eighth Avenue in Manhattan, and the headquarters for the corporation were located there.

Frankie had been working for the Short Stop Corporation for over ten years; he had been one of their first employees. He was making decent money, but he felt he should be earning more by now. The owner of the corporation, Paddy Leer, paid himself quite nicely; Frankie knew everyone's salary since he maintained the books for the entire corporation.

Paddy's son Freddy was a driver for FoodCo, a large food distribution company. His main route was located in Manhattan and he often stopped in at the Eighth Avenue Short Stop for lunch. Whenever he stopped by, he would check upstairs to see if Frankie would join him. Many weekends, Freddy traveled the country searching for new Short Stop locations and was paid as a consultant since he also held another job.

On this particular day, Frankie was not in the mood for Freddy. He was tired of hearing about his great travels, parties, girls, and more—all while getting paid for his time. During the last year, Freddy had traveled 14 weekends and found exactly one new location. The money the corporation was spending on his travels was ludicrous. Frankie thought to himself, "I work so much harder, and I make so much less, and I don't have half the fun. Where is the justice here?"

Frankie eventually went downstairs and listened to Freddy's escapades. But when he went back upstairs, he decided to do something about his own predicament. He put a second consultant on the books, John Jones. He decided to pay John Jones only half of what Freddy made and would keep him on the books for only a few months so no one was likely to notice. What no one would know was that John Jones was Frankie's three-year-old nephew. Frankie had set up a bank account for him when he was born and Frankie would have no trouble cashing the checks made out to John Jones. In a few months, Frankie would take John Jones off the books. No one would be the wiser since Frankie handled all the books.

Case Questions

1. Construct the best utilitarian rationalization of Frankie's behavior you can, then analyze your argument to see if it holds up. Can his behavior be condoned by utilitarianism? Why or why not?

2. Apply a Kantian analysis to Frankie's behavior. What do you conclude? Why?

3. Take a look at Frankie's moral character, from what you know about it from the case study. What do you conclude? What virtues or vices can you find?

 # Case Study—Bonus Miles

Ralph Edmondson is the chief executive officer of corporate giant Laslo, Inc., which is ranked one of Fortune 500's best companies to work for. The company offers many employee benefits, such as childcare and school reimbursement. The corporation also has great perks for corporate-level employees. One of Edmondson's many corporate perks is the use of the company's private jet for business travel.

On one of Ralph's recent trips, he read an alarming newspaper report about an executive from his company who was using the company's jet not only for business travel, but also to fly family and friends. Ralph immediately wanted to know who this person was and, as soon as he landed at his destination, he called Laslo, Inc., headquarters to open an immediate investigation into the matter.

After a thorough investigation, it was found that the chief financial officer of Laslo, Inc., Manny Arroyo, had arranged for the company's corporate jet to be available for family and friends. The jet had been used on a number of occasions to fly to Europe, South America, and Asia and, in some instances, Arroyo did not even accompany the group.

After Ralph read the report, he knew he had to make some decisions as this situation raised troubling governance questions within the company. He wondered why he did not know what was happening earlier and whether there were any other issues that he did not know about. He particularly questioned what he should do with his chief financial officer. Most of all, he wanted to know how he could make sure this never happened again.

Ralph did not have an immediate answer to some of his thoughts. However, he knew exactly what he would say to the chief financial officer when he met with him.

Case Questions

1. What should Ralph do about Manny Arroyo? List some different possibilities, and argue which of them is the ethically correct one to follow.

2. Do you see any compensatory justice and/or retributive justice issues here? Explain why or why not.

3. From what you know, make an assessment of the moral character of Manny Arroyo. How do you assess it?

This case was authored by Samer Hassan, Ph.D., Associate Professor of Hospitality Management at Johnson & Wales University, Florida campus.

23

Applying Ethics to Maintain an Environmentally Sound Hospitality and Tourism Industry

We abuse land because we regard it as a commodity belonging to us. When we see land as a community to which we belong, we may begin to use it with love and respect. —Aldo Leopold

EACH YEAR MORE THAN 150 MILLION TONS of pollutants are pumped into the air we breathe, more than 41 million tons of toxic wastes are produced, and 15 billion gallons of pollutants are dumped into the nation's waterways.[1] Total annual U.S. energy consumption is equivalent to about 2,134,960,000 tons of oil.[2] On average, each American produces more than four pounds of garbage each day.

The hospitality and tourism industry does not exist in a vacuum. There are specific environmental areas that relate to this industry: water pollution, noise pollution, deforestation, depletion of species and habitats, solid waste management, recycling, and more. The entire hospitality and tourism industry depends on one form or another of the natural environment for the energy it uses, the material resources it needs, and for waste disposal. The environment, in turn, is affected by the industry's commercial activities.

Guestrooms can produce large amounts of waste, ranging from a half pound to 28 pounds per day, depending on the number of occupants and the type of property. Aluminum cans, bottles, newspapers, and magazines—typical guestroom refuse—are all recyclable. Other waste materials produced by a lodging facility include cardboard boxes, cooking oil, and office paper.

Additionally, any type of construction project can produce yard waste and debris from demolition.[3] Water is wasted when a facility launders linens and towels that have barely been used for guests staying over.

Companies are citizens in their communities. Hospitality and tourism businesses can exert influence on their communities, including in the environmental arena. Managers, employees, shareholders, guests, and the community are all environmental actors—whether they understand their roles or not. Businesses

223

have a responsibility to conduct their affairs in a manner that sustains the environment upon which we all depend.

 ## Case Study—The Fishing Trip

Lester Montego lives in Gransen, Florida, a small fishing village on the west coast of Florida. He owns and operates Montego Fishing Charters, Inc. The charter has been in Lester's family for more than 50 years. Lester's father Leroy and grandfather Lamont had owned the charter previously. Lester was proud to carry on the family tradition.

The village of Gransen sends out bulletins to the local newspapers when the fishing is particularly good. Lester likes to write the bulletins, and a few days ago, he turned in the following report.

> I fished 17 miles out of Newton's Pass on Thursday, 8/23, with Paul Knobley, Jasen Hardy, Christina Dixon, Red Leahy, and Buddy Masters. We caught seven keeper mangrove snapper, a few Spanish mackerel and porgies, and released two goliath grouper, each about 20 pounds, before we hit the jackpot with a 24-pound cobia. We had hooked a small remora on a shrimp, and the cobia was hanging around trying to eat the shrimp protruding from the remora's mouth (cobia tend to swim with remora.) With a little coaxing, the cobia swam boatside. I grabbed my gaff, and hitting it lucky, got the fish dead-on. A green cobia is notorious for its power and ability to tear up everything in the boat, and I was prepared for the worst, but I was lucky. The way the gaff caught him, he never knew what got him.

What Lester didn't mention was that the fishermen also came across a group of manatees and that the boat had hit one of them. There was no doubt in Lester's mind that the manatee had been hurt very badly and may have been killed.

Manatees had been put on Florida's endangered species list because their numbers had dropped alarmingly due to motorized boat propellers striking them. Florida law also required that motorboats travel at speeds of five miles per hour or less when operating in areas known to be populated by manatees. Since the group of manatees was large, Lester thought they would probably be around this location for the next few days or even longer. It bothered Lester because the fishing there was great and he had a sizable group who wanted to go back there the next day.

Case Commentary: Utilitarianism

A utilitarian would consider the harms and benefits that would come from different courses of action. On the benefit side, Lester would make money by saying nothing about the manatee colony while proceeding to book a fishing cruise for the next day. The fishermen would benefit by having a fun fishing trip. But weighing against these positive outcomes is the likelihood of harm or even death to more manatees if he should proceed with the fishing cruise.

While it may take a number of complicated calculations, most people would probably agree that the potential harms to the manatees would outweigh any of

the benefits that Lester and the fishermen might enjoy. Because all of the consequences must be considered when calculating the benefits and harms of an action,
a utilitarian would have to consider the intricate interconnected nature of all life
on the planet and the unknown but potentially disastrous impact when a particular species is eliminated. Extreme caution is required when considering doing
anything that might potentially be harmful to a species. In short, it would require
strong measures to ensure the safety of members of that species.

There are also questions about how much to value the pain and suffering
of non-human animals. To discuss this at length would take us too far from our
present focus, but those utilitarians who extend their concern about harms and
benefits beyond the realm of human beings to include harms to animals who are
able to feel pain and suffering would also weigh heavily the harm to the manatees,
independent of any impact on human society.

Therefore, either an act utilitarian or a rule utilitarian would probably condemn Lester if he simply fails to report the manatee colony and proceeds with
his fishing trip as normal the following day. From a utilitarian perspective, Lester
needs to fashion a course of action that provides the maximum benefit with the
minimum harm.

Several alternatives may be possible, depending on facts and circumstances.
For example, one alternative would be to cancel the trip for the next day, while
slowly (five miles per hour or less) going out to see if the manatees were still in
the area; only after noting that they were gone could Lester resume fishing there.
This option would likely entail some loss of income to Lester in the short run, but
utilitarianism requires that the "big picture" be the center of one's ethical focus,
not merely one's immediate self-gain.

A second possibility would allow Lester to take the fishing trip the following
day, but require him to proceed to the great fishing spot at a pace of only five miles
per hour while in the manatee "danger zone." This may considerably shorten the
fishing period for the fishermen and cause disappointment, but that sacrifice is
necessary and justified by a utilitarian calculus under the facts as we presently
have them.

A third possibility would be to try to convince the fishermen to fish the next
day in an area less likely to yield a large amount of caught fish but also out of
the area of harm to manatees. Again, this may yield some disappointment to the
fishermen involved and/or a loss of income (either immediately or long-term) for
Lester, but these are outweighed by the harm of fishing in a manner likely to seriously injure or kill manatees.

Other possibilities may be suggested. In any case, the ethically right thing
to do would be to pursue the possibility that maximizes benefits and minimizes
harms.

Case Commentary: Kant's Categorical Imperative

Any form of deception that denies others the ability to be morally autonomous,
rational decision-makers would be immoral according to Kant's categorical imperative. Lester's duty is to be honest about the manatees. To not do so is to use others

for his own self-gain. If Lester continues his deception by withholding information about the manatee colony, he is using a variety of others: the fishermen, who are denied the moral autonomy to decide their own preferred course of action; the government officials, who are denied the opportunity to act rationally and ethically to set temporary rules and regulations for the area; and members of the public at large, who are potentially denied the positive right to live in an environmentally sustainable world. Thus, Kant would focus on the deception of other human beings involved rather than focus directly on the harm done to the manatees.

Case Commentary: The Ethic of Justice

There could be some justice issues involved in this case, as well as legal issues. If the law requires that Lester report manatee colonies, and he fails to do so, he is breaking the law. The same holds for any failure to keep his speed down to five miles per hour when that is the legal requirement in areas with manatee colonies. However, if Lester was not caught by the Coast Guard or other regulatory authorities, and was only seen breaking the law by the other fishermen on his boat, we might encounter the issue of whether or not one of the fishermen would report him. The duty of others to report him brings up another set of ethical issues worth discussing, but which we will not address in this short commentary.

Aside from the legal issues, there may also be distributive justice issues. If Lester fails to report the manatees and recklessly endangers them by fishing in a normal way in their vicinity, he may be broadly distributing risks and rewards in an unjust way. He would be maximizing his rewards (income) while distributing the risks through environmental degradation to the broader society in a manner that would never be condoned by people behind the veil of ignorance. This is, however, a rather complicated argument, and it is probably more expedient to consider the morality of Lester's conduct by using the utilitarian or Kantian lens rather than the lens of distributive justice.

An additional justice issue in the case would concern the proper punishment or retribution if Lester is caught illegally fishing or illegally speeding. Punishment could include paying a fine or worse, depending on the laws that he has broken or the seriousness of his offense. Lester's punishment might involve some form of compensation to those harmed by his actions; in this way, compensatory justice issues also enter into and may be combined with the retributive justice issues involved.

Case Commentary: Aristotle and the Ethics of Virtue

According to Aristotle, a virtuous person is one of good character. Lester's character will be found to be lacking if he withholds information from the fishermen and the public. The vice of dishonesty is being displayed and the virtue of honesty is absent. Lester would be exhibiting the vice of greed, since he would be acting solely for his own desire for money. He would be severely lacking in the virtue of generosity. We could also question his wisdom (or prudence): his ability to know what is the right thing to do is deficient. Thus, virtue or character ethics would judge Lester's character by the actions he takes under these circumstances.

Case Study—All Roads Lead to the Resort

The Escape Now Resort Conglomerate (ENRC) has been searching for a new resort and spa location. The company finally decided on a pristine beach on the island of Madreha in the Caribbean. Madreha is a small island, hardly known outside the immediate vicinity, with very high unemployment. The local government has been seeking a remedy to the work problem and has high hopes for the new resort.

The new resort will host 300 guestrooms, two Olympic-sized swimming pools, and six lighted tennis courts. Golf will be offered at a local course two miles inland. At present, there is only one two-lane road that leads out to this area of the coastline, because the only inhabitants are a small group of retirees. Other than that, the area is enclosed by natural forestation.

People First, a local activist group, has researched ENRC. People First claims that the ENRC has a history of not fulfilling its promises to the communities where they build. It wants the local government to set up a contract that delineates any consequences that will result if ENRC does not keep its word on all the promised measures.

People First called a meeting, which was attended by 250 people. This was a very large turnout for such a small island. The guest speaker was Ronald Avery, an engineer specializing in construction management.

Mr. Avery stated that the basic infrastructure of Madreha would not support the type of resort that ENRC was proposing. New roads would have to be built. "Consider where these roads will be built," he emphasized. "And the sewage system is not appropriately set up for such a large structure," he continued. He further discussed noise issues, electricity, water, and a host of other topics the islanders had to consider.

"But the jobs! We will all have jobs!" someone in the crowd shouted out.

People First representative Claire Muller called the meeting back to order. "We have to consider all sides of this equation. Maybe it is possible to have it all."

"But the island will suffer," another person stated. "It will become noisy and overrun with tourists and we'll all have $6 per hour jobs. That's not much better than we have now."

"At least we'll all have jobs," another islander said.

It went on and on. Finally, it was decided that the group would put together a community contract. A group from People First would speak with local government officials, insisting that ENRC sign the contract. Consequences would be clearly defined.

The group met with Archibald Sander, assistant to the governor. Their requests to ENRC included the following:

1. Eighty percent of all construction jobs, including construction management positions, would go to islanders.

2. Eighty percent of all resort positions would go to islanders.

3. Jobs would pay, at a minimum, $7 per hour.

4. All sewage, water, and electrical systems would be appropriately updated in order to support 1,000 more people per day after the resort was completed.

5. Noise ordinances would be put into effect.

6. Two new roads into and out of the planned resort area would be built. The roads would each be two-lane roads in keeping with the area's present forestation. A minimal number of trees would be cut down. People First would be involved in the selection of the tree paths, as well as the acceptance of the trees to be cut.

Archibald Sander agreed with all the provisions in the document. He brought the contract to Governor Landon Lamar. Governor Lamar knew it would be difficult for ENRC to agree to all of the requests, but he said he would meet with them and see what he could do.

The following week, both Mr. Sander and Governor Lamar met with Rad Hopkins, director of construction for ENRC. Surprisingly, Mr. Hopkins agreed to most of the provisions. He said he would give 75 percent of jobs to the islanders and he would pay the $7 per hour job rate. He said he would meet with People First and the governor's advisors regarding road building, but he had to maintain the final say, as he was the expert in the area. Concerning sewage, water, and electricity, he guaranteed that all systems would be brought into compliance with the local codes.

Six months later, a People First member, Jan Eberley, awakened fellow member Claire Muller shortly after dawn. Jan was quite upset. During the night, ENRC had removed all of the trees from a three-acre parcel of land. Furthermore, when Jan and a group of People First representatives had gone out to the spot, the construction workers, none of whom were islanders, just laughed at them.

When Claire joined them at the site, the deforestation was complete. Mr. Hopkins was nowhere to be found. The new director of construction, Harmon Harper, had been hired only a few days earlier. "I was just following orders," he claimed.

Eighteen months later, the resort had been completed for several months. Occupancy rates were high. So were the town noise levels.

The islanders were divided over their opinion of the resort. Some, allied with People First, went to the governor's office. The governor was unavailable. The assistant to the governor was unavailable. During the next month, 40 of the 275 islanders who worked at the resort were laid off. Some islanders tried to bring sanctions against ENRC, but were unable to establish the legality of the contract. People First led a series of demonstrations outside the resort, causing a drop in the number of tourist visits.

Islanders found themselves bitterly divided. Some, appreciating the jobs, supported ENRC. Others, noting environmental degradation, opposed ENRC.

Case Questions

1. From a utilitarian perspective, how would you evaluate this case? How would you balance the benefits and harms?

2. Make a case that People First, although it may have been well-intentioned, acted unethically.

3. Make a case that ENRC, whatever its intentions, acted unethically.

4. What is your own perspective? How do you ethically evaluate this situation? Why?

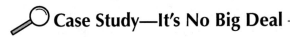

Case Study—It's No Big Deal

Doug Cagney is the owner and manager of Dougie's Diner in Middlefork County. He has recently joined the Middlefork Restaurant Owners Association (MROA). The group's bylaws include a section on protecting the environment. The MROA has been pressuring the Middlefork County government to start a recycling program for the county, but has not been successful.

At the most recent meeting, the association voted to voluntarily salvage all possible recyclable items at their respective establishments, such as aluminum soda cans, cardboard, Styrofoam containers, etc. The group planned to pay local college students to pick up the recyclables and haul them to a local reprocessing plant. The money that would be earned for the effort would go back to the association to be used for scholarships for local students studying food service management at Middlefork Community College.

The clientele at Doug Cagney's diner comprised three main groups with different rush hours. The largest group contained hundreds of local high school students. There was a very busy two-hour lunch rush and a second rush at 3 P.M. when school ended. The other busy times included breakfast for truckers who were always in a hurry and early evening dinner specials that started at 5 P.M. for senior citizens. The diner, which was a weekday operation only, closed each evening promptly at 7 P.M. after a typical 13-hour day.

For several weeks after Doug joined the MROA, he valiantly tried to collect aluminum cans. He handed out flyers to all the students asking them to drop their cans in special receptacles. He spoke with truckers and senior citizens personally to ask for their assistance. He asked his employees to sift through the outside garbage for the aluminum. But the situation seemed hopeless. The only cans they were able to recover regularly were the ones that were served at the tables that the servers retrieved on their own. There was just not enough time in the day to salvage the cans when the customers would not assist. His employees refused to go through the garbage any longer.

After two months, Doug gave up. He didn't even bother recycling cardboard and Styrofoam any longer. He thought, "Why should I do this for everyone else when they won't even help themselves? Besides, how much harm can my little place be doing anyway?"

Case Questions

1. Does Doug have any responsibility to recycle in this situation? Why or why not?

2. What does a utilitarian analysis say Doug should do? Explain your answer.

3. What does a Kantian analysis say Doug should do? Explain your answer.

4. What do you think of Doug's explanation? Is he right in thinking that "his little place can't do much harm anyway"? Would Aristotle agree or disagree with you? Explain your answer.

5. If he chose to do something, Doug could concentrate primarily on his own restaurant's practices, or he could focus on broader attempts to change the public's habits through education, cooperative programs with other merchants and the county administration, etc. Is there any ethical reason to prefer one course of action to another? Whatever your answer, explain why you think so.

Case Study—Safety First

The City of Bridgeview, located on Long Island directly on the Atlantic Ocean, has recently opened a public swimming area adjacent to a boating area that has been operational for five years. In order to ensure the safety of both the boaters and the swimmers, the city's community relations director, Damon Bailey, has suggested that rules and regulations be instituted. He has drafted the following statement, which includes safety statistics, for his colleagues in community relations to consider:

1. Persons boating must be licensed.

   a. People can receive boating licenses only after taking and passing a course on boating safety. The Office of Community Relations will offer such a course for a small fee. Licenses can also be obtained from outside concerns authorized by the Office of Community Relations; a list of such places will be made available.

   b. Persons boating without a license are subject to substantial fines.

   c. Allowing only licensed boaters on the water has been shown to decrease deaths and serious injuries by 78 percent.

2. Prohibit alcohol in boating and swimming areas.

   a. People who are impaired by alcohol do not make good swimmers.

   b. People who are impaired by alcohol do not make good boaters.

   c. The costs to the community involved with this measure could be substantial; costs could include loss of income if the location is used mainly for adult party purposes.

   d. Statistically, limiting alcoholic beverages in swimming and boating areas has shown to decrease deaths and serious injuries by 80 percent.

3. Ban swimming when rip currents are present.

   a. Rip currents are the most threatening natural hazard to be found along any coastline. The United States Lifesaving Association estimates that the annual number of deaths due to rip currents exceeds 100. Rip currents account for more than 80 percent of rescues performed by surf beach lifeguards each year.

   b. If swimming when rip currents are present is not banned, the cost to the Community Relations Office will include increased death and injury liability insurance.

    c. Statistically, this measure has been shown to decrease deaths and serious injuries by 40 percent.

4. Do not allow any glass containers in swimming and boating areas.

    a. Broken glass causes injuries and increases exposure to liability.

    b. All beverages for sale should be in non-breakable containers. Presently there are some items sold that are in glass containers. These are sold because they are less expensive than the beverages in plastic containers (because the glass containers are recyclable and there is a substantial return for the recycled glass).

    c. Statistically, this measure has been shown to decrease all injuries by 30 percent.

5. Ban beach fires.

    a. Beach fires destroy the natural environment. Debris from beach fires is difficult to clean.

    b. Beach fires cause injuries and increase exposure to liability.

    c. The Office of Community Relations will lose income if beach-goers choose other locations.

    d. Statistically, this measure has been shown to decrease death and serious injury by 65 percent.

6. Prohibit scuba diving.

    a. Scuba diving can cause serious medical conditions including inner ear barotraumas, pulmonary barotraumas, arterial gas embolism (AGE), and decompression sickness ("the bends").

    b. The estimated annual death rate is 90 per year worldwide.

    c. Statistically, this measure has been shown to decrease death and serious injury by 88 percent.

A meeting was called to debate Mr. Bailey's suggestions. Heated discussion took place regarding whether or not to adopt any or all of the suggested measures.

Case Questions

1. What ethical issues are involved in this case? Explain your answer.

2. Which measures would you argue should be followed? Explain and defend your answer.

3. Going measure by measure, list the ethical arguments for adopting or not adopting the proposed rule. Which type of ethical analysis are you using?

Endnotes

1. Manuel G. Velasquez, *Business Ethics: Concepts and Cases*, 5th ed. (Upper Saddle River, N.J.: Prentice Hall, 2002), p. 206.

2. Lester Brown, "Challenges of the New Century," in *State of the World 2000* (New York: WW Norton & Company, 2000), pp. 5-8.

3. Rhonda Sherman, "Waste Reduction and Recycling for the Lodging Industry," North Carolina Cooperative Extension Service, AG-473-17 WQWM-128.

24

Ethics and Public Policy in the Hospitality and Tourism Industry

A law is something which must have a moral basis, so that there is an inner compelling force for every citizen to obey. —Chaim Weizmann

THIS CHAPTER EXAMINES the relationship between ethics and public policies regulating the hospitality and tourism industry. While issues in this area can be complex, the basic outlines of some of the major disagreements will be laid out in this chapter.

By *public policy*, we are referring to laws and governmental regulations of business affairs. Public policy questions are inherently *political* in the sense that they concern what public officials should do. In a democratic society, public policy questions are openly debated public issues that engage politicians, political parties, and legislatures.

Because public policy questions are political, they immediately get tangled up in issues that we do not think of as simple ethical issues. The phrase "It's all politics" often indicates the speaker is so cynical about politics and the political process that he or she does not believe rational perspectives can be applied. Instead, the person believes that self-interested, power-grabbing individuals or groups are bending things to their own interest. While this cynical viewpoint about politics may or may not be correct, it does not move political issues entirely outside the reach of ethics. As with all human activities, political activities have ethical consequences, and therefore they can be judged ethically.

Ethical issues that are also political issues are complicated by the fact that views of them inevitably are dependent on *ideology*. An ideology is a system of beliefs that are both factual and value-laden about the way the world works. Ideologies implicitly or explicitly answer basic questions about human nature (are we inherently selfish? benevolent? etc.), about the purpose of government (to protect private property? reduce inequality? enforce majority will? protect individuals' rights? etc.), about the "good society" (free? equal? just? conforming to the will of one's God or deity? etc.), and the like. Our ideologies, or outlooks, enormously influence how we see the world and inevitably make us more sensitive to certain aspects and perhaps less sensitive to others.

233

Thus, in many political arguments, because of ideological differences, two sides are talking past each other, discounting or not seeing "facts" to which the other side is appealing. Especially in politics, emotions can run high, and sensitivity to the point of view or factual considerations of one's opponent is often lacking. Therefore, it is important, when doing an ethical analysis of public policy debates, to exercise a certain degree of humility about ethical claims made for your side. This does not mean that morality is irrelevant in public policy discussions—different policies have different motivations and consequences, and those differences are just as subject to ethical debate as any others.

Ideological views about governmental relations with business activities vary widely. At the one extreme is the perspective that there should be no governmental interference in the private affairs of businesses—an unregulated market should govern all aspects of business affairs. From this perspective, any government intrusion is immoral because it curtails freedom and inevitably leads to inefficiency and injustices. This ideology is often labeled "individualistic," with individuals and businesses allowed to acquire as much as possible, free from government restraint or control.

Milton Friedman argued that businesses have no obligation of any sort beyond the obligation to make as much money as possible as long as they live within the basic rules of the game set up by society. Friedman believed that there should be few rules regulating business, other than certain basic ones enforcing contracts and preventing monopolistic, deceptive, or unfair business practices. However, the real question is, "How far can the government go in setting up the rules of the game?" Even Friedman did not argue that there should be no rules; only that rules should be minimal. Others may see a greater need for governmentally enforceable rules on a wider front if they believe that corporate behavior will not likely achieve socially desired ends simply on a voluntary basis.

At the opposite extreme, socialist ideology argues that economic activities should be controlled by the government because this is the only way such basic values as fairness and general equality can be protected from private plundering entities like large corporations. The private market is seen as a mechanism whereby the rich and powerful control and take advantage of those with less wealth. Freedom is conceived as freedom from hunger, freedom from insecurity and deprivation, etc., rather than freedom from societal ties and obligations.

Between the extremes of unregulated "pure" capitalism and socialism is the ideology of a mixed economy—a capitalist market economy that is primarily run by private enterprise, but with more or less extensive governmental intervention into that economy to protect public interests. Virtually all advanced industrial capitalist economies are of the mixed variety, including that of the United States. There are many differences among nations, with the United States having one of the less regulated economies, while many European (especially Scandinavian) economies are considerably more regulated.

Within society, different groups with varying interests and ideologies tend to take opposite attitudes toward government regulation of business for extraneous (i.e., non-business) purposes. Environmental groups, women's rights groups, civil rights groups, organized labor, consumer protection groups, and others tend to favor government regulation of business activities to protect the various interests they represent. These groups lobby government for laws on environmental protection, banning discrimination against women or minorities, minimum wage, occupational safety, consumer protection and "truth-in-advertising", etc., laws that require businesses to adhere to certain standards.

Industry and business organizations tend to oppose most regulations over business conduct, or at least those that cost money or restrict a company's freedom of action. While certain minimal regulations may be acceptable, industry and business groups generally feel that governmental regulation is unneeded, unduly cumbersome, expensive, and highly inefficient. They lobby government against any new regulations or against expansion of existing regulations. The general outlook put forward by these groups is that businesses will be able to do much more for society if they are left to themselves to pursue profit-making ways to serve the public. The following case study provides an example.

Case Study—The Public Exposure Debate

A coalition of organizations has been operating in the state of Wisconsin for quite some time. It is composed of consumer groups, labor unions, women's organizations, environmental groups, civil rights groups, activist student groups, gay rights groups, some religiously based social action groups, and low-income community organizing groups. It is known as the Wisconsin Coalition for Progressive Action, (WCPA). WCPA has pursued an active agenda in the state for the past eight years, organizing constituencies and lobbying the state legislature to pass a number of bills, including ones to provide healthcare for all children in the state, to tighten the environmental regulatory process for new building developments, to ban state contracts with companies found guilty more than once of violating anti-discrimination employment laws, and to require businesses doing business with the state to remain neutral in the event its employees wish to form a labor union. The group has been moderately successful, winning at least partial victories in a number of these campaigns.

WCPA has just unveiled a new campaign. Under the slogan, "All Business Is the People's Business," it is pushing for a law requiring all businesses that are registered in the state and have more than five employees to file yearly forms with the state's commerce department. These forms are to be open to the public. They will list a number of things about the business that ordinarily might be kept private: the compensation of all top company officials making more than $100,000 per year; the number of employees, average wages paid to each category of company employee, how many of the company's employees receive health care insurance (and for those that do, what percentage of premiums the individual employee must pay), how many employees have a company-provided pension, any business done by the company for the state or any other public entity within the state, and any violations of law the company has been found guilty of in the past ten years.

WCPA spokesman Milo Danver issued a press release stating that companies are artificial creations that exist solely for the benefit of the people. Therefore, the people have the right to know how these entities are behaving. Danver argues that this law would in no way restrict the freedom of companies in their behavior; it is simply a "sunshine law" requiring them to be transparent so that citizens can judge their overall impact on the community. Those who shift various obligations to the public, such as health care costs and costs of maintaining people in their old age (pensions), or who pay wages so low that their employees qualify for food stamps and other forms of public assistance should be exposed for what they are doing. In that way, citizens (both as participants in public policy formation and as consumers) can decide in an intelligent and informed manner how they wish to relate to companies. Danver argued that this bill, if passed into law, would reward companies that raise living standards, provide health care insurance and pensions, and the like. The only companies that would be punished, he claimed, are the "bad apples" that drag down living standards in the community. The law would not affect the many businesses who abide by standards making their employment practices beneficial to society as a whole.

Oliver Standifant, the spokesperson for the Wisconsin Food, Beverage, and Entertainment Association (WFBEA), immediately sent out an "Alarm Memo" to all the members of his association. Portions of Mr. Standifant's memo follow:

> "The misguided idealists are at it again! We have just received word that they will be lobbying for a drastic change in state law that would have horrible consequences for every member of this association, not to mention the general public.
>
> [At this point, the memo relates the details of the proposed law.]
>
> This fundamental attack on our free enterprise system would harm the very people it is supposedly trying to help. If businesses can't set wages according to what the market dictates as fair and just compensation, but instead has to satisfy government bureaucrats and socialist-minded do-gooders, many businesses will be forced out of business. Efficiency will suffer enormously.
>
> We also know that any bill like this will drive businesses away from our state. No one wants to invest and operate in a state that would treat its business citizens in such a hostile manner. I can think of no other measure that does a better job of destroying job creation in our state.
>
> Each and every one of you will no longer be able to run your business as you see fit. Jobs will be lost by the tens of thousands. Those who were earning an entry-level wage will be left with no job and no wage at all.
>
> The clammy hand of government bureaucracy is threatening us as never before. You must all contact your legislators to stop this proposed bill immediately.
>
> In addition, we will need to double our political fund assessment of each association member, so that we can increase our ability to elect legislators who understand the needs of businesses in our industry. I will be calling an emergency meeting of our executive committee with the aim of instituting an immediate doubling of our political fund assessment to fight this insidious attack upon us."

Milo Danver obtained a copy of this memo and circulated it to all of the members of the WCPA coalition. In a letter accompanying the memo, Danver made the following assertions:

(1) Absolutely no "dictating" of wages, healthcare coverage, pension coverage, or anything else is contained in the proposal.

(2) Transparency and accountability to the public are the real issues here, not an attack on the private enterprise economic system.

(3) There would be no loss of jobs if this bill were to pass, but there may be a number of embarrassed businesses that would improve the wages and/or healthcare coverage and/or pension coverage of their employees.

(4) The constituency of the organizations making up this coalition would benefit enormously if the law were passed, because the "underdog" and the "have-nots" would have a basis to expose mistreatment, and a way to appeal to the public for policies ensuring better treatment.

(5) The WCPA feels that the ferocious counterattack of the WFBEA means that political efforts will have to be increased greatly in the coming year, so that the "power of the people" is able to counter the "power of the moneyed inter-ests" in their attempt to sway legislators.

Case Commentary

If we attempt to analyze this case from an ethical perspective, it immediately becomes clear how ideological and political the case is. No ethical analysis is pos-sible until a number of factual issues are cleared up, and these factual issues are deeply embedded in ideological viewpoints. In this text, we have no intention of reviewing different political ideologies and pronouncing one correct and another wrong. But we can show how dependent our ethical conclusions are on our beliefs about factual matters, as well as how ideological our factual beliefs actually are.

In this case, there are a number of highly disputed assertions about what the facts are. Is it really true that this measure will not harm the state's business cli-mate and its ability to attract and retain businesses? If so, aren't there a lot of rea-sons for supporting the proposed legislation? Alternatively, is it really true that this legislation would distort the workings of the market in a way that impedes business efficiency and leads to increased unemployment? If so, isn't that a reason to strongly oppose this legislation? Is this an assault on private enterprise that will likely lead to ever more government meddling and an end to a vibrant economy? If true, this is a reason to oppose the measure. Or, is it a noble attempt to force pri-vate corporations to deal honestly and openly with the public citizens upon whom it depends for so much, simply by being transparent in its behavior? If true, this is a reason to support the proposed measure.

We could continue to contrast the "facts" that are strongly believed by pro-ponents on each side, to show how each would likely sway our ethical judgment about what is the best stance to take on the proposed legislation. But we stop here, simply to note that these factual beliefs, bolstered by (and, in many ways, depen-dent upon) an ideological outlook, can make all the difference in how one ethically sees matters of public policy such as this.

Mr. Danver and most of those who lead the organizations in his coalition sin-cerely believe that many (not all) corporations receive all sorts of corporate welfare (tax abatements, provision of public utilities, social welfare supports for low wage employees, favorable zoning and other treatment, etc.) from the public without providing equal value in return. They believe that strong governmental regulation of the market is absolutely necessary to ensure beneficial and fair treatment of individuals, especially those who are poorer or who are from vulnerable populations such as minorities, immigrants, women, etc. They believe that corporate entities, left to themselves, will cheat those who are more vulnerable and despoil the environment unless they are *required* (with sanctions backing up the requirements) to not do so—not because the individuals running those corporations are bad or evil, but simply because the market rewards only profit-making, not ethical behavior. They also believe that governmental regulation of the sort envisioned by this measure will have no negative unintended consequences of any great importance.

Mr. Standifant and most of those who lead the businesses in his association sincerely believe that corporations are the productive element in the economy—the lynchpin that creates all the wealth that all citizens enjoy. They believe that corporations, far from receiving unduly favorable treatment, are often besieged from all sides by those trying to squeeze ever more out of the "goose that lays the golden egg." They believe that the business environment is already hard enough, and that further government intrusion into business matters is bound to wipe out a lot of productive businesses. They believe that a free market, unfettered by government or other constraints, produces the best possible outcome to a society. They believe that most (although not all) businesses are run ethically, and that only minimal oversight is needed to ensure ethical behavior. For the most part, the market will weed out those that do not adhere to basic ethical standards.

Simply by looking at these contrasting beliefs, one can see that a utilitarian analysis, for example, would arrive at diametrically opposed conclusions, depending on which of the two ideological worldviews the analyst adhered to. Using the same ethical perspective, but holding different factual beliefs, two utilitarians could easily end up on opposite sides of the issue. The same is true for a Kantian: Who would be violating the categorical imperative if the measure does or does not pass thanks to the strenuous efforts of the proponents on one side or the other? A Kantian of one ideological worldview may see violation of the humanity of others (i.e., a violation of the categorical imperative) on one side or the other, depending on which set of facts he or she believed to be true. The same is true for a follower of justice ethics—which side is likely to lead to greater injustices? It all depends on the facts. And a virtue ethicist who is judging the character of Mr. Danver and Mr. Standifant would also have to sort out these ideological factual issues before making a good judgment of character.

The point of this is not to argue that ethical judgments about political matters are impossible, but rather to point out how important it is to establish what is factually true if we are to arrive at an agreed upon ethical judgment. And that becomes hard to do regarding political matters if we have different ideological outlooks that make us see a different set of facts in the world.

One thing to note is that here, as is often the case, each side seems to ideologically view the world as if what is best for *its own members* is also what's best for *society as a whole*. The private interests of each side's constituents are seen as identical to, or virtually identical to, the public interest. This is a very common tendency. That fact alone should warn us to carefully examine our own perspectives and look for biases toward seeing our own self-interest as always what's best for others. It is very hard to notice these biases, but we all should make the effort.

Minority viewpoints within the organizations on both sides are also possible, and perhaps even likely. For example, certain organizations that might normally operate within Mr. Danver's coalition may not join it on this particular issue, because they consider the legislation unduly intrusive into the private affairs of businesses, unlikely to achieve its goals of aiding workers' wages and treatment, or other reasons. The leaders of a few businesses within Mr. Standifant's association might find the proposed legislation entirely unobjectionable because they are proud of their practices and would be happy to expose them to public scrutiny, while they consider some of their competitors to be bottom feeders taking unfair competitive advantage by substandard employment practices and whose poor records they would be happy to see exposed. The interest groups mentioned in the case would probably not be unanimous in the stance they took, but we believe the predominant sentiment would divide along the lines sketched out in the case.

For associations of businesses within the hospitality and tourism industries, the question regarding what stance to take toward various public policy issues often becomes: what is the most enlightened self-interest position to take? That is, which policy is likely to lead to the most beneficial consequences for the industry in the long run? They must determine what the long run is, and how to best calculate results over that period of time. When associations do this, they are clearly applying a utilitarian ethic, looking for the greatest benefits for the greatest number in the industry. However, if they take only an industry standpoint, they are simply acting as an interest group, not as a guardian of what will necessarily lead to the greatest good for the greatest number in society as a whole. Therefore, from the standpoint of society as a whole, their position must be measured in terms of its impact on everyone. If it still measures up as best, it is the ethical position from a utilitarian perspective. Of course, justice and rights considerations may enter into the calculations also, if the particular issue being considered involves questions of rights and fairness.

Because public policies affect us all in major ways, it is important to apply an ethical perspective to them, hard though that may be. The difficult thing is to get to enough common ground in terms of political ideology to be able to make sound and widely acceptable judgments.

Case Study—A Fair Price to Pay

Christopher Hopkins is a state representative from Louisiana, one of the states without a minimum wage law. This has not been an issue in the past as the federal minimum wage laws cover most workers.

Recently, a group of activists began advocating for the passage of a Louisiana minimum wage law. To complicate the issue, they want the state law to be 65 cents per hour higher than the federal government requires.

The Louisiana Food, Beverage, & Entertainment Association (FBEA) has made it clear to Mr. Hopkins that they are against the passage of a state law. They believe that such a law will cut into profits so drastically that many small businesses will have to close and that even larger businesses will undoubtedly suffer.

The activist group The People's Wage Society (TPWS) disagrees. They have statistics showing businesses will not be so drastically affected. They also show how a person living in Louisiana, earning the minimum wage, could not possibly support a family of even two people. It would be hard enough to support one person, they vehemently argue.

Mr. Hopkins is conflicted. He is up for re-election in six months. The FBEA has donated quite a bit of money to his campaigns in the past. He has rarely had a disagreement with them. However, he can certainly see the points being made by TPWS. He must make a decision in the next week because his constituents will be asking him questions while he is out campaigning for re-election.

Case Questions

1. Which side should Mr. Hopkins support? Explain your answer.

2. Formulate the fundamental principle on which each side would base its moral argument.

3. Would your decision depend on factual matters or moral conviction? Explain your answer.

4. Can political issues like this be based on moral premises? Explain your answer.

 Case Study—Secondhand Rose

Neptune County passed an anti-smoking ordinance in 1993. Three years later, the County Office on Law interpreted it to allow smoking in all bars, while restricting smoking in restaurants to separate rooms. Presently, there are 70 eating and drinking establishments countywide that allow smoking. The number of places that allow smoking appears to be growing instead of diminishing.

Rose Manson had been a bartender for 12 years when she decided that working around secondhand smoke was hurting her lungs. She left Orly's Bar and Grille in Neptune County in 2004 under friendly circumstances. She jokingly promised to return to work for Orly when he banned smoking at the bar.

Rose decided that she was going to assist the no-smoking effort in Neptune County. She wanted to help close the loophole that allowed a health hazard such as smoking to exist in separate restaurant dining rooms and in bars. She attended county council meetings and lobbied with other concerned citizens. Three of five council members signed a pledge saying they would introduce or support legislation that made workplaces and public places completely smoke-free. Strangely, Mr. James Gladhand, the councilman who was most supportive and outspoken about the county's law to prevent tobacco sales to those under 18, would not sign onto the smoke-free effort.

Rose was disturbed about Mr. Gladhand's lack of support. She felt that if she could get his support, then they could not possibly lose. She delved into his background, trying to find common ground for discussion. During her research, she discovered that he was a silent partner in two of the neighborhood bars where smoking was presently permitted.

While she was at it, Rose looked into another local politician she thought she could get help from, Victor Shadder. Mr. Shadder had long been a proponent of the smoking ban. During her research, Rose discovered that Mr. Shadder received very large sums of money for his campaigns from smoking opponents.

Case Questions

1. What are the major arguments that support Mr. Gladhand's position? Explain your answer.

2. What are the major arguments that support Rose's position? Explain your answer.

3. In light of your answers to questions one and two, are there any factual issues that need to be clarified to help settle the question of whose position has a better ethical justification?

Case Study—Fishy Facts: The Good, the Bad, and the Ugly

You decide. The following are facts about fish as a food product.

GOOD	BAD	UGLY
Low in saturated fat	Leading route of exposure to methyl mercury	Mercury impairs fetal brain development
High in protein	Women who eat fish more than three times per week have mercury levels that are seven times higher than women who eat no fish	The Environmental Protection Agency (EPA) estimates one in six U.S. babies is born yearly with unsafe methyl mercury blood levels
Excellent source of omega-3 fatty acids	Fish are vulnerable because, in water, toxic substances can reach higher levels due to the longer food chains	Top predatory fish, like tuna, can have extremely high levels of mercury—much higher than the water level it is swimming in
Omega 3 FAs reduce blood pressure and build healthy brains in children	The placenta cannot filter out methyl mercury	Methyl mercury halts cell division in the fetal brain

Source: Sandra Steingraber, "How Mercury-Tainted Tuna Damages Fetal Brains," *In These Times*, Jan. 2005, pp. 16–17, 29.

Case Questions

1. Should factory emissions of methyl mercury into the environment be limited? If so, what would be the cut-off point for the cost?

2. How do we balance the cost to the industry against the brain damage? Should there be a trade off or should emissions be cut drastically *no matter what the cost*?

3. Apply utilitarianism, Kantian duty ethics, and Rawlsian justice ethics to questions one and two above.

4. Should women eating in restaurants be warned about eating fish, especially fish at the top of the food chain, such as tuna and swordfish? If so, who is responsible for doing the warning and why?

 Case Study—Loyal Beyond the Letter of the Law

A recent study by Victuals Insurance, an insurance company that specializes in insuring restaurants, found that slips, trips, and falls by patrons are the most common general liability insurance claims filed by full-service restaurants. Furthermore, slips, trips, and falls represent about 27 percent of workers' compensation claims. The Victuals Company mailed an informational notice to its clients suggesting that an extra focus on safe flooring, adequate lighting, and quick clean-up of spills could help operators cut insurance costs.

The notice from Victuals intrigued Edna Beckman, the owner of Variety Delicatessen and Restaurant in Novo City. She followed all of the advice: she had the flooring changed (at great cost), she had the lighting upgraded (at further cost), and she fervently monitored any spills, including rain, snow, and mud that were tracked inside when the weather was poor.

Within two years, she noticed a definite drop in insurance claims. She compared claim costs from five years earlier to the cost of the previous year, and she was delighted. Furthermore, her insurance premium was lowered.

Two weeks after doing her personal comparative study, Crenshaw, one of Edna's most loyal chefs, fell in the kitchen. He suffered severe back strain and was told that he needed complete bed rest. Six months later, workers' compensation insurance and sick days had been exhausted for Crenshaw. He started using up his accrued vacation time. His back was still severely strained. Nine months later, Crenshaw was still unable to return to work as a chef. However, Edna thought she might use his talents in the office. She spoke to Crenshaw and they agreed that he would come in two mornings per week to do some bookwork. Edna continued to pay Crenshaw his full salary.

Later that month, Edna's lawyer and business partner, Frank Malloy, came by to discuss an upcoming audit. When he saw that Edna was giving Crenshaw his full salary, he became angry and shouted, "Why are we paying him? And, why are we paying him full salary? We are not required by law to pay him. Why do you think we have laws governing these types of issues?"

Case Questions

1. What should Edna do? Explain your answer and base it on at least one of the theories we have studied.

2. Explain Malloy's point of view. What is his reasoning?

3. Develop a policy for handling situations of this type that you feel is fair to all concerned. Is this policy based on any of the ethical theories we have studied?

 Case Study—Menu Management

Adrian is the cashier at the Hi Ho Burger Shop. The small boutique restaurant specializes in different types of burgers, including vegetarian burgers. One evening Stephanie, one of Adrian's friends who is a vegetarian, came into the restaurant and ordered the whoop-de-do, a soy burger.

Within one minute of Stephanie's first bite, she began choking. Adrian, who is trained in first aid, jumped up and immediately began to slap Stephanie on her back. But Stephanie fought her off and instead, reached into her purse and pulled out a needle, which Adrian later learned was a strong antihistamine. As soon as she had started coughing, Stephanie realized that the burger must contain nuts; she is severely allergic to nuts.

Stephanie settled down and left shortly afterwards. She promised to see her doctor first thing in the morning.

The next day, Adrian spoke to her boss Leonard about the matter. She suggested to Leonard that the menu should contain labels of all the ingredients that are used, so that there would be no more incidents. She told Leonard how scared she was for her good friend Stephanie.

Leonard listened politely, but then he explained why he would not list the ingredients. He made it clear that it is the customer's responsibility to ask if certain ingredients are used in a menu item. He added, "Customers know when they have problems. If we start with nuts, it will never stop. Next it will be milk, then eggs. Then people will want to know how many calories. I won't have it."

Case Questions

1. Whose point of view do you agree with in this case? Explain your answer.

2. Which theorist would agree with your rationalization? Explain your answer.

25

Ethical Issues in Research and Academia

The foundation of every state is the education of its youth. —Diogenes Laertius

EDUCATION SETS THE STANDARD for different human endeavors and this is no less true for the hospitality and tourism industry than for other areas of human activity. While a primary aim of education is to teach facts, skills, reasoning, and the like, education also bears some responsibility for helping those being educated to behave in a manner that comports with the ethical expectations of our society and our institutions. While education (and educational institutions) cannot bear the entire burden of teaching people how to know right from wrong, this nonetheless remains one of its many functions.

In particular, those engaged in educating students have a responsibility to behave in an ethical manner. They should be role models, serving as an example for students to emulate. Just as is true of managers and owners, educators are in a position of authority and, thus, carry a responsibility along with that authority.

Case Study—Who Is the Professor, Please?

Waldo Reed was asked by his department chair, Jesse Armstrong, to accompany a group of students to Aspen, Colorado, for a one-week ski/study trip during spring break. The purpose of the trip was to give the students a great experience and an opportunity to write a journal. Each of the students enrolled in the one-credit course was also enrolled in a journal writing class on campus.

Since he was an avid skier, Waldo really wanted to go on the trip. Waldo requested that his wife, Honey, be allowed to accompany him, and the department chair reluctantly agreed. "Remember," Armstrong said, "You are the instructor. Your wife is not to take on any responsibilities for the students." Waldo agreed and when he proposed the trip to his wife he explained that to her as well. Even though she wasn't a skier, Honey was very excited and she readily agreed.

Waldo met with the students two weeks before departure. He explained travel and hotel arrangements, and ended by saying, "Bear in mind, you are receiving college credit for this trip. Your only assignment is to keep a journal of your activities and impressions for the week; your grade will be based mostly on this journal. If you get out of hand, you will lose points but, otherwise, that's it. If you don't abuse this great situation, we'll all have a wonderful time."

245

The week went well. Waldo was out on the slopes early every day. Honey kept herself busy by shopping, going to the salon, soaking in the hot tub, and more. They were both having a great week and could not believe Waldo was receiving extra pay for the assignment.

On day six of the trip, the journals were due. Waldo was overwhelmed when he saw the pile. "I think I have a lot of Dickens wannabes," he thought to himself. He also knew how much work was waiting for him at home because he was due back in class on Monday and he hadn't done any preparation. Over breakfast before he went out to the slopes for his last day, he moaned and moaned about the journals to his wife.

Suddenly he smiled. "Honey, what are you doing today?" Waldo asked.

"Packing and not much else," she answered.

"Why don't you read over the journals? You can tell me if there are any students who didn't do the assignment or if there are any odd or unusual entries. If you'll do this for me, I'll buy you that shawl that you want in the gift shop downstairs."

Both Honey and Waldo knew that she should not read the journals. But Waldo wanted to ski and he also needed the time home on the plane to prepare for his Monday classes. Honey wanted the shawl, so she agreed.

After Waldo left for the day, Honey readied herself at the desk in the hotel room. At noon, she decided to call room service because she wanted to keep reading the journals and didn't feel comfortable taking any of them with her to lunch in the hotel dining room. At 12:30 P.M. there was a knock on the door. It was room service with her lunch. She had the waiter place it on the desk and, as soon as he left, she sat down to continue her reading while she was eating.

Two minutes later, there was another knock on the door. Honey assumed it was the waiter returning for something he had forgotten. She was surprised to see Sara, one of the students, standing there. Sara was just as surprised to see her journal in Honey's hands, but she didn't say anything.

"I sprained my ankle and I remember you said that you kept bandages. Can I borrow one?" Sara asked.

While Honey pulled out her first aid kit, Sara took in the scene. It was obvious that Honey was reading the students' journals, but Sara didn't say anything.

"Here you go. Would you like some help?" Honey asked.

"No thanks. I've done this before. And I'm meeting Sam for lunch at the skiers' café in just a few minutes."

Sara left immediately feeling very uncomfortable. She pondered, "I wonder what the school was thinking. Reed is out every day skiing and hanging out with the students. Mrs. Reed is reading our journals. How does she know what to look for in a journal? We spent a whole course on journal writing; that's why we were offered credit for this trip. Who is the professor, please?"

Case Commentary: Utilitarianism

Neither an act utilitarian nor a rule utilitarian would consider Honey's reading and grading of the student journals acceptable. An act utilitarian would ask "is this the greatest good for the greatest number of people?" Any good coming from this situation is very narrowly for the Reeds: Waldo has the opportunity to do more skiing and has extra preparation time for his upcoming classes, while his wife gets a new shawl. The numerous possible harms follow.

A rule utilitarian would know that a universal rule allowing fraudulent instructor roles could not possibly lead to the maximum benefits over harms. Many negative consequences could flow from a situation such as this. Sara is on her way to the skier's café. Since she is bothered by seeing her journal in Honey's hands, it is likely that she will tell a friend, who will tell another friend and so forth. Back on campus, she might report the incident to Armstrong, the department chair. The consequences include loss of respect and general cynicism about people (especially those in authority) actually performing the duties expected of them. Additionally, the department might be harmed if Sara decides to take it further than Armstrong. Other possible consequences, all of them having to do with a general deterioration of ethical expectations, could be listed. Utilitarianism would not find the behavior of the Reeds to be ethically justified.

Case Commentary: Kant's Categorical Imperative

As is typical in cases of deception for purposes of self-gain, Kant would find the behavior of the Reeds to be unacceptable. Applying the first formulation of the categorical imperative shows that universalizing a deceptive practice of false instructorship would undermine the very practice of assigning and contracting for teaching duties and, thus, would be self-contradictory. It would be irrational and unethical.

Waldo is not living up to his duty as the professor. His motive (extra time to ski and prepare for classes) is self-serving and he cannot universalize the deception involved; he is acting in a way that he could not and would not allow others, were they to desire to treat him in the same manner.

The second formulation of the categorical imperative states that each person should be treated as an autonomous, rational, thinking individual. Here again, Waldo is dehumanizing his students by not playing straight with them. He is using them for his own pleasure and he is cheating them of his expertise. As is always the case for Kant, being deceptive for self-gain is not treating others (in this case, the students) as ends-unto-themselves; rather they are being used.

Case Commentary: The Ethic of Justice

Once again, fraudulent transactions violate Rawls's principles of distributive justice, because they distribute rewards and burdens unfairly in a manner that people behind the veil of ignorance would never condone. Waldo is acting unjustly and his behavior could never be turned into general societal arrangements that satisfy the requirements of justice.

If Waldo is caught reneging on his responsibility, there will probably be retributive measures taken. If it is a first offense, measures might consist of nothing more than taking away his right to ever escort students on future tours. However, if he has acted inappropriately in the past or if he attempts to cover up his behavior and is caught, he may be brought up on charges by the university or denied payment for work not performed. The seriousness of the punishment should be proportional to the seriousness of his offense. He probably has not done anything illegal, but it is unethical.

Students like Sara may demand compensation for the damage done by being graded by an incompetent (and hidden) instructor. In this way, compensatory justice issues may arise. She might request a refund for the course since she was evaluated by an incompetent grader; but a much more likely form of compensation would be making the students "whole" by having a real professor read and comment on their work.

Case Commentary: Aristotle and the Ethics of Virtue

Virtue ethics would view Waldo's character as lacking. He shows the vice of self-indulgence. He wants to have lots of play and little work, while being generously paid for escorting the student group. He is also lacking in moderation, thereby exhibiting the vice of overindulgence. He does not know when enough is enough. By skiing up to the last possible moment, while ignoring his responsibilities, he is not acting in moderation. Additionally, he is dishonest. By having Honey grade the students' papers, but acting as if he has completed the task himself, he is exhibiting the vice of dishonesty. From the point of view of character ethics, Waldo would be found wanting.

 ## Case Study—Dreams of the Prado

One winter afternoon, Dr. Harvey Dolan, a tenured professor at Hungry Hollow University, was thinking about his plans for the forthcoming academic year. He was eager to attend the upcoming conference, Issues in Solid Waste Management for the Food Service Industry, in Madrid the following September. He pictured himself ambling down the sun-soaked city center while the music of street musicians hummed in the air. He dreamed of strolling through the Prado and the Palacio Real. He drooled at the thought of eating tapas as he listened to flamenco music.

However, there was one major obstacle. Hungry Hollow University did not fund conference trips unless the attending professor was presenting a peer-reviewed research paper. Unfortunately, Harvey was not in the mood for writing a research paper. In fact, Harvey had not been in the mood for quite some time. Essentially, Harvey had not been disposed to doing research since he had been promoted to full professor.

But Harvey really wanted to go on this trip. Colleagues from various professional organizations would be in attendance. Several of his industry contacts would also be there and he had to keep up with those contacts. How else would he continue to receive complimentary meals, spa packages, and hotel nights? Finally, when would he ever have the opportunity again to visit Madrid without personal cost? What could he do?

Throughout the next day, Harvey pondered his dilemma. How could he convince the university to send him on the trip without doing a research paper? What he really needed was an idea for an abstract, but the abstract was due in just a few days, and Harvey hadn't a clue about what he might investigate, even if he was willing to do the research.

Suddenly, a light bulb went on in Harvey's brain. He remembered that he had worked with his colleagues Janet Moore and Dorothy Vega from other universities on a project about environmentally friendly hotels just last year. He knew for a fact that, to date, the paper had not been submitted anywhere because Janet's portion was still in progress. Her mother had become ill and Janet had asked Dorothy and Harvey to give her an extra few months to complete her portion. Harvey knew that Janet's mom was near death and that Janet was very devoted to her. In fact, Janet had recently requested that she not be scheduled for classes during the spring semester; in essence, she was taking a leave of absence to care for her dying mother.

Harvey mulled over the possibilities. He knew Janet was scarcely paying attention to her classroom responsibilities. She certainly wasn't planning on going to the conference in Madrid. Harvey wasn't too concerned with Dorothy, a colleague from LaRosa State College. She was hundreds of miles away. Besides, Harvey thought of Dorothy as being scatterbrained and provincial; she would do inconsequential work on many different projects with negligible outcomes. As far as Harvey knew, Dorothy had never attended an international conference. At least, he had never seen her at any.

A few days later, after considering the possibilities, Harvey decided to submit an abstract for the Madrid conference based on the research that he had done with Dorothy and Janet. However, he decided that since Janet was so busy with her mom and Dorothy wouldn't care, he would just do it on his own. In his mind, there was no need to include their names on the abstract.

Harvey submitted the abstract and it was accepted. Within the month, he had finished off Janet's portion of the paper, which did not amount to much work after all, and submitted it for the conference proceedings. One month later, Harvey received a letter of congratulations from the symposium paper-review committee. He immediately called his travel agent and began his plans for the Madrid trip.

Unfortunately for Harvey, Erma Lane, a good friend of Dorothy's, was also attending the Madrid conference. Erma had carefully read over all of the conference materials as she was getting ready for her trip. When she spotted Harvey's name, she recognized it immediately because she had remembered Dorothy speaking of him. Her recollections were that Dorothy had not been at all pleased with Harvey's work on the research project. In fact, she felt that Harvey was a leech because he had not done much work at all and was getting his name on yet another publication. Most regrettably for Harvey, Erma also recognized the title of the research project, as Harvey had not even bothered to change the title of the presentation. Erma, understanding exactly what had happened, immediately called Dorothy to ask her why her name was not on the paper.

After speaking with Erma, Dorothy called Janet. Together, they decided to contact Professor Lewis Engles, the symposium paper-review coordinator for the Madrid conference. Professor Engles asked Dorothy and Janet to submit their previous research, which they did. After comparing their submissions with Harvey's paper, Engles recognized that Harvey had unfairly submitted work that was not entirely his own. Consequently, Harvey was contacted by Professor Engles and asked to withdraw his paper. Engles informed Harvey of the investigation regarding the previous research that had been written by Dorothy and Janet. He also stated that if Harvey quietly excused himself from the conference, no further action would be taken.

Case Questions

1. Name the major ethical issues involved in this case.

2. How would a utilitarian analyze this case? Explain your answer.

3. How would a Kantian analyze this case? Explain your answer.

4. Look at the case from the point of view of just distribution of rewards and burdens. What would John Rawls say? Explain your answer.

5. Do an analysis of the moral characters of Harvey, Erma, and Engles. Do your analysis in terms of the virtues and vices.

6. What would you do if you were Engles, the symposium paper-review coordinator? Explain your answer.

 Case Study—The Ugly American —————————————

Elmer Askins and his wife Sugar were very excited about their upcoming study abroad trip to Spain, France, and Germany. Elmer, a professor at Hodgkins University in Loontown, Nebraska, and his wife had been on one prior study abroad trip. The previous year, they had escorted a group of students to Manchester, England. The major difference between the two trips was that in England the group remained in the same location but took day trips for sightseeing purposes. On the upcoming tour, there would be more travel involved. The group would be moving several times over the three-week period.

Neither Elmer nor his wife spoke Spanish, French, or German. However, Elmer was not worried; he knew that people spoke English in the large cities. He also hired several tour operators in the various cities to assist with the tours, so he felt that when he was around town with the students, there would be no worries.

However, things do not always go smoothly when traveling with a group of students. Because Elmer had not been strict regarding tardiness, the students were appearing later and later every day. Now that they were in Paris, the situation was out of control. By the time the last stragglers had arrived in the hotel lobby for the day's touring, the group had already missed one tour that still had to be paid for. Elmer and Sugar decided to try to squeeze the tour in for the afternoon and, by the time the day was over, they were running more than four hours behind schedule. Originally, the group was supposed to take a train at 5 P.M., arriving at 8 P.M. in Verlet du Lac, a tiny village in Provence. The last train left at 10 P.M. and Elmer was determined to be on it.

When they arrived at the train station, the ticket master tried to explain to Elmer that at 2 A.M. the station in Verlet du Lac would be closed. There would be no one at the train station and there would be no transportation available. But Elmer didn't understand; he grabbed the tickets and told the students to head to the train. A kindly passenger who had overheard the ticket master stopped Elmer as he was herding the students onto the train. "Monsieur, you should really wait until morning. There is nothing available to you at two in the morning in Verlet du Lac. You are risking your students' health."

But Elmer did not listen; he herded his students onto the train. Verlet du Lac was the last stop. The students, as well as Elmer and Sugar, were mostly sound asleep as the conductor went around rousing everyone. They grabbed their luggage and trudged off the train. There was nothing there but a few benches and a concrete slab. The doors to the stationhouse were locked tight and there was no town in sight.

"Well, group, this is your fault, so make yourselves comfortable. Maybe you'll start setting your alarm clocks." Most of them fell asleep, lying on coats and using backpacks for pillows. But, somehow during the night, several backpacks were stolen.

Case Questions

1. Does Elmer bear responsibility for the plight of the students, including the stolen backpacks? Why or why not?

2. Does either the ticket master or the conductor bear any responsibility? Why or why not?

3. Apply a utilitarian analysis of what Elmer should have done.

4. How do culture and cultural differences enter into this case? What ethical responsibility does one have (or not have) to understand the culture of others when one travels?

5. Analyze the character of Elmer from a character ethics or virtue ethics perspective.

 Case Study—How Much Is the Rent?

Jethro Browning is the director of admissions at Capulet College in Chicago. Capulet admits approximately 500 new students per semester. They have dormitory space for almost 2,000 and have been trying to purchase appropriate apartment buildings near the campus to supplement the number of sleeping rooms for students.

Ted McFooley, president of Capulet College, held a meeting with his executive council to discuss the issue. The first topic on the agenda was the housing problem. He said, "One of the major complaints that students have is that it is difficult to find housing. A survey was done during the previous academic year and students overwhelmingly supported university rental apartments as the number one choice for housing. The major reasoning was that if the student could select housing from already pre-selected apartments and/or rooms, the start and end of the school year would be much smoother."

A few weeks after the meeting, Jethro Browning got married. He and his bride began looking for a home to purchase shortly after the wedding. They found the perfect house; it was a small one-family home located only 15 minutes from the campus. They put in a bid and asked to be notified within 48 hours if the bid was accepted.

Two days later, on Monday, Jethro was sitting in his office at Capulet telling his student assistant Sybil about his potential new home. While they were talking, his wife called to tell him their bid was accepted. Sybil congratulated him and told him he was very fortunate to have a nice place to live so close to campus. "That's the major complaint of students on campus these days, and I understand. Each year, I have to spend the first week of school scrounging for an apartment. Either that or I have to come early to find an apartment. But I need to work and live at home as long as I can so I don't pay rent when I'm not in school. And by late summer all the decent stuff is gone anyway. You should see the hole I'm living in now!"

After Sybil left, Jethro started thinking. While house hunting, he and his wife Lanelle had looked over many duplexes, triplexes, and condos. They still had money from the wedding and could afford a down payment on a few condos at least. These days, you don't even need a down payment. He could buy a few places and rent them out to students. If the rent was high enough, he wouldn't even have to worry about them staying for only nine months instead of twelve. And who would be better than the director of admissions to offer students housing before they even looked over the lists of official college housing? He could have his personal units filled up in no time. His finishing thought was that the college would always rent out all of their units because there was such a shortage.

The next week, President McFooley had a follow-up meeting regarding the student housing issue. All members of the executive council were present. Jethro told the group of his idea. Dagwood Burns, director of physical plant, spoke first. "You've got the entrepreneur spirit we love to see, Jethro. I think I might squeeze out the purchase of a condo or two, myself." Marie, McFooley's assistant, chimed in: "This is great! Duane and I have been looking for some good investing opportunities. I know he'll be interested, especially when I explain how it will be impossible to have any empty apartments."

Their excitement was contagious. By the end of the meeting, every member of the executive council had announced his or her intention to purchase condos in the neighborhood for student use. They decided to hire an apartment rental agency to handle the rentals of their apartments, so that the ownership would be disguised and no irate parents or snoopy newspaper reporters would accuse them of a conflict of interest, even though they were all certain that there really were no conflict of interest violations involved here.

Jethro made sure to give all newly-entering students the list of apartments owned by him and his colleagues before he gave them the name of the one new college-owned apartment. Thus, each new student received in their welcome packet a list of dormitory options and off-campus apartments owned by Jethro and his colleagues. Only after the dormitory was filled or students came inquiring for other available apartments would Jethro give them an additional list containing the college's apartment building plus a few others in the neighborhood. He and his colleagues were finding that they could rent their apartments out for about the same as comparable dorm and local apartment rental rates and still make a profit. The mortgage payments were being covered by the rent, with money left over even after repair and maintenance costs. "Pretty good deal," he thought to himself. "We're getting our new properties paid for and then some."

Because of all the new apartment possibilities open to students, the college was finding that its dorms were emptying out and they were unable to fill all dorm rooms. Also, the college's newly-acquired apartment building was not completely filled by students, so the college was forced to open the building up to anyone who wanted an apartment in the neighborhood or else it would be leaving a significant portion of its apartments empty.

Case Questions

1. Is there a conflict of interest here? Explain your answer.

2. Apply a utilitarian analysis to this case. Is the behavior of Jethro and his colleagues ethical from this perspective? Why or why not?

3. Apply a Kantian analysis to this case. Is the behavior of Jethro and his colleagues ethical from this perspective? Why or why not?

4. How would you characterize the moral character of the leadership of Capulet College?

 Case Study—The Private College ————————————————————

In 1960, five men decided to open a private, not-for-profit post-secondary educational institution in Madison, New York. The facility was to be a professional business college. Frank Gilford, a local hotel entrepreneur, became involved in order to diversify his holdings. Marvin Tesh became involved because he wanted to be affiliated with a university; he had just lost his bid for promotion and tenure at Madison Community College. The other three shareholders, Leonard Patrick, Al Daley, and Darius Doolittle, jumped on board because they were friends of either Frank or Marvin. Their areas of expertise included accounting and finance.

While searching for properties, the men found an operating secretarial school that was for sale. They purchased the school in April 1960; the facility was remodeled over the summer, and in September 1960, the school reopened as the Gilford & Tesh College. It was incorporated as a private, not-for-profit institution and advertised itself as a small specialty college, focusing on business studies. The five men were the shareholders of the GTC Corporation. All profits were to be returned to the corporation, and salaries were to be paid from the corporate accounts. Rent for the property would be paid from the GTC account to a separate account, the GTPDD Corporation. At the end of each year, 80 percent of the monies in this account would be paid out to the owners as bonuses.

Over the years, the school became a great success. In 1968, Gilford & Tesh opened a second campus in Montpelier, Vermont; in 1975, the third campus was opened in Indianapolis, Indiana; in 1982, the fourth was opened in San Diego; and the fifth campus was opened in 1990 in Jacksonville, Florida. The strategy of the five shareholders was to continue to open campuses based on local real estate values, as that was how their bonuses were obtained.

However, in 2000, the campuses began to falter. Too many local community colleges and state universities were offering the same courses and degrees as Gilford & Tesh, while tuition at Gilford & Tesh was more than double what a state university would cost. Different strategies were employed, but by 2005, the men realized that they would have to cut back in order to stay solvent. Memos went back and forth between the five men. They had narrowed down their choice of potential cutbacks to either cutting their bonuses from the rental income or reducing a variety of employee benefits, such as retirement and health care. They could not cut back on faculty as they were operating with too many adjunct (part-time) faculty members already, and thus were in danger of losing their accredited status as a college.

Gilford and Tesh went over the various proposals and then called an emergency executive committee meeting. Gilford chaired the meeting. He gave a detailed update of the financial situation and asked the group to consider the following, "We have earned good money over the years and I know that each of us has put away a substantial sum for the future. Both Tesh and I would be willing to receive smaller bonuses this year if each of you would consider the same."

"I have another idea," Leonard Patrick announced. "I have been giving this a great deal of thought. I have researched our retirement plans for the staff and faculty, and we are spending entirely too much on these plans. If we dump all the money from the current retirement plan into AGM Associates and change the type of plan that we offer, we can save millions. I have all the research right here."

Gilford asked, "What do you mean change the type of plan?"

Patrick explained, "We would change from a defined benefit to a defined contribution pension plan. Most people don't understand the difference. We can explain it in a way so that it sounds like we are doing it for their benefit. And here's the kicker: we end our presentation by telling them we are supplementing their raise for the coming year with a one year bonus for good performance. That will probably stop any questions."

The group looked over the numbers that Patrick presented. It was apparent that the changes proposed would do two things. First, it would shift all the risk in the plan from the college to the individual faculty members. The new plan guaranteed only a set amount would be paid per year into the plan, not a guaranteed pension for every year of service. Depending on how well the investments performed, the pensioners might or might not end up with a reasonably good-sized pension—the risk would now be on the individual faculty members. The college would have no obligation to provide any particular pension to a 30-year employee, for example; pension size would depend on how much the invested pension money had earned. Second, because most employees would be cut off from the old pension plan while they had fewer years of service, most employees would end up with smaller total pensions (old plan plus new plan added together) than they would have had if the old plan had been continued, based on reasonable market assumptions. In other words, the changes would result in a cut in pensions, averaging about 22 percent for the average employee (although different employees would experience larger or smaller cuts, depending on how long they had been with the college.)

In the end, the five men realized that they would save a great deal more money by changing the retirement plan than they would by shortchanging themselves on their bonuses. At that point, the decision to change retirement plans became an easy one. They immediately decided to change pension plans, while sugarcoating the change to convince faculty they would not be harmed and might actually do better if the stock market prospered. They also decided to give all faculty a one-time bonus of one percent.

Case Questions

1. Analyze this case from a distributive justice perspective. Would people behind the veil of ignorance approve of the decision made by these five men? Why or why not?

2. From a utilitarian perspective, will the decision lead to the greatest good for the greatest number? Try to come up with all the arguments you can that might argue for a "yes" answer or a "no" answer. Which one is convincing? Why?

3. Apply a Kantian analysis to this case. Are these five men applying the categorical imperative? Why or why not?

4. What does virtue ethics tell us about the character of these men? Explain your answer.

Index

257